The New Shell Guides
South and Mid Wales

The New Shell Guides
South and Mid Wales

Wynford Vaughan-Thomas

Series Editor: John Julius Norwich

Photography by Nick Meers unless otherwise stated

Michael Joseph · London

First published in Great Britain by
Michael Joseph Limited, 27 Wrights Lane,
London W8 5TZ 1987

This book was designed and produced by
Swallow Editions Limited, Swallow House,
11–21 Northdown Street, London N1 9BN

© Shell UK Limited 1987

British Library Cataloguing in Publication Data:

Vaughan-Thomas, Wynford
   The new Shell guide to South and Mid-Wales.
   1. Wales, South — Description and travel
   — Guide-books 2. Wales — Description
   and travel — 1981 — Guide-books
   I. Title
   914.29′404858   DA740.S65

Cased edition: ISBN 0–7181–2762–5
Paperback edition: ISBN 0–7181–2767–6

Editor: Georgina Evans and Raymond Kaye
Cartographer: M L Design
Production: Hugh Allan

Filmset by Wyvern Typesetting Limited,
Central Trading Estate, 277 Bath Road,
Bristol BS4 3EH
Printed in Great Britain by
Purnell Book Production Ltd, Paulton, Bristol

The name Shell and the Shell emblem are registered
trademarks

Shell UK Ltd would point out that the contributors'
views are not necessarily those of this company.

The information contained in this book is believed
correct at the time of printing. While every
care has been taken to ensure that the information
is accurate, the publishers and Shell can
accept no responsibility for any errors or omissions
or for changes in the details given.

A list of Shell publications
can be obtained by writing to:
Department UOMK/60;
Shell UK Oil
PO Box No.148
Shell-Mex House
Strand
London WC2R 0DX

*Front cover photograph: Cerrig Samson cromlech, near
Abercastle, Dyfed, see p. 40.*
*Back cover photograph: Detail on the Town Hall,
Llanidloes, Powys, see p. 136*

*Title page: Newport Sands with Dinas Head in the
background, Dyfed, see p. 156*

John Julius Norwich was born in 1929. He read French and
Russian at New College, Oxford, and in 1952 joined the
Foreign Office where he served until 1964. Since then he has
published two books on the medieval Norman Kingdom in
Sicily, *The Normans in the South* and *The Kingdom in the Sun*;
two historical travel books, *Mount Athos* (with Reresby
Sitwell) and *Sahara*; an anthology of poetry and prose,
Christmas Crackers; and two volumes on the history of Venice,
Venice, the Rise to Empire and *Venice, the Greatness and the
Fall*, now published in one volume as *A History of Venice*. He
was also general editor of *Great Architecture of the World* and,
more recently, author of *The Architecture of Southern England*.

In addition, he writes and presents historical documen-
taries for BBC television and frequently broadcasts on BBC
radio. He is chairman of the Venice in Peril Fund, a Trustee of
the Civic Trust, a member of the Executive and Properties
Committees of the National Trust.

Wynford Vaughan-Thomas was a Welshman who took a
particular interest in exploring the natural beauties of his
native land. He travelled through it in a remarkable variety of
ways – on foot, on a bicycle and on horseback.

He was born in Swansea and was educated at Swansea
Grammar School where Dylan Thomas's father was his
English master. He went to Oxford and after graduating
served for a spell as a Keeper of Manuscripts and Records in
the National Library of Wales at Aberystwyth. He joined the
BBC in 1936 in the Outside Broadcasts department. With the
outbreak of war he became one of the distinguished band of
BBC war-correspondents, covering air raids over Berlin, the
Anzio landing, the liberation of the south of France and the
final assault on Hitler's Germany. After the war, he travelled
extensively throughout the Commonwealth and became a
well-known commentator on many major royal and public
occasions.

He returned to Wales as a Director of HTV, the independent television company for Wales and the West and took a
special interest in programmes on the countryside. He
retained his connection with the company and was the
co-presenter of the major television series on the history of
Wales, 'The Dragon has Two Tongues', shortly before his
death in 1987.

In 1986 he was awarded the CBE.

Nick Meers born in Gloucestershire in 1955, gained a
diploma from Guildford School of Photography in 1978. He
brings to the New Shell Guide experiences gained from
landscape and wildlife assignments ranging from Canada's
National Parks to the Cayman Islands, from Ireland to Israel,
from Wisconsin to West Africa.

In 1986 he won first prize in the 'Events' catagory of the
British Photography Competition organised by the Sunday
Telegraph Magazine and the National Trust.

Martin Dohrn was born in Christchurch, New Zealand in
1957. He moved to England with his family 10 years later. His
interest in landscape and natural history stemmed from his
schooldays where he took up photography as a humane
alternative to collecting insects.

Contents

Introduction

Then and Now

Writing a guide book to a part of the country where you were born and brought up is a voyage of exploration into your own past. As you carefully list the modern attractions of each town and village, vivid memories assail you of the time when you first saw them through the eager eyes of youth. How have they changed, and have the changes all been for the better? Or has that early charm of a place, which seemed so magical when you were young, faded with the passing years?

When I was born in Swansea – more years ago than I care to admit – South Wales was most definitely not a tourist area. If it had any image in the outside world, it was of narrow mining valleys overhung with smoke, from which long trains heaped with coal rattled down incessantly to grimy ports, where steelworks and tinplate works added to the industrial squalor. Even as late as the 1930s, the poet W. H. Auden could write that

> . . . Glamorgan hid a life
> Grim as a tidal rock pool in her glove-shaped valleys.

We, who lived there, knew how wrong he was. Why, on the very doorstep of my native town was a secret that we hugged to ourselves – the unspoiled, enchanting Gower peninsula, with its beaches of golden sand backed by bright, clean limestone cliffs and, inland, the curlew-haunted commons and downs crowned with mysterious cromlechs and romantic castles. Here we spent the first holidays I can remember – at Port Eynon or Rhosili, reached in the rickety buses that crawled once a day along the white, dusty roads. And we could fish in rock pools still crowded with prawns and even crabs and lobsters.

As I grew up, I found that there was a wider world beyond Gower to explore, and the bicycle was the perfect means of exploring it. It is hard to imagine how traffic-free were the roads of rural South Wales even in the days after the First World War. On our bicycles we first ventured into the mountains north of Swansea, into the then unvisited and lonely Brecon Beacons and Carmarthenshire Fans. The only people we met on the high summits were the shepherds on their sturdy Welsh ponies, rounding up their flocks like the patriarchs of old. There were no aircraft to disturb the silence; only the quiet sound of the wind whistling among the rocks. It was here that I first learned the charm of solitude.

My father was a distinguished musician and composer, who was much in demand as an adjudicator in the numerous eisteddfodau that then took place all over the countryside. This was still a world into which the cinema had not penetrated, radio and television were undreamed of, and the motor car still a luxury which only the rich could afford or the local doctor drive. Welsh was still the dominant language and the chapel the centre of village life. The local eisteddfod would be the highlight of the year. Competition between rival choirs had an intensity only seen at cup finals today, and an enthusiasm we now reserve for pop festivals. The classic Welsh joke about the

The Montgomery Canal, near Welshpool, see p. 181

two conductors meeting after a particularly close contest sums it all up. 'Yes,' admitted the losing conductor, 'I admit that you beat us hands down on "Lift up your Heads, Ye Gates of Brass", but in "Love, Perfect Love", we gave you Hell!'

Life may not have been very rich and varied in those villages of South Wales on the eve of the First World War, but it was lived with a peculiar intensity. The local poet who won the chair at the National Eisteddfod became a national hero, and the eloquent preachers in the chapel pulpits set the standard of speech. No one could accuse the average South Walian of being tongue-tied. Over this basically Nonconformist and Liberal Wales loomed the charismatic figure of David Lloyd George. True he was a North Walian, but the whole country regarded him with pride even when they disagreed with his politics. It really was an astonishing achievement in those Edwardian days: the rise of this cottage-bred boy from an obscure corner of Wales to become Prime Minister and War Leader of Great Britain. Even the colliers in the Rhondda, who were beginning to turn to the rising Labour Party, declared, 'Well, he showed 'em, didn't he; he showed 'em!' I, myself, was lucky enough to see Lloyd George in action on the platform at the height of his powers. I was ten at the time, and my aunt had taken me to the National Eisteddfod at Neath in 1918. 'What is he saying, Auntie Bess?', I inquired. 'Never mind what he is saying,' my aunt replied. 'Doesn't he say it beautifully?'

Perhaps I look back on my early days in South Wales with far too romantic an eye. There must have been dark shadows somewhere in the perpetual sunshine of my early memories, but, of course, I have long forgotten them. Even after I had gone up to Oxford, I still saw South Wales as a place of romance rather than reality. I spent one blissful Long Vacation on Ramsey Island in 1927. It was still farmed in those days, although the sheep were the wildest animals I had ever seen. I remember the words of an old farmer in the lonely country behind Tregaron, when I remarked that his sheep seemed difficult to control. 'Bachgen, Welsh sheep aren't really sheep. They're antelopes in woolly pullovers.' There was even an eagle soaring over Ramsey, one of a pair that had been originally released on Skomer in the hope that they would breed and re-establish the golden eagle in Wales. Unfortunately both birds turned out to be females. The buzzard remains the largest bird that soars over the moorlands of Wales.

In all my early explorations of the wilder parts of South Wales, I either camped out or stayed in farmhouses. The place was not tourist-orientated in those days. There were friendly, old-fashioned coaching inns in the small towns, where the menu was not exactly varied. One wanderer over the hills behind Brecon was moved to write in the hotel book:

> Mutton chop by night
> And mutton chop by day;
> Till, when you meet a mountain sheep,
> You turn the other way.

Tourism was confined to a few, long-established centres. The miners from the Rhondda poured down to Barry Island for day trips, and the more prosperous people from the Valleys took their holidays at Porthcawl. Tenby, away in the West, retained a slightly exclusive Regency charm, while Aberystwyth drew on the English Midlands for its clientele. The Wells – Llandrindod above all – were reputed, by those who did not have the money to go there, to be secret centres of power politics.

The Brecon Beacons, see p. 81

As the socially and politically ambitious took the waters, and the band in the Pump Room Gardens played selections from 'The Arcadians', promotions were quietly arranged and reputations made or unmade. How far away and innocent it all seems now! For this was still strongly Nonconformist Wales – Liberal and high-minded. At least, on the surface. This was the Wales which, in the 1880s, had insisted on every pub being firmly shut on the Sabbath day. The Welsh Sunday became notorious among thirsty travellers and hardly an encouragement to the tourist trade. In the rural areas, however, ingenuity outflanked legality. There was always a back entry into the pub for those in the know. I remember taking a reviving glass in the back room of a pub on a Sunday in a little town in West Wales. 'What about the licensing laws?', I nervously inquired. The landlord reassured me. 'Don't worry, Mr Thomas. Around here we shut but we don't close.'

I have one final, overriding memory of that now vanished rural society: it was still dominated by the horse. In the industrial areas, the train and the tram gave working people their mobility. In the country areas, until well after the First World War, the pony and trap – or the 'gambo', as one version of this indispensible mode of transport was known in parts of South Wales – was the way the farmer and his family went to market. Market day was the big day of the week, the moment when everybody met and gossip and news were exchanged. Even today, Thursday in Fishguard – market day – is known in Welsh as 'shwd i chwi hedde' day: 'How are you today' day!

The horse was the sole power unit on the farm. The tractor did not become common in the Welsh countryside until after the Second World War. And what a wonderful variety of horses there were, from the sturdy Welsh cob to the tireless little wiry Welsh mountain pony. The great shire horses were confined to the richer, flatter lands of places like the Vale of Glamorgan and now you only see them once a year at the Royal Welsh Show at Builth. As they go by in their beribboned pride, I seem to see the passing of that old rural South Wales I grew to know and love.

How completely that world has disappeared! In the Valleys, King Coal has long since been deposed by Oil. Two Depressions and two World Wars have profoundly changed the whole structure of industrial South Wales. I find it hard to accept that, today, not a single ton of coal is mined through the whole length of the Rhondda. At Blaenavon, they have even turned a pit into a tourist attraction. The small tinplate works, which were once so busy in every little township around Swansea and Llanelli, have all been swallowed up by the giant steel and strip mill complex of Port Talbot, with its apanages of Trostre and Velindre. In common with every other industrial area in Britain, South Wales has turned to new industries to meet the challenge of the future. A second Severn Bridge has now been approved, which will bring South Wales in closer touch with world markets. A giant barrage across the Severn has also been proposed, to harness the swift-flowing tides of the Bristol Channel. If the scheme is carried out, it will alter the whole Welsh side of the Severn estuary, from Penarth to Chepstow.

The changes in rural South and Mid Wales may not be quite as obvious on the surface. The landscape retains its charm. The pattern of small fields on the hillsides has not been destroyed – as in East Anglia – by ripping up the hedges to create vast prairies growing unwanted wheat. The sheep are still in possession of much of the moorlands. True, there are some innovations which I find it hard to accept. Parts of the coast have not escaped the caravan blight, and the Forestry Commission has covered the high ground with too many conifers for my liking. I must admit, however, that the Commission has mended its ways and is now managing its plantations in Wales with a more sensitive eye on the landscape; and, at the same time, the South Wales coast has been better protected in recent years. South and Mid Wales still remain the delightful surprise packets of British tourism.

The social changes may lie below the surface, but they have been equally profound. The chapel has tended to lose its place as the undisputed centre of social life in the villages. The car, radio and television have, between them, severely dented the authority of the pulpit. Even the teetotal Welsh Sunday has disappeared over most of the country. There are still a few TT strongholds left in parts of north-west and mid-west Wales, but even they may disappear when the next referendum comes round. The Welsh language is also under pressure, but there has been a sustained and increasingly successful effort to support and restore it. Everyone who loves Wales will surely wish the language well, Wales without Welsh seems inconceivable.

Does all this mean that South Wales is losing its distinctive character – is it slowly being merged into the mass-produced, standardized society that has taken over so much of urban Britain in recent times? Happily I can report that, as I looked again at South and Mid Wales in preparation for this guide, I could still see, under all the modern developments and so-called improvements, the warm-hearted, distinctive country of my youth. It awaits your exploration and you will not be disappointed.

The Big Pit Museum, Blaenavon, Gwent, see p. 163

The Face of the Land

Our guide covers the six counties of South and Mid Wales – Gwent, South, Mid, and West Glamorgan, Dyfed and Powys. To the visitor, travelling through the Principality for the first time, South Wales comes as an unexpected and delightful surprise, while Mid Wales is still an unspoiled and undiscovered country as far as the average tourist is concerned.

Maybe this is because South Wales has inherited a totally misleading image from its industrial past. In some quarters it still presents a picture of a landscape scarred by coalmines and blackened by the smoke of steelworks. Industrial Wales is still there, of course, and is vital to the wellbeing of the nation, but it covers barely a third of the country. The rest is a rich amalgam of fertile farmlands set in green valleys, backed by lonely mountains and ringed, in the West, by an incomparable coastline. The valleys of the Wye, the Usk, the Tywi and the Teifi can hold their own for pastoral beauty with the finest in Britain, while the high hills of the Brecon Beacons rise to nearly 3000 ft. There are comparatively uncrowded and unpublicized sites to explore. Is there a more astonishing castle than Carreg Cennen near Llandeilo, perched on its limestone crag like an illumination from a medieval manuscript? Where will you find such a necklace of elegant waterfalls to rival the white cascades that adorn the upper Neath valley?

If South Wales has its surprises, Mid Wales is a land of consoling peace. You can still lose the hurry of the modern world in the lonely wilderness of Plynlimon or among the hidden, wooded waterways of northern Powys. Naturally our area has all the impedimenta of contemporary 'development', from motorways and caravan parks to the bungaloid growth around the larger towns. But we can be surprised and thankful that so much remains unspoiled.

The whole landscape is sterner and more varied than its carefully tended counterpart in southern England. The key to the character of a countryside lies in the rocks out of which it has been fashioned through the long, slow passage of time. The chalk, clays and Oolitic limestones of southern England were laid down in comparatively undisturbed layers and inspire the celebrated garden-like quality of the landscape that we admire in the paintings of Gainsborough and Constable. The rocks of South and Mid Wales are far more contorted and in many areas create a dramatic landscape that has a Turneresque quality.

When they crossed the Welsh border, the early fathers of geology like Murchinson and Sidgwick were quick to seize on the contrast between the brushed and combed farmlands of south-east England and the wild countryside of Wales. They gave the names of the old Celtic tribes of Wales – the Silures and the Ordovices – to the rock systems they were carefully defining for the first time, and they applied the Roman term for Wales, Cambria, to what they felt were among the oldest rocks of all. Thus the terms of Cambrian, Ordovician and Silurian entered the language of international geology. South Wales can show older rocks than the Cambrian of the early pioneers. There are strata near St David's that are pre-Cambrian and geologists have

The Usk Valley, near Abergavenny, Gwent, see p. 170

estimated that these rocks took the almost unimaginable age of 4000 million years to form. Serious scientists will smile at the suggestion but the very age of these ancient rocks seems to give a strange quality of romantic remoteness to the magical landscape of this corner of north Pembrokeshire, the Land's End of Wales, with its tempestuous coastline and rocky outcrops that look like miniature mountains.

Geological magic is even more necessary when we come to Mid Wales. The grey, unfertile slates and shales of the Ordovician and Silurian periods that underlie the wide moorlands and lonely, rounded summits of the Plynlimon range, invest them with a special quality of isolation from our sophisticated world. No wonder that this is the most sparsely inhabited part of the whole Principality. The main roads are still compelled to make a wide circuit around it. This Plynlimon wilderness proved an impassable barrier in the railway age. Optimistic promoters once sought to link industrial Lancashire with the splendid but under-used harbour of Milford Haven. The whole scheme foundered in the wild mountains of Mid Wales, leaving a small completed section along the easier levels of the Teifi valley to bear, for many years, the splendid but totally misleading title of the Manchester and Milford.

This central knot of intractable mountains has had an important effect on the history of Wales and on the character of its people. It made communication between North and South Wales difficult and time consuming. Thus, although they have a common language, a North Walian can feel as different from a South Walian as a Yorkshireman does from a Man of Kent. Part of the wilderness has been somewhat tamed in our own day by the spread of forestry and the construction of huge reservoirs like Llyn Brianne and Llyn Clywedog, but the sheep is still king over wide stretches of undisturbed moorland. The power of Plynlimon to divide north and south continues in our modern age.

There is a second barrier across South Wales but, curiously enough, it has always lacked the divisive power of Plynlimon. This is the impressive escarpment of Old Red Sandstone rocks that stretches for over 50 miles, from the valley of the Tywi to the valley of the Wye. The summits are all over the 2000-ft mark, beginning with the Black Mountain behind Llangadog, continuing with the Carmarthenshire Fans and on to the Brecon Beacons. The great escarpment ends with the Black Mountains of Monmouthshire, now in Gwent, that look out over the English plains on the very border. The Old Red Sandstone really does live up to its name, as you can see when the farmers plough the fields at the foot of the mountains. The Usk cuts through this long line of high hills just south of Abergavenny; the town is surrounded by summits with intriguing names like the Blorenge, the Sugar Loaf and the Skirrid and it lives up to its popular title of the Gateway to Wales, although the border lies many miles to the east.

Every part of the range has its own characteristics. The Black Mountain looks fiercely dark under storm clouds, while the Carmarthenshire Fans hold two fascinating lakes under their layered red cliffs. The Brecon Beacons have the highest summits of the escarpment with Pen-y-Fan reaching 2907 ft. Somehow this does not seem an impressive height when you look it up on the new Ordnance Survey map and see it marked as 886 metres high!

But no matter how you measure them, these hills remain a challenge to the mountain walker. The summits are not difficult to reach in summer weather and the

Previous page: The wilds of Plynlimon, see p. 161

rewards are great – almost the whole of South Wales is spread at the climber's feet and the view extends from Exmoor in Somerset to the summit cairn of Cader Idris in Gwynedd. Winter is another matter. Under snow the Brecon Beacons and the cliffs of the Carmarthenshire Fans become serious mountaineering expeditions. This great Old Red Sandstone range is South Wales's equivalent of Snowdonia.

The cliffs, lakes and steeper slopes are all on the north face of the escarpment. On the southern side, the hills fall more gently to meet the first rocks of the coal measures. Surprisingly to the layman, the first strata that geologists classify as belonging to the dark Carboniferous system are composed of that clean, glittering and most attractive of rocks, limestone. The limestone underlies all the coal measures and thus outcrops on both the northern and southern edges of the coalfield. The northern outcrop, in particular, makes a dramatic contrast to the sombre mining valleys, and this contrast is seen at its best in the top end of the Tawe valley. The Tawe runs up from Swansea to its source under the summit of the Carmarthenshire Fans. For most of its course it cuts through the coalfield, and although the mines have now closed, the overgrown tips and straggling mining villages are still there. Beyond Abercrave the valley takes a sharp turn and all traces of industry disappear. The limestone cliffs look down on the clear, unsullied Tawe running through the woodlands with the high summits of the Old Red Sandstone in the background.

The great Victorian 'diva', the singer Adelina Patti, once lived here, in the Tawe Valley. In 1878 she was at the height of her fame and could command a fee of £1000 a night at the New York opera: an enormous sum even for these days. But although she had triumphed on the stage, she had been unlucky in love. She, and her new lover, the tenor Signor Nicolini, needed a refuge from the prying eyes of the world. Patti built a baronial castle at Craig-y-Nos, the Crag of Night, and here she settled down to happiness after her marriage to Nicolini, who had become a keen trout fisherman. The castle is still there, together with the small private opera house Patti built, complete with a painted curtain showing her in a chariot in her favourite role in Rossini's 'Semiramide'. The Queen of Song became the Queen of Swansea as well.

The whole area is riddled with caves. The Dan-yr-Ogof caverns at Craig-y-Nos are open to the public and rival those of Cheddar with their stalactites and underground lakes. Indeed the whole of the limestone outcrop along the northern edge of the coalfield has become classic caving country, with huge underground systems that are still being explored. This exploration, however, is for experts only.

The scene changes dramatically when you leave the limestone and turn south. You enter the darker, underground world of the coal measures – those rocks that have left their indelible stamp, not just on the coalfield but on the whole of South Wales. The mining valleys thrust up into the hills like the probing fingers of a grimy hand. They are astonishingly deep-cut and close together. They are choked with terraced houses and dominated by the tall winding gear of the pit shafts. This must be the most surprising industrial landscape in Britain and once held three-quarters of the population of the whole of Wales. At the end of the 18th century, at the time of the Industrial Revolution, the peasants began to flock in from the country to the settlements that were growing up along the northern outcrop of the coal seams. Here, on the bleak moorlands, deposits of iron ore are found in conjunction with the coal and the iron masters established their works at Aberdare, Hirwaun, Dowlais and Merthyr Tydfil and there was a time when Merthyr was the fastest growing town in the world. The old miners gave the picturesque name of the Farewell Rock to the

Above: The Carmarthenshire Fans, from near Llandeusant, see p. 96

lowest layer of the coal measures immediately above the limestone. Once they hit it, they knew that it was no use driving their shaft any deeper.

Alas, the ironworks have long since disappeared and even the coalmines are now saying 'farewell' to the land where they once nurtured a strange, unique yet vigorous community life. The coalfield reaches its widest extent in Gwent and the three Glamorgan counties, but it also stretches westwards, getting narrower and lower as it goes. The coal measures dip under the sea in the wide estuaries of Carmarthen Bay to re-emerge in Pembrokeshire, now in Dyfed. The character of the coal alters as it goes towards the west. The steam coal changes into the harder, more compact anthracite – so compact that you can pick up some of it without getting dirt on your hands and even polish it into ornaments. The coal measures finally disappear under the waters of the Irish Sea at Broad Haven and Little Haven on the far west coast of Dyfed, where the seams of the wide coalfield have become squeezed into a few square miles of cliffs, looking down on sandy beaches crowded with holidaymakers in summer. A curious contrast to the deep and once smoky valleys of Rhondda Fawr and Rhondda Fach nearly 70 miles away to the east.

The younger Triassic and Liassic rocks stand next in age to the Carboniferous coal measures. They are represented in South Wales in one area only – the Vale of Glamorgan to the west of Cardiff and bounded by the Bristol Channel. The Vale has much in common with the landscape of Somerset just south across the water. It is a pleasant, fertile and rolling landscape – comparatively low lying and reminding us that, in spite of so many popular Welsh songs, not every part of the land is mountainous. The low-lying Vale offered an easy pathway to invaders and both the Romans and the Normans marched this way to conquest: the geology of the region once again influencing the course of history.

The younger rocks, like the chalk that covers so much of south-east England, are all missing from South Wales, but there remained one final, powerful force that

Opposite: The Brecon Beacons, Powys, looking east from Pen-y-Fan, see p. 81 (Martin Dohrn)

shaped the face of the countryside – ice. About a million years ago, the climate of Europe started to deteriorate and grow steadily colder. Glaciers formed on the high ground of the Radnor Forest, Plynlimon and the peaks of the Great Escarpment and poured remorselessly down on to the lower ground, grinding the face of the earth as they moved. Moving ice possesses astonishing power. The glaciers deepened the valleys and cut their slopes to create a characteristic U-shaped profile. The ice continued to accumulate until the whole of Wales was buried in its chill and deadly shroud. The ice also formed on the high summits of western Scotland, Cumbria and on the Irish mountains. These glaciers poured into the Irish Sea to combine into the greatest and most powerful ice sheet of them all – so powerful, indeed, that it was able to override Pembrokeshire and cross the Preseli Hills to push far eastwards along the line of the Bristol Channel, penning back the local glaciers to the valley mouths as it went. Thus you can walk on the beaches of the Gower Peninsula and pick up rounded stones that have been carried from the far distant Ailsa Craig in the Firth of Clyde in Scotland.

Through the long years of the Ice Age, the glaciers ebbed and flowed but, in the end, there was not a single corner of the land that had not felt the transforming power of the ice. You can stand on the summit of Carn Ingli in the Preseli Hills today, and as you look down on the pattern of fertile fields and the cliffs of the coastline warm in the summer weather, you can feel a slight cold shudder when you picture the scene as it was, say, 20,000 years ago with the chill wind blowing off cliffs of ice that were over 1000 ft high.

Ten thousand years ago the first glaciers were finally melting in the high hills, after carving out deep, cliff-lined hollows called in Welsh *cwms*, where small lakes formed behind the abandoned moraines. The melting ice left behind it a savage landscape, plastered with the boulder clay ground from the scarred rocks and with the river courses diverted by the glacial debris into new courses across the original lie of the land.

Slowly its green mantle returned to the bruised earth. The climate became warmer – so much so that the woods of mountain oak, alder, birch and hazel eventually clothed the highest mountain tops. When the climate once again deteriorated, this vegetation decayed to form the wide deposits of peat that cover much of the high ground of South Wales. The level of the sea also changed and the roots of old woodlands, the so-called submerged forests, can be seen in the sands of Swansea Bay and in places along the coast of Dyfed. By this time, our remote ancestors, the earliest hunters, had appeared on the scene, following the vast herds of game that occupied the tundras finally freed from the ice. They have left traces of their presence in the caves of the Gower coast. But the sea, in the course of time, covered their hunting grounds.

We have now reached the point, roughly 4000 years ago, when the face of South Wales had taken the form that, in general outline, we can recognize today. Modern man has since stamped it with his factories, roads, railways and ever-expanding towns, but beneath this contemporary dress lies the old landscape of mountains, lowlands and coastline that have not been structurally altered since the land recovered from the onslaught of the ice. Of these three elements that compose the countryside, the coastline is probably the least altered. Over the centuries ports, breakwaters and dykes have been constructed on an ever-increasing scale. In our own day proposals have been put forward for a huge barrage across the upper section of the Bristol Channel that would harness the fierce tides for electricity. Next to the

Bay of Fundy in North America, the Bristol Channel has the highest tides in the world. But, for the moment, the general outline of the South Wales coast is unaltered.

That coastline is very varied, including every sort of coastal formation from high cliffs to wide, sandy estuaries. The first section, from the Severn Bridge to Cardiff, is a surprise for here is the last type of coastline you would expect to find in Wales. It is a miniature fenland, complete with a hinterland of drainage channels and protected from the waters by a high impressive dyke. The area is below sea level and, as a result, suffered disastrous flooding in Elizabethan days. The drowning of the Wentloog Levels was lamented in many a pathetic ballad, and you can still see the highest level of the invading sea marked on the church towers.

From Cardiff westwards, the Triassic rocks of the Vale of Glamorgan form low, layered cliffs, but at Porthcawl the sand dunes begin and to the west the Kenfig Burrows form a wilderness of sand that, between the 14th and 15th centuries, buried the old town of Kenfig. Industry takes over at Port Talbot, where the dunes are backed by the giant steelworks, and, in effect, industrial development and port installations dominate the scene to Swansea, where the white headland of the Mumbles announces the beginning of the Gower Peninsula, with its splendid sequence of sandy bays backed by bright limestone cliffs – an unexpected surprise packet, indeed, to find in what, after all, is marked on the map as part of the coalfield. Carmarthen Bay is the land of the wide estuaries with winding river courses through vast sandbanks, rich in cockles and alive with great flights of wading birds. The poet, Dylan Thomas, looked out over it from his boathouse at Laugharne and christened it his 'heron priested shore'.

The limestone returns in south Dyfed in a coastline that rivals that of Gower in its sequence of shining cliffs and golden sands. The line is broken by the great winding fiord of Milford Haven, which stretches far inland and offers one of the finest and most neglected harbours in Britain. The wide sweep of St Bride's Bay marks the point where the coast looks directly westwards to the open Atlantic. Offshore lie the small and bird-haunted islands that are the glory of this part of the coast and which have already given a foretaste of their charm at Caldey, near Tenby. Skokholm, Skomer and Grassholm are the bird islands and Ramsey is the paradise of seals. Furthest out of all is the lonely rock crowned with the Smalls lighthouse.

The highest cliffs in South Wales come in the wild section that runs from the ancient rocks of St David's Head, past Fishguard to the mouth of the Teifi. Cemaes Head touches the 600 ft mark.

The final section of the South and Mid Wales coastline runs from Cardigan town and the estuary of the Teifi to the estuary of the Dyfi (Dovey), beyond the elegant coastal resort and university town of Aberystwyth. The cliffs are mainly composed of slates and shales but there are sandy beaches at Llangranog and delightful little harbours at New Quay and Aberaeron. Modern planners have decided that our part of the coast should have its boundary along the Dyfi as it winds out over its sandbanks to the sea; and, indeed, as you look across the estuary to the high hills beyond, the countryside already has the feel of mountainous North Wales about it. But before it yields to the north, this section of South and Mid Wales has one final geological

Overleaf: Pwlldyu Head looking across Hunt's Bay, Gower, West Glamorgan, see p. 115
(Martin Dohrn)

curiosity to offer – the great bog of Borth, in Welsh Cors Fochno.

Over the long passage of time, the scouring action of the waves on the cliffs and on the boulder clay left by the glaciers has led to the formation of constantly growing spits of debris at the mouths of the estuaries of Cardigan Bay. Behind these embankments, the sediments brought down by the rivers have accumulated to form boglands, where the acid and peaty soil has defied the most enterprising agriculturalist. Cors Fochno, however boldly it may defy the farmer, gives a compensating delight to the naturalist and birdwatcher. A similar area of untamed bog lies just north of Tregaron in the upper valley of the Teifi. Here an old glacial moraine has dammed the river to form Cors Caron, another splendid bird-haunted boggy wilderness. How refreshing it is to find these free and beautiful sanctuaries in Wales, where the birds and the animals seem more at home than humans.

Wild life, together with the trees that shelter it and the vegetation that nurtures it, is a vital component of the Face of the Land: as vital as the rocks that underlie it and the coast that encircles it. In our own time, important changes have taken place throughout Britain in our farming methods which have not always been helpful to our flora and fauna. Above all, forestry has spread on a big scale in Wales and changed the appearance of the landscape over wide areas. The lonely moorlands between the Tywi and the Teifi used to be known as the Green Desert of Wales, the undisputed realm of the sheep farmer; but now, seemingly endless plantations of fir trees have replaced the sheep, and many of the farms, inhabited through long centuries, are abandoned and falling into ruin. Forestry has also spread further north and the solid phalanx of fir trees has advanced from the Clywedog valley almost to the summit ridge of Plynlimon. In Gwent and the Glamorgans, the high ground between the narrow mining valleys – once the breathing space for the pent-up population in summer and the open ground where the miners trained their whippets – is buried deep under conifers, and these monotonous growths have invaded parts of the Great Escarpment and buried the northern slopes of the Radnor Forest.

The very title of forest is a misnomer in some parts of the South Wales hills. The map marks the long ridge of the Great Escarpment between the Carmarthen Fans and the Brecon Beacons as the Fforest Fawr, the Great Forest, but this has always been open moorland. The term 'forest', in the Middle Ages, indicated a royal or princely hunting ground.

This spread of forestry has been strongly opposed by conservationists who fear its effects on wild life and on the fishing in lakes and rivers as well as on the appearance of the countryside. But the existing forests are here to stay, even if a limit is eventually placed on their expansion. The Forestry Commission may have been somewhat ruthless in its planting in the early days in South Wales but it now pays more attention to the deciduous trees that are the natural, historic cover of the ground and has adopted a more enlightened policy on public access to its plantations.

The conservationists have also been concerned with the effect of fir plantations on wild life, but the South Wales countryside still harbours a rich variety of birds and mammals. There have been many changes over the centuries and the bigger animals have died out. The bear was certainly present in the Roman period, but seems to have departed soon after the legions left. The red deer was hunted by the native princes but there is no mention of it after the end of the Middle Ages. The famous Welsh chronicler Geraldus Cambrensis has left us a vivid description of the beavers on the banks of the Teifi in the 12th century but they, too, followed the red deer into the darkness. The last wolf in Wales was claimed to have been killed near Abergwesyn in Mid Wales in Tudor times.

A whole range of smaller animals, however, still remains to delight us, from the badger and the fox to the polecat, which finds a refuge in the forests. Rare birds include the Cornish chough, the red-legged member of the crow family, which has almost disappeared from its native county but has found a new, safer home on Ramsey Island and the adjacent coastline. Even rarer is that magnificent bird, the red kite, with its forked tail and soaring, thrilling flight. Only a few years ago its numbers had been reduced to a few pairs, breeding precariously in a lost valley near the headwaters of the River Tywi in the Green Desert of central Wales. The red kite seemed destined for oblivion in the hands of those pestiferous spoilers of our natural heritage, the egg collectors. This noble bird was saved, however, by a remarkable community effort involving the whole countryside. The inhabitants of the valley – from the schoolchildren to the sheep farmers – formed themselves into a voluntary Watch Committee. Every suspicious stranger was immediately reported and the secret nesting sites watched day and night. The battle to save the kite was won and the birds have now spread into neighbouring valleys. Long may the red kite soar over the windswept moorlands in this still lonely landscape.

There are other areas of the South and Mid Wales countryside where conservationists hope that our natural heritage may be protected. The Brecon Beacons National Park includes most of the Great Escarpment, while the Pembrokeshire National Park protects the incomparable coastline and the romantic Preseli Hills. Gower has long been designated as an Area of Outstanding Natural Beauty, while there are numerous nature reserves in places like the Tregaron Bog, the Oxwich marshes and part of Llangorse Lake. No one can be certain about what the future may bring. We can only hope that we shall be able to hand on the Face of Wales unblemished to future generations.

Llangorse lake, Powys, with the Black Mountains of Gwent behind, see p. 133

The Princes of Wales

In the summer of 1969, with all due ceremony in the noble setting of historic Caernarfon Castle, Prince Charles was invested with the honour of Prince of Wales. The Queen had already taken the occasion of the Commonwealth Games at Cardiff in 1958 to announce that she had granted him the title and the ceremony at Caernarfon was the formal, public presentation of the Prince to the people of Wales. It was a splendid occasion, when the Prince swore fealty to Her Majesty and then came out to the balcony on the Queen Eleanor's Gate to receive the cheers of the crowd. On the face of it, this was a traditional ceremony, following long-established precedents, but, in truth, it was a modern re-creation of an almost forgotten past.

The Investiture had been first suggested in 1910 by the Bishop of St Asaph's and had found a quick response in the fertile mind of Lloyd George. He convinced King George V that the man who bore the title of Prince of Wales ought to assume it in Wales itself. No public ceremony had attended George V and Edward VII when they, in their turn, had become Princes of Wales. King George V willingly agreed and the Investitute of 1911 was a glittering occasion, enjoyed by all concerned except perhaps Prince Edward, who was embarrassed by being dressed in what he described afterwards as a 'preposterous rig'. The guests were blissfully ignorant of the anxieties of the principal actor in that memorable scene. There may have been some disapproving voices in the Investiture of 1969 but there were none in 1911. This investiture seemed to be the apotheosis of that confident, successful Edwardian Wales. And who could then foretell the future?

The organizers had got the past wrong for they based their claim to hold the ceremony at Caernarfon Castle on the celebrated story of Edward I presenting his infant son to the conquered Welsh. Edward, after defeating the last Welsh Prince of Wales, Llywelyn, gathered the dejected Welsh barons together at Caernarfon and, to gain their allegiance, promised them a new prince to replace the dead Llywelyn – and one who could not speak a word of the hated English tongue. Whereupon he produced his infant son, Edward, who had just been born in the castle and most certainly could not speak a word of English – or any other language for that matter!

Alas, this pretty fable will not stand up to the harsh scrutiny of the professional historians. Caernarfon Castle was certainly being built in 1282 as part of the iron ring of castles that Edward was throwing around Snowdonia to hold down the still restive Welsh, and his queen, Eleanor of Castile, gave birth to a son there, in temporary apartments behind the still unfinished circuit of the walls. That son became known as Edward of Caernarfon but there is no evidence that Edward I was in residence in the castle at the time of the birth. Young Edward was not invested with the honour of the Principality of Wales until 1301. He was then at the mature age of 19 and the ceremony took place at Lincoln not Caernarfon. Furthermore, Edward was not the eldest son. This was Prince Alphonso, who presented the trophies of his father's Welsh campaign to the Church at Westminster Abbey. But in 1284, Alphonso

The investiture of H.R.H. Prince Charles as Prince of Wales, Caernarfon Castle, 1969
(Camera Press, London)

The investiture of 1911 with George V, Queen Mary and Prince Edward later Duke of Windsor
(Syndication International)

suddenly died and Edward of Caernarfon took his place as heir to the throne. It was a near-run thing but Wales nearly had an Alphonso as its first Prince – a thought that almost persuades you to believe the old story of Edward I presenting his infant son to the unhappy Welsh barons, although this yarn did not appear in print until Tudor times, in such somewhat fanciful volumes as Dr David Powell's *Historie of Cambria*.

Poor Llywelyn was consigned to slow oblivion. His own bards had lamented him in one of the most moving poems in the Welsh language:

> O God! that the sea may engulf the land.
> Why are we left to long-drawn weariness?

Thereafter, the first and last native Welsh Prince of Wales faded from history. Owain Glyndwr outshone him in the memory of the nation, and it was left to Thomas Gray, the forerunner of the Romantic movement in the mid-18th century, to put in a good word for the fallen hero and pronounce a resounding curse on his ruthless supplanter, Edward I. In his poem 'The Bard' Gray pictures a hoary-headed minstrel, perched on a crag which 'frowned o'er old Conway's foaming flood', who thundered:

> Ruin seize thee, ruthless king!
> Confusion on thy banners wait!

After his multi-versed prophecy the old bard obligingly plunged to his death in the Conwy. In our own day, Welsh nationalists have turned again to Llywelyn. Ceremonies have been held in his honour at the memorial at Cilmery outside Builth, near the spot where he was slain. They certainly approved of the prophecy of Gray's bard that confusion waited for Edward. His son, the first English Prince of Wales, proved a disaster as a king. He was defeated by the Scots at Bannockburn, and, as he was a homosexual, eventually incurred the fury of his wife, Isabella, a regular 'she-wolf of France'. She with her lover the Marcher lord, Roger Mortimer, led the final revolt against her unhappy husband. Edward fled to South Wales but was captured near Tonyrefail in Mid Glamorgan, in a little valley still known as Pant y Brad, meaning the Dingle of Treachery. He was dragged off to his shameful death in Berkeley Castle, but in his flight through South Wales he had scattered his treasure and even his records. A hoard of his coins was recently dug up at Neath Abbey and, strangest survival of all, his marriage contract with Isabella was found hidden in the thatched roof of a farm in Gower. It is now in the museum at Swansea.

The only ray of kindness shed on the whole sad story comes from the Wakefield chronicler who recorded, 'Where the Scots would rebel against him and all England would rid herself of him, the Welsh in a wonderful manner cherished and esteemed him, and as far as they were able stood by him . . . composing mournful songs to him in the language of their country.' Perhaps there may be some truth, after all, in that old story that Edward I gained the allegiance of the Welsh by presenting his infant son to them at Caernarfon.

There have been twenty-one Princes of Wales since Edward of Caernarfon, if we ignore the unfortunate Llywelyn, and they present an extraordinary variety of characters, Warriors, statesmen, frustrated artists and spectacular sinners all have their place in the roll call. Their fates were extraordinarily varied as well. Some, like the eldest sons of Henry VII and James I, died as Princes of Wales and were never crowned king. Others, like the Prince Regent and Edward VII, waited an intolerable time in the wings before stepping on to the centre of the stage. Princes of Wales have been slaughtered on the battlefield, secretly murdered and ruthlessly removed from their inheritance. Many were married against their will. All, from their birth, were bound to be pawns in the great game of politics. The larger part of their story belongs to the wider history of Britain but it is intriguing to note how many of them worked in, or even visited, the country from which they took their title.

Edward of Woodstock, better known to history as the Black Prince, was the next royal son to receive the honour after Edward of Caernarfon. There is no record that he ever visited his Principality, although he valued it as a fruitful source of soldiers. Welsh archers played a big part in his great victory at Poitiers. He did, however, have a rival claimant to his title in the person of Owain Llawgoch, who was the last of the line of Gwynedd and the grandson of Llywelyn the Last's younger brother. The French knew him as Yvain de Galles and he built up a great military reputation on

Above: A nineteenth-century interpretation of the Princes in the Tower, 1483, by P. Delaroche
(Wallace Collection, London)

their side. He was murdered before he could effectively press his claim.

Henry V had an even more formidable rival when he was Prince of Wales, for Owain Glyndwr had been formally recognized as the true prince by the kings of France, Scotland and Castile. Henry was the prince who had to fight hardest for his own inheritance. After him there was no further claimant of Welsh origin to dispute the title, but there was trouble enough for Princes of Wales in England itself. The Wars of the Roses began, largely due to the weak government of the saintly but incompetent Henry VI, and it was left to his fiery wife, Margaret of Anjou, to fight like a tigress for the rights of her son Edward. Of all the Princes of Wales, he had the most troubled and tragic tenure of the office. When he was a mere child he had been forced to fly for refuge to Wales after the Lancastrian defeat at Northampton in 1459. At Malpas, near the Welsh border south of Wrexham, the little party of royal refugees fell into the hands of a band of robbers, and they were only saved by Margaret's impassioned plea to the youngest of the robbers, 'Save the son of your king.' The robber was moved by her entreaty and succeeded in getting her and the

Opposite: Prince Henry, son of James I as Prince of Wales, c. 1610, by R. Peake
(National Portrait Gallery, London)

Prince away in secret to take refuge in Harlech Castle. Poor Edward did not survive to inherit the throne. He was killed at Tewkesbury in 1471.

Soon there was more blood to stain the princely tapestry. On the death of Edward IV his son, another Edward, was in residence at Ludlow, where, as Prince of Wales, he was presiding over the newly formed Council of Wales and the Marches. Richard, the brother of Edward IV, is supposed to have kidnapped him and his younger brother as they were being brought up to London for the coronation. They disappeared into the Tower of London and never emerged.

Richard, now Richard III, hastened to make his own son, Edward of Middleham, Prince of Wales. The boy was invested with the title in an elaborate ceremony at York Minster. In the letters patent, the king praised his son for 'the singular wit and endowments of nature wherewith, his young age considered, he is remarkably furnished'. We are reminded of another Prince of Wales, only a year before, who was equally well endowed. Edward of Middleham is a wraithlike figure in the procession of the Princes of Wales. In April 1484, he suddenly died, to the intense grief of his father.

The year 1485 is a date that everybody knows – or at least every Welshman. Henry Tudor defeated Richard III at the battle of Bosworth; and he lost no time in strengthening his somewhat shaky claim to the throne by marrying Elizabeth of York, daughter of Edward IV, within four months of his victory. In September 1486 their eldest son was born, named Arthur as a gesture to his Welsh supporters. As soon as possible, Henry made him Prince of Wales. There was a splendid ceremony in which the young man came in procession down the Thames to Westminster, and Garter King-of-arms floridly compared his arrival by barge to the return of King Arthur from the island of Avalon. He was married to Catherine of Aragon and the young couple went to Ludlow where Arthur would gain experience in the business of government as head, or nominal head, of the Council for Wales and the Marches. But he soon fell ill and died.

Henry VII, however, was noted for his tightness in money matters. Arthur's death might involve the king returning Catherine's dowry. He solved the problem by calming his grief and marrying Catherine off to Arthur's younger brother, Henry. He saved more money by forgoing any ceremony and making Henry Prince of Wales by letters patent. There were no further Princes of Wales for over a hundred years. Henry's daughters were occasionally addressed as Princesses of Wales but this was mere court flattery. Henry never issued letters patent, and in that predominantly male society it is inconceivable that he could ever have done so. He probably felt his sickly son Edward was too young to go through the ceremony. The Tudors, who owed their first steps on fortune's ladder to a successful love affair, proved singularly impotent when it came to providing male heirs to the throne.

The Stuarts did better. James I made his eldest son Prince of Wales when he reached the age of 16. Henry, a lad of great promise, unfortunately died, and once again a younger brother was promoted to the honour. There is no record of either Henry or Charles visiting Wales when they held the title, although after he had ascended the throne Charles was glad enough to turn to the Principality for help in his war with Parliament. He brought his son, young Charles, to Raglan where he left him in the care of the Earl of Worcester. Here young Charles gave early proof of that tact and skill in charming men that distinguished him as Charles II. The local gentry had poured out their gold and silver for the royal cause in the Civil War and the humbler farmers had brought their gifts of cattle and poultry. The young prince was greatly moved and made his first recorded speech: 'Gentlemen, I have heard formerly of the true affection and meanings of the ancient Brittainies – but my kind entertainment hath made me confide in your love, which I shall always remember . . . You may be sure of that, and of my favour as long as I am Prince of Wales.'

Charles II had no heir and he was succeeded by his brother, the unpopular and Catholic Duke of York who became James II. The crisis of his short reign came when his wife, Mary of Modena, unexpectedly produced a son and heir, a future Prince of Wales. The Protestant nation was profoundly alarmed. Was a Catholic line now to occupy the British throne permanently? Wales had a curious connection with this complicated business. In her anxiety to produce the long hoped-for Catholic heir, Mary made a pilgrimage to the shrine of St Winifred's at Holywell in North Wales. The saint did not bring much luck, for when the infant eventually arrived, the Protestants declared that he had been smuggled into the royal bed in a warming pan. The poor child was swiftly carried into exile in France with his parents. With the childless William of Orange and Mary jointly occupying the throne, the only person who could claim to be a Prince of Wales was in exile. When Queen Anne succeeded she and her husband produced children at regular intervals but not one survived long enough to be made Prince.

The Hanoverian princes were singularly unattractive and were not remotely interested in Wales. The only one who ever came near the place was the Prince Regent, 'Prinny', afterwards George IV. He once rode over the border near Welshpool to be greeted by the assembled gentry of Montgomeryshire. He drank a toast and departed hurriedly back to the more congenial social scene at Brighton. The Prince's Oak still stands at the side of the road to prove that the Prince set foot in his own Principality.

In the Victorian age, the Princes of Wales paid more attention to duty. Edward VII, as prince, may not have been exactly a model of propriety, but he never shirked the now-obligatory royal round of hand-shaking, public appearances and ceremonial openings. George V and the Duke of Windsor followed the same course.

The present Prince of Wales has brought far more than a sense of duty to his office. Of all the Princes of Wales, he is the one who has striven hardest to identify himself with the ordinary life of Wales. He spent a term at Aberystwyth University College, and while he would not claim to have mastered the language, he learned enough, and his pronunciation was good enough, for him to make a public speech at the Urdd Eisteddfod. It surprised and delighted everyone present. He must be the only member of the royal family ever to accomplish this linguistic feat. If any man can match the ancient office of Prince of Wales with the increasing and testing demands of the modern world, it is surely Prince Charles.

In these days of equality for women, can a woman become Princess of Wales in her own right? In the old French monarchy the Salic law prohibited the accession of a female to the throne but no such rule has ever existed in Britain. The honour is in the absolute gift of the sovereign and, in theory, he or she can give it to anyone. Queen Victoria's first child was a daughter, Victoria, but it never occurred to her or the Prince Consort to make her Princess of Wales. Instead the princess married the heir to the German throne and became the mother of Kaiser William II. But times are changing. Who knows what will happen in the future? At the moment the only way a woman can become Princess of Wales is to follow the happy example of Lady Diana Spencer and marry the most successful Prince of Wales in modern history.

The Pembrokeshire Coast Path

The Pembrokeshire Coast Path in Dyfed ranks with the finest of those public trackways through the choicest scenery of Britain that are our most imaginative legacy from the transient idealism of the immediate post-Second World War years. The route was first prospected by the distinguished naturalist, R. M. Lockley, as far back as 1951 and was finally officially opened in 1970 after many years of patient and complicated negotiations over points of access and rights of way. Wales has no equivalent to the Pennine Way through the mountains from north to south, and Offa's Dyke Path, as it passes through South Wales, lies mainly on the English side of the Wye until it reaches Mid Wales. But the Pembrokeshire Coast Path is one of the glories of the walker's Wales. The track keeps as close as possible to the cliff edge or the seashore. There are a few diversions from the coast, especially around the wide inlet of Milford Haven and through the small coastal towns of Fishguard and Tenby. The army still has its tank firing range at Linney Head which prohibits access at certain notified times. But by far the greatest part of the path goes through lonely coastland, alive with the clamour of sea birds and with great views out over a wild, island-studded sea. Thus the walker who tackles the whole length of the path gains an unforgettable experience. It is also possible to walk selected sections of it, for there are convenient access points along the way.

The track surface is not hard to negotiate and anyone used to mountain walking will find no difficulties but it is not suitable for young children and elderly people. The visitor still needs good stout boots or shoes and adequate protection from the vagaries of Welsh weather. The path is well signposted and its official length is 167 miles (269 km). There are, however, many tempting diversions which can greatly, if delightfully, increase the distance covered. No walker will stick firmly to the coast at St David's where the splendid cathedral and the Bishop's Palace are only a few short miles inland. Day trips to the attractive islands of Ramsey and Skomer start from points on the path itself. Accommodation varies from the big hotels at Saundersfoot, Fishguard and Tenby to more modest farmhouse lodgings, and there are, in addition, some Youth Hostels. There are a few stretches where no lodgings are available for some miles but, on the whole, accommodation is not a problem (further information is available from the South Wales Tourism Council, Gloucester Place, Swansea). A glance at the map will show you that the path is far from level; it ascends hills and descends into valleys, some of which are distinctly boggy in places. In the northern section especially, there is plenty of hard up-and-downhill work but experienced hill walkers will take it all in their stride.

The conscientious visitor will also obey the Country Code and remember that, although the path is a public right of way, this does not imply public ownership of the land. The goodwill of the landowners and farmers is essential to the well-being of the path. Small sections are already in the hands of the National Trust.

The attractions of the path vary with the seasons. The sea birds are at the height of their breeding activities in the early summer and in certain places are an astonishing

Plaque commemorating the gift of Ceibwr Bay to the National Trust

St David's Cathedral, see p. 171   *(Martin Dohrn)*

sight, with colonies of guillemots, razorbills and kittiwakes all struggling for space on the narrow cliff ledges. The rare puffins, Manx shearwaters and gannets can be glimpsed occasionally from some sections of the path, while the black-suited cormorants go scudding low across the surface of the sea or perch on the rocks, extending their wings to dry until they look like as many miniature Draculas. To see the rarer sea birds in all their glory, however, you must make a trip to the offshore islands, although the birdwatcher is offered ample compensation without leaving the path. In the northern section he will be unlucky if he does not see the rare Cornish chough or the raven. The buzzard is well re-established now that myxomatosis no longer ravages the rabbit population. Even in winter, the Pembrokeshire coast has its fascinating migrants. The geese fly from the increasing chill of the North to the warmer marshes behind the pebble beaches. Of Pembrokeshire and its bird population, the naturalist John Barrett claims with justice: 'Very few localities in Britain rival the variety and perhaps only the north coast of Norfolk exceeds it.'

The same praise can be given to the flowers of the Pembrokeshire Coast Path. They are seen at their best in spring and early summer, with the golden gorse leading the show on many of the cliff tops. The plants on the exposed sections have to be tough and wind resistant for gusts of over 90 mph have been recorded at St Ann's Head. Of the bigger animals, the fox and badger live along the path but both take care not to be easily seen by the daytime visitor. The seals are bolder and there is a chance of seeing them outside the breeding season at places like Ceibwr Bay. From late August to October the seals are much more in evidence, especially along the coast north of the mouth of Milford Haven to the Teifi estuary. At Strumble Head, if you are lucky, you may hear the haunting, keening sound they make in the caves, but to see the Atlantic grey seal in impressive numbers you must make the trip across the sound to Ramsey Island. Here the beaches and caves are crowded with seals, especially in September, with the white-furred pups lying on the rocks. The young seals, when they reach maturity, can sometimes travel long distances for their fishing. Seals marked on Ramsey have turned up on the Saltee Islands across the Irish Sea, near Wexford; in Cornwall; and, in a few cases, in Brittany.

Seals are not the only animal attraction on Ramsey. Attempts are being made to establish a herd of red deer in the southern section. Perhaps the smallest and most charming animals associated with the path are the tiny Skomer voles which have become so gentle that you can pick them up in your hands. On Cardigan Island there is a herd of Soay sheep which seem as wild as any deer.

Cardigan Island is not strictly part of the Pembrokeshire Coast Path, for it lies on the north side of the Teifi estuary, the starting point of the path, but it is a prominent part of the fine view from the summit of Cemaes Head. This is the first test of a walker's stamina if you are following the path from north to south, for it rises to 600 feet behind the little village of St Dogmaels where most people begin their journey. The cliffs on the headland are remarkable. The Silurian strata at Pen-yr-Afr have been thrown into extraordinary twisted curves. They are also extremely friable and it is well to warn the visitor at the very beginning of his long walk that cliff climbing is for experts only, and the best rocks for the sport are the limestone cliffs in the southern section. The sensible walker will not venture needlessly on exposed and slippery rock faces.

The whole coastline for the next 50 miles between Cemaes Head and St David's is a splendid landscape composition of high cliffs, noble headland, hidden beaches and romantic inlets, broken by strange rock formations like the Witch's Cauldron near Ceibwr, which looks like a miniature Lulworth Cove, connected to the open water by a dark cave. As you tramp south-west along the path, you become aware of the presence of the high Preseli Hills in the background. Between Newport and Fishguard they sweep down to the sea like the Mountains of Mourne in Ireland and create a succession of fine, prow-like heads, all of which touch the 500-foot mark. Dinas Island is one of the finest of them, but the title of island is a misnomer: the headland is firmly connected with the mainland by the now dry channel formed, thousands of years ago, from the force of the melt waters of the giant glacier that occupied the Irish Sea.

There is history a-plenty. The little town of Newport on its sandy estuary has proudly retained its medieval charter in defiance of all modern administrative reshuffling. At Cwm yr Eglwys, the ruined seaman's church of St Brynach is a memorial to the fury of the great gale of 1859. The delightful little yacht-packed harbour of Lower Town in Fishguard was the scene of a daring raid by the privateer Paul Jones in the American War of Independence, when he held the town to ransom. As a result, the local gentry built themselves a private fort on the point, which still contains 18th-century cannon. These old guns only once went into action when they fired a few shots at the French ships which then retired to land their troops at Carreg Wastad for the celebrated Last Invasion of Britain in 1797. The fine circle of Fishguard Bay is now protected by the great breakwater that guards the harbour of Goodwick, from which the ferry boats leave for Rosslare, 54 miles away across the restless western sea to southern Ireland. The path climbs up the steep hill behind the harbour station to emerge on the lonely cliff edge, where a memorial stone marks the spot where the French landed in 1797. As you look down the steep, rocky slopes of

Above: The folded rocks of Pen-yr-Afr, Caemes Head, see pp. 37 and 94

the ironically named Carreg Wastad – meaning the level stone or rock – you wonder how the French ever succeeded in landing at all.

Strumble Head is marked by the fine, white tower of the lighthouse, which presides over a wild, foam-flecked sea when the notorious Strumble race is in full flood against a strong wind. Like Dinas Island the headland faces north and before you leave it, pause for a moment and take a last look in a northerly direction. You may be lucky to be there on one of those rare days of exceptional visibility when, for a few brief hours, the whole world around you can change dramatically. Across the northern horizon the mountains of North Wales appear, marching in impressive and diminishing procession down the long Lleyn Peninsula, from Snowdon itself to the full stop of Bardsey Island. If you follow the horizon still further westwards, another island magically emerges from the sea. This, in reality, is the 3000 ft summit ridge of the Wicklow Hills in Ireland – a vision that might have inspired the old legend of Tir-nan-Og, the island of Eternal Youth lost in the western sea. Alas, the vision is rare and transient but the person who is lucky enough to see it will never forget it.

There are plenty of compensations, however, in the section of the path that leads from Strumble to St David's. The cliff scenery rises to an impressive climax at Pwllderi, one of the few places along the path where the motorist can savour its real, wild character without having to move from his car. The conscientious walker, however, will continue to be rewarded by splendid cliff scenery as he comes down to the cove of Aber Bach. If he arrives at a moment when the sea mists are blowing in he can readily believe the local tradition that, as late as the 1820s, a fisherman caught a mermaid here and brought her back to the nearby farm of Treissyllt. She wriggled back to the sea but not before she had laid a curse on the farm that no child would

Opposite: On Caemes Head (Martin Dohrn)

The beach at Aber Bach, Strumble Head, see pp. 38 and 175

henceforth be born there – a spell happily broken in 1906 when the baby arrived before the doctor or the ambulance.

The track now takes you past the attractive inlets of Abercastle and Porth-gain to the point of St David's Head, guarded by its two impressive rocky outcrops of Penberi and Carnllidi. The character of the rock has now changed. The shales and slates of the Silurian and Ordovician series are left behind and do not reappear along the path, which for short stretches now traverses the ancient Pre-Cambrian formations. The walker has the satisfaction of having some of the oldest rocks in the world under his feet. On the headland of St David's he is also standing on the oldest named feature on the coast of Wales. It appears on the oldest known map of the world – the celebrated map of Ptolemy from the second century BC.

Again the site is worthy of its history. Beyond the wide sands of Whitesand Bay lies Ramsey Island, and still further out, the remarkable scatter of rocks and islets known as the Bishop and the Clerks. South Bishop has a fine lighthouse but these dangerous reefs can still claim their victims. Old George Owen, the Tudor historian who wrote a classic description of the Pembrokeshire of his day, gave an eloquent description of them. 'The Bishop and those his clerks preach deadly doctrine to their winter audience and are commendable in nothing but their good residence!'

St David's is one of the important turning points of the path. Once past Ramsey Island the coast changes direction and opens out into the wide sweep of St Brides Bay. Here the waves come thundering in direct from the Atlantic and a new island vista appears. At the end of the southern arm of the bay, the bird islands of Skokholm and Skomer offer their rare treasures of bird life during the breeding season, including the delightful, parrot-like puffins and the far-travelling Manx shearwaters. Eight miles further out, beyond Skokholm, is Grassholm, the site of one of the largest gannet colonies. In early summer, they rise from their nesting places in a white, swirling cloud of clamouring birds, then plunge like dive bombers into the sea

– one of the most thrilling natural spectacles Britain can offer. Still further out, past the sinister shoals of the Barrels and the Hats, rises the lonely tower of the Smalls lighthouse, crowning the most westerly speck of rock that can call itself part of the land of Wales.

Solva is the biggest village on the northern arm of St Brides Bay. It has become very much a yachting centre and a place of second homes for visitors or retired people, but the restored lime kilns at the head of the winding harbour remind us that, not so very long ago, all the small villages and tiny harbours along the Pembrokeshire coastline were busy centres for the sailing craft that brought up the limestone as ballast from the southern half of the county – an essential ingredient in the old agricultural economy before the spread of artificial fertilizers. The advent of the car and lorry eventually killed the busy, centuries-old coastal trade and changed the character of the little harbours along the Pembrokeshire Path.

Another dramatic change of character occurs a few miles beyond Solva. It is marked by the wide sands of Newgale, backed by the remarkable pebble bank and open to the full force of the Atlantic winds – a thrilling sight in a storm. You are now crossing that invisible line called the Landsker, which still separates the northern Welsh-speaking half of the county from the southern English-speaking half. The division was established over 700 years ago, when the Anglo-Norman barons and their Fleming mercenaries drove out the Welsh and settled the area with immigrants from Somerset and Devon. From now on the place names along the path are predominantly English – Nolton Haven, Broad Haven and Little Haven, all popular in the summer holidays, and Martins Haven, where you embark to cross the racing waters of Jack Sound to the birds of Skomer.

St Ann's Head marks the entrance to the winding, complex reaches of Milford Haven. Its richly coloured Old Red Sandstone rock emphasizes another major geological change. The coal measures are exposed along the inner sweep of St Brides Bay, while to the south of the Haven lie the bright, clean limestone rocks that are the special attraction of the south Dyfed coastline. Before he reaches them, the walker has to make the long detour around the shores of the Haven, which are crossed near Neyland by the impressively high road bridge. The wild sea coast is left behind for the moment. Here the attractions are architectural and historical although the waterway of the Haven remains impressive, in spite of the oil refineries that in recent years have clustered around Milford and near Pembroke Dock. You feel the romance of the past history as soon as you turn towards the Haven after leaving St Ann's Head. You are now walking in the footsteps of Henry VII who landed at Mill Bay, on 7 August 1485, on his way to the victory of Bosworth. Henry's presence remains with you when you have crossed the Haven by the road bridge for he was born in Pembroke Castle, one of the finest of the many medieval castles of Wales and a magnificent example of the art of fortification before the days of the great leveller, gunpowder.

Fortification has been a constant theme on this long detour away from the open sea around the winding waters of the Haven. The Victorians built a series of remarkable thick-walled forts on many of the promontories and islets, all with an eye to possible attack by the French. You pass the last of them on Thorn Island just after leaving Angle but you are not yet out of the range of the army and guns. After you have rounded the headland to the open, breezy beach of Freshwater West you approach the zone which is part of a big firing range. It occupies the coastline around Linney

Head, and the walker has to make a long detour through Castlemartin. When he comes back to the coast again, he finds that it has made its final change of direction along the path. The thrilling line of limestone cliffs now looks due south towards the entrance to the Bristol Channel.

Compared to the strenuous ups and downs of the path in the northern section, the route in the south is easier going. The cliff-tops are extraordinarily level, being part of the celebrated 200 ft South Pembrokeshire platform cut by the sea at the end of the Tertiary period and then uplifted by more recent earth movements. The coast presents a remarkable array of stacks, blowholes and caves, including the spectacular natural arch known as the Green Bridge of Wales.

Near the bluff prow of St Govan's Head, now much frequented by rock gymnasts, the little St Govan's Chapel is wedged into a crack of the rocks – a moving witness to the early days of Christianity in Britain. A few miles further on near Bosherston are the beautiful lily ponds, created by the Earl of Cawdor after his marriage to the rich heiress, Miss Lort. These winding lakes are embowered in trees and although Stackpole Court was demolished in 1967, the lily ponds are safely in the hands of the National Trust. The path also goes past the curious harbour of Stackpole Quay, built by the Earl for his private yacht, the *Speedwitch*.

The coast continues to be deeply indented as it runs eastwards, but it must be admitted that it has lost a little of that wildness that gave it such a unique character north of Milford Haven. The army installations intrude a little around Manorbier and caravans are prominent at Lydstep and as you approach Tenby. But there are still plenty of unspoiled delights even though you have to share them with more visitors than the comparable pleasures of the north. There are fine views out to Caldey Island from Giltar Point, although the bungalows of Freshwater East are an intrusion. The island makes up for it all with its atmosphere of tranquil retirement from the world and its modern monastery which maintains the long traditions of Christian worship on this lonely spot.

Tenby gets distinctly crowded in high summer but in all other seasons retains its Regency charm behind its ancient town walls. The coast between Tenby and Saundersfoot has been described as the most sheltered in the old Pembrokeshire (now in Dyfed) with the woodlands coming down to the sea. Saundersfoot owes its harbour to the now vanished anthracite coal trade and the carboniferous rocks form the final section of the path. It comes to its official end on the long beach at Amroth on the very boundary of the old county of Pembrokeshire. It is also a fitting place to end our long journey, for eastwards the character of the coastline changes. You are entering the estuary country of Carmarthen Bay, a landscape of wide sands and dunes and winding tidal rivers. It has its own charm but the world of the high cliffs and the thundering Atlantic waves, the rare seabirds and seals has been left behind. This belongs alone to the enterprising walker who has covered those exciting 167 miles between Caemes Head and Amroth.

This has perforce been a very short account of a very long and amazingly varied journey. But the walker will discover a whole series of surprises on his way, from the Iron Age forts on so many of the headlands to the submerged forest disclosed at low spring tides at Amroth; from the remarkable Nectarium at Solva, where tropical butterflies are bred, to the charming little museum at Tenby, roosting in the walls of the castle. There is an excellent guide to the path by John Barrett, published by the Countryside Commission.

Pembroke Castle Dyfed, see p. 160

Tenby Harbour, see p. 178

(Martin Dohrn)

The Image of Wales

'Wales', the tourist brochures proclaim, 'is different.' But how different? The tourist may be intrigued on arriving at the border to be greeted by a sign in Welsh, *Croeso i Gyrmu* – Welcome To Wales. And it is certainly remarkable that in these crowded islands within 70 miles of great conurbations like Liverpool and Birmingham, you can find yourself in a country inn where the locals are all happily conversing in a language that does not remotely resemble English. Of course, the Principality has not escaped the increasing pressure of the media of mass communication. Radio and television, combined with the ease of travel brought about by the car and the aeroplane, have profoundly altered the way we all live in the modern world. Does this mean that the Welshness of Wales has been lost in our new standardized surroundings? Far from it! The visitor of today will not expect to find the image of the old, pre-First World War Wales – strongly radical, chapelgoing and teetotal on Sundays. There may still be a few areas in Gwynedd and North Dyfed which remain 'dry', but the spectacular sabbath trek of the thirsty across the border to the first pub in England is a thing of the past. Modern permissive Welshmen, however, remain as emotionally committed to their Welsh nationality as their fathers and grandfathers before them. No one can doubt this who has attended the National Eisteddfod or found himself among the crowd at Cardiff Arms Park when Wales fights its annual rugby battle against England.

The old pattern of country life in Wales has profoundly changed in recent years, although some special local customs survived into surprisingly modern days. There are still plenty of people, for example, who remember Phil Tanner, the last folk singer of the English-speaking part of Gower, reciting his invitation to a bidding wedding. In a bidding wedding all the guests arrived with handsome presents and they expected to receive equally handsome gifts when they, in their turn, had a wedding in their own family. Phil had a patriarchal beard, twinkling eyes and a glorious tenor voice linked with an infectious chuckle as he went through his invitation ritual:

> I'm a messenger to you and the whole house in general.
> To invite you to the wedding of Morgan Evans and Nancy Hopkins.
> The wedding will be next Monday fortnight.
> The wedding will be at the Ship Inn, Port Eynon,
> Where the bride will take breakfast on plenty of good beer,
>   butter and cheese,
> Walk to Port Eynon church to get married, back and take dinner.
> Then I'll see if I can get you some good tin meat and
>   some good attendance.
> And whatever you wish to give at dinner table the bride
>   will be thankful for.
> There will be a fiddle in attendance and plenty of music there,
>   and dancing if you will come along and dance.
> There'll fiddlers, fifers, drummers and the devil knows what besides.

The Mari Lwyd, St Fagan's Folk Museum, Cardiff

I don't know what. There'll be plenty of drinkables there
   so they tell me, but I haven't tasted.
And if you come to the wedding
I'll do everything in my power that evening if required,
To get you a sweetheart, if I don't get drunk.
But the bride is wishful that you should come or send.

What a marvellous evocation of the old country pleasure of a bygone Wales! Not all the delights enumerated by Phil Tanner have departed from the Gower scene, and they still have the habit, at some weddings, of greeting the bride with a joyous volley from the shotguns of the male guests as she leaves church.

The strange ritual of the Mari Lwyd, enacted on Twelfth Night and in some areas around Christmastide as well, survived far longer than the bidding wedding, and in Glamorgan and Pembrokeshire there were still a few parties making the traditional tour of the houses right up to the outbreak of the Second World War. Folklore enthusiasts have even revived it occasionally in our own day. The Mari Lwyd (Grey Mary) was a horse's skull, decorated with ribbons and hoisted on a pole, which was carried around by a man hidden in a white sheet. The skull had been whitened by lime and kept buried when not in use. The carrier of the Mari Lwyd was accompanied by a small band of fiddlers and singers, also decorated with ribbons and sashes. Outside each house they sang the traditional rhyme announcing their arrival:

> *Wel, dyma ni'n dwad,*
> *Gyfeillion diniwad,*
> *I 'mofyn am genad -i ganu.*

'Well, here we come, simple friends, to ask your permission to sing.'

And sing they did, but each verse had to be challenged by the folk inside with impromptu replies in rhyme. The poetic battle went on until, at last, the members of the household admitted defeat and the mummers entered amid laughter and rejoicing. The Mari Lwyd's jaws had been fitted with a spring which set them snapping, and as the girls ran into the dark corners in mock horror, the younger members of the party stole kisses while the older folk regaled themselves with a draught from one of those beautiful and elaborate wassail bowls for which the old Ewenny Pottery in the Vale of Glamorgan was famous.

Learned archaeologists have speculated upon the origins of the Mari Lwyd, and some have even suggested a pre-Christian link with the old Celtic cult of the horse god. Equally remote origins are ascribed to the curious custom of Hunting the Wren which was especially common in Pembrokeshire, although it was not unknown in other parts of Wales as well. Wrens were captured and carried around by children in specially constructed little 'wren houses', which were decorated with ribbons. Again, this was a Twelfth Night custom and one which ornithologists are probably glad to find discontinued.

All these activities took place in the period that the old folk regarded as the 'back end' of the year – when the midwinter weather limited outside work and the farmer and his farmhands sat around the kitchen fire, repairing the wooden tools in preparation for the first signs of spring. The wood turner was an important man in old agricultural communities and his craft still has its practitioners today. This was

Welsh National costumes (The Wales Tourist Board)

also the time for less practical activities, when the young men took pride in carving those beautiful and elaborate love spoons, to be presented eventually to the girl of their choice. No one has yet produced a satisfactory explanation as to why amorous young Welsh farm servants should have chosen the spoon as their symbol of undying affection. The earliest surviving example is dated 1667, but the tradition of the love spoon must go back to the Middle Ages.

It was also a convenient form of valentine in the days before writing became a common skill. The written valentine seems to have appeared in Wales in the mid-17th century, and the rhymes were probably written by the local poet – a figure of importance and respect in every Welsh community since the days of Celtic Britain, and still influential in Welsh-speaking villages today. There is a particularly charming one from northern Powys which may be translated: 'It is easier to collect the sea in a spoon and to place it all in an eggshell than to turn my mind from my little

Love spoons, St Fagan's Folk Museum, Cardiff   *(The Wales Tourist Board)*

South Wales type of Welsh dresser, Brecknock Museum, Brecon, Powys   *(The Wales Tourist Board)*

darling.' And here is one specimen in Gower English:

> Streams of pleasure, rivers of wine,
> Plantations of tea – and a young girl to mind!

We can picture the farmer, his family and his workers busy repairing their broken rakes and spade shafts, carving their love spoons, laboriously copying their valentines and listening to the stories told by the old grandfather or grandmother as the firelight flickered on the well-polished Welsh dresser. An over-idyllic picture, of course – country life in rural Wales was hard going right up to the advent of the tractor. Nevertheless, it had a quality about it, and the Welsh dressers, now so much sought after, can remind us of that.

The Welsh dresser, like the love spoon, has a long history. It started life in the halls of the gentry in Elizabethan and Jacobean Wales as a display case for the family silver and china on important occasions. It lost caste as the gentry found it easier to buy more sophisticated and elegant furniture, and the dresser found its last refuge in the farmhouse kitchen. It was still an article in which to take pride, even if the farmer's wife only had pewter to display; and the local carpenters took pride and devoted skill to making it. The North Wales type always had cupboards beneath the 'apron', while in the South Wales variety the latter was supported by arches. Montgomeryshire dressers sometimes had two small cupboards on either side of the upper tier.

We turn now from the dresser which was the pride of the farmer's wife to the dress she wore as she lovingly polished it. This varied in style from area to area and did not always conform to the standardized outfit of a tall black hat set on a white, frilled cap, blouse covered by a shawl, and red skirt with a white apron made familiar by tourist advertisements. The black tall hat was certainly worn in most parts of the country, for it was reasonably cheap and had Puritan connections. Its adoption as a national symbol owed a great deal to the enthusiastic advocacy of that remarkable character, Lady Llanover. She had married Benjamin Hall who, as Commissioner of Works, was responsible for installing the great bell (Big Ben, of course) in the tower of the Houses of Parliament in London. Lady Llanover was an enthusiast for everything Welsh and, among her many services to the nation, made a collection of paintings depicting the types of dress worn in every part of Wales. The emergence of the female national costume reflected her own preferences and she made it fashionable.

One other dress shares with it the popular image of things Welsh – the white robes of the bards of the Gorsedd at the National Eisteddfod, headed by the Archdruid with his golden crown, his sceptre and his golden breastplate in the shape of an old Celtic torque. In its present form, the bardic robe is even more recent than the national costume in which fond and patriotic Welsh mothers delight to dress their little daughters on important occasions. The whole concept of the Gorsedd of Bards of the Isle of Britain, now so closely associated in pageantry with the national Eisteddfod, originated in the fertile mind of a remarkable Glamorgan man at the very end of the 18th century. Iolo Morgannwg (Edward Williams) began life as a stonemason but he acquired a profound knowledge of early Welsh poetry and of the sources of Welsh history. He was a central figure in what Welsh historians have called the 18th-century Renaissance. By the time Iolo was born in 1742, the old Welsh culture and bardic traditions had gone into eclipse. The troubles of the Civil War had hastened the complete Anglicization of the gentry and Wales itself, so highly regarded under the Tudors, had almost disappeared again into the mists. A character in one of Sir John Vanbrugh's plays – called, as we might expect, Quaint – announces that he has a Welsh mother. 'A Welsh woman,' his friend inquires, 'pray of what country is that?' He receives the enlightening reply, 'That, sir, is a country at the World's Backside!'

Against such bland dismissal of Welshness Iolo and his friends reacted violently – so violently, indeed, that Iolo felt free to doctor the records of the past to increase the glory of his newly restored Wales. His inventions have bedevilled Welsh historians up to our own day. He seized avidly on the Druids, the embodiment of Celtic wisdom, and followed the lead of men like the pioneer archaeologist William Stukely, who associated the much later Druids with the far earlier Neolithic cromlechs and stone circles. Iolo's imagination ran riot and he had no hesitation in claiming that the early Welsh bards had inherited the secret wisdom of the Celtic

The Archdruid at the National Eisteddfod (The Wales Tourist Board)

Druids. He staged the first meeting of his revived Gorsedd of Bards – Gorsedd means throne – in 1792 in the last place you might expect to find such grave, mystic figures in conference, at Primrose Hill in London. By the 1820s Iolo's Gorsedd had found its place in the National Eisteddfod and gained in credibility, for the Eisteddfod's pedigree goes back to the Middle Ages and by the middle of the 19th century it had become the most important Welsh national festival, when poets and musicians met annually in competition, in a centre alternately in north and south Wales. A Gorsedd circle of undressed local stone is set up in every town where the National Eisteddfod meets. As a result, there is scarcely a place of importance in the Principality that has not now got its stone circle tucked away somewhere in a public park or convenient common. Iolo's fantasy has set a puzzle for the archaeologists a thousand years hence as well as bewildering the unsuspecting tourist of today.

The Gorsedd, however, has now been in existence for nearly 200 years and has gained in dignity and respect as well as capturing the affection of the ordinary people of Wales. Other nations have their orders of knighthood or chivalry. Wales is happy to have an order that honours, not just social success, but achievement in the arts.

There is one art on which Wales has always prided itself – music. In Dylan Thomas's 'Under Milk Wood', Organ Morgan exclaims with fervour, 'Thank the Lord, we are a musical nation.' Far back in the 12th century, Geraldus Cambrensis, in his celebrated description of Wales written after he had travelled the country with Archbishop Baldwin to preach the Third Crusade, noted that the Welsh were skilled in part singing, a rare accomplishment in the Middle Ages. Welsh harpists were employed at the English court under both Edward II and Richard II, and the harp has remained a favourite Welsh instrument. Welsh choirs, especially the male voice variety, were the central feature of Welsh musical life in the 19th century. The orchestra hardly existed and opera, in general, met with stern Puritan disapproval. All in sharp contrast to the state of things today, when the Welsh National Opera has an international reputation, Welsh composers have made impressive contributions to the orchestral repertoire and, in St David's Hall, Cardiff possess one of the finest concert centres in the country. A hundred years ago the scene was far more restricted. Wales was a relatively poor country and the choir was the least expensive form of mass music making. This choral tradition received a powerful boost from the chapels, where it played a vital part in the act of worship. It has ensured that a group of average Welshmen can burst into a hymn, in four-part harmony, at the drop of a hat. Even today, when the influence of the chapel has steadily declined, Wales remains the only country where the people sing hymns for pleasure in public houses and at football matches.

The spontaneous mass singing at Cardiff Arms Park has been a source of inspiration to the Welsh team and a powerful discouragement to their opponents. Welsh rugby has always had a more democratic and even nationalistic quality than the game as played in England. The game was first brought to the big towns of South Wales by men who had imbibed its spirit at their English public schools but it underwent a subtle change of character when it spread to the mining valleys and the small tin-plate villages in the western section of the coalfield. Here it became an expression of local pride.

Keen modern Welsh nationalists are quick to point out that South Wales had a predecessor of rugby in the game of Cnappan, so vividly described by old George Owen in his survey of Tudor Pembrokeshire:

The crowd in full cry at Cardiff Arms Park   *(The Wales Tourist Board)*

> Cnappan is a game used in one part of this shire among the Welshmen both rare to hear, troublesome to describe and painful to practice.

A game would be arranged by two prominent gentlemen who rallied whole parishes to support their side. Each team, if you could describe a huge swirling crowd of footrunners and horsemen armed with clubs as such, strove to hurl the round, wooden ball, as far as possible in opposite directions. There were no goals and the struggle swayed happily backwards and forwards across miles of the countryside for hours, in fact until the players were exhausted.

Says George Owen, 'They contest not for any wager or valuable thing but for glory and renown . . . which they esteem dearer to them than worldly wealth.'

The boys in the local rugby team, happily drinking their well-earned beer with their opponents after the match, might be a little surprised to find themselves hailed as bearers of a great tradition going back into the Welsh past, and rugby is perhaps a light-hearted example of the need many modern Welshmen feel to safeguard the legacy of that past and adapt it to the needs of the future – especially when it comes to the question of the survival of the language. Welsh has been increasingly under pressure, and Welsh speakers feel passionately that Wales's special contribution to that successful amalgam of cultures that we call Great Britain is linked to the survival of the language as a living, vital part of everyday life. Their persistent advocacy has created a separate television channel for daily transmissions of programmes in the Welsh language, and perceptive visitors will surely wish them success.

No one can foretell the future but modern Welsh nationalists can take inspiration from the defiant words that Giraldus Cambrensis records as being spoken by a brave old Welshman at Pencader in Dyfed to the powerful and formidable King Henry II of England, back in the 12th century. These words are now engraved in stone at Pencader.

> Nor do I think that any other nation than that of Wales . . . shall, on the day of severe examination before the supreme Judge, answer for this corner of the earth.

South Wales in History

A witty writer once claimed that the history of man in South Wales could be summed up by the three C's – cromlechs, castles and chapels. This curiously assorted trio certainly strikes the visitor as a special feature of our region, but the history of South Wales is a little more complex than this brisk summary implies. We can conveniently begin our account with an event that caused intense excitement in intellectual circles just over 160 years ago.

In 1823 that pioneer archaeologist, the celebrated Dean Buckland of Oxford, began his excavations in the Paviland caves in Gower. He was astonished to uncover a human skeleton in association with long extinct animals like the mammoth and the cave bear. The good Dean was convinced that the skeleton was that of an ancient British priestess, buried in Paviland long after the animal bones were first swept there by Noah's Flood. The priestess achieved immediate fame as the Red Lady of Paviland.

In 1912, however, Professor Sollas proved that the skeleton was that of a youth of the Cro-Magnon race, first identified in southern France and the creators of those magnificent cave paintings that are the first masterpieces of European art. We are tempted to call the young man of Paviland our first Welshman; this is a pardonable exaggeration. It was to be another 15,000 years at least before the Celtic ancestors of the modern Welshmen trod the soft turf on the cliff top above Goat's Hole. Through the long centuries that slowly passed after that strange burial in a Gower cave, only small bands of hunters and food gatherers wandered over the rough, post-glacial landscape of South Wales.

Around 10,000 BC, however, in the distant Middle East, a dramatic change in the fortunes of mankind was taking place, which archaeologists rightly call the Neolithic Revolution. Man had learned the art of domesticating animals and raising crops. By 4000 BC the first farmers had entered Britain and even penetrated to the remote fastnesses of western Pembrokeshire. Traces of their simple huts have been found on the rocky knoll of Clegyr Boia, within sight of the tower of the present cathedral of St David's. These were the men who first tamed the wilderness that was Wales. By 3000 BC they had grown in power and organization, and were ready to give Wales its first architecture. We have reached the 'cromlech' period!

These early farmers began to bury their important dead with impressive ceremony and evolved the technique of constructing burial chambers out of massive, undressed stones – hence the term 'megalith' or 'big stone'. The whole construction was finally covered with a mound of earth or small stones. With the passage of time these covering mounds were worn away, leaving the stones of the burial chamber in impressive isolation to form what we now call cromlechs. South Wales can offer a whole series of them, including the biggest of all, Pentre Ifan on the slopes of the Preseli Hills.

Side by side with the cromlechs stand the stone circles. There was surely some powerful religious motive driving our ancestors to undergo the back-breaking labour

Kidwelly Castle, Dyfed, see p. 122

of setting up these heavy stones in such lonely places. How else can we account for the extraordinary story of the Bluestones from the Preselis? In the mid-1920s, a Welshman, Dr H. H. Thomas, proved beyond doubt that the Bluestones that stand in the inner circle of Stonehenge came from the rocky outcrop of Carn Meini on the Preseli Hills in Pembrokeshire. No wonder that the remarkable stone circles and cromlechs have stirred the imagination of Welshmen throughout the ages. The peasantry were convinced that they were the work of King Arthur. In the 18th century the great stones were erroneously associated with the Celtic druids.

The age of the cromlechs lasted a very long time indeed – 3000 years at least; but by 500 BC, the face of society in South Wales had changed again. Bronze gave way to iron, and the Men of Iron were the latest newcomers to Welsh scene, the Celts. The Celts have always had a key place in Welsh history and culture. Rightly or wrongly, modern Welshmen still talk of themselves as Celts, sharply divided from the neighbouring English, who look for their Anglo-Saxon roots to the Germanic world. The Celts had their origin in central Europe, and the Romans depicted them as a warrior race, recklessly brave in battle, great eaters, drinkers and orators, a fighting aristocracy whose art, full of sensuous curves, we can admire in the gold torques, fire dogs and drinking cups we can see in the National Museum of Wales at Cardiff. In the centre of their religion stood the druids, guardians of secret, esoteric lore and called by the classical authors 'the wisest of men'.

Apart from those beautiful artifacts in the museum at Cardiff, what sort of legacy have the old Celts left to the modern Welshmen? Their forts still remain on the hill tops to remind us that they were a fighting race, but their most important legacy was their language. Old Brythonic is the ancestor of Welsh. These were the people who had to face the full military power of Rome when the legions invaded Britain in AD 43 in the reign of the Emperor Claudius. In a short time, the Roman armies overran the lowlands of southern Britain. Celtic *élan* went down before Roman discipline. The Silures of South Wales were a tougher proposition, but in the end the Romans bound the country in an iron network of forts and military roads, powered from the great legionary base of Isca, the modern Caerleon outside Newport, Gwent. The tribes eventually came to accept and even to take pride in Roman rule. But after 400 years of being part of the imposing structure of Imperial Rome, the unbelievable happened – the Empire's defences started to crumble under the increasing pressure from the barbarians outside the 'limes'. The legions were withdrawn and South Wales, like the rest of Roman Britain, was left to fight for survival against the invading Saxons on the east and the Irish crossing over the sea from the west. The Dark Ages had begun.

Whatever may have happened in the east, the Celts in the west put up a strong and in the end a successful resistance to the Saxon advance on the land that was to become Wales. Could they have had a leader called Arthur?

As the mists slowly clear, we can see an independent Wales emerging. The Roman administrative structure had disappeared with the legions. In its place, the old Celtic tribal structure partly re-emerged, with the rulers giving themselves the grandiose titles of kings, although their 'kingdoms' were the size of a modern county. The memorial stone of the ruler of Dyfed, the old territory of the Demetae, has survived, bearing the inscription to Vortipor, 'Protector'. But it is doubtful if these kinglets gave their people much protection, for if they were not at war with the Saxons or the Irish, they were busy fighting each other. A saving ray of light, however, falls on this murky scene. The sixth century was the period when Wales finally became Christian

– this is the Age of the Saints.

Christianity eventually conquered the whole of the country and some of the leading personalities in the process came from the south. St Illtud, whose monastery gave its name to Llantwit Major, was even famous on the Continent as 'the Wisest of the Britons'. David, the other great South Wales saint, was a man of a different stamp. His disciples were attracted to him by the strict austerity of his life – he was Dewi Ddyfrwr, David the Waterdrinker, the first teetotaller in Welsh history. After the Norman Conquest, his cult eclipsed that of Illtud. It was the ascetic not the scholar who became the patron saint of Wales and the day of his death, 1 March, is celebrated as the National Day.

While the saints were at work, the Anglo-Saxons were also busy. Their advance had been temporarily checked by the battle of Mount Badon around AD 500, and the Britons had been given a breathing space to recover, but by the beginning of the 7th century, the Anglo-Saxon pressure became stronger, fiercer and more successful. They penetrated into the lower Severn valley and, in the north, cut the connection between the Britons in Wales and those in Cumbria and Scotland. The Britons of this western peninsula were on their own. At last we can speak of a separate country called Wales whose inhabitants called themselves the Cymry – 'fellow countrymen', but who were termed by their Anglo-Saxon enemies the *Wealas* – the 'foreigners' or the Welsh.

The isolation of the Welsh was completed when the leaders of the Celtic church met St Augustine at Aust, on the English side of the Severn, in AD 602. Augustine was fresh from his success in converting the pagan rulers of Kent in eastern England and demanded the immediate submission of the Welsh to the Roman church. The Celtic church was proud that it had kept the light of Christianity shining in Britain through the darkest part of the Dark Ages. They were deeply hurt by Augustine's attitude. Saints have many qualities, but tact is not conspicuous among them. The Celtic church leaders withdrew with a feeling of hurt dignity. The isolation of Wales was now total.

The rise of the powerful state of Mercia on the border brought a new menace to the Welsh. Slowly they were driven back from their last strongholds in the fertile Severn plains into the foothills of the western mountains. Here they made their final stand – desperately but successfully. Their success was marked, at the end of the 8th century, by the great dyke built by the strong Mercian ruler, Offa. It runs the whole length of the border, winding over hill and dale like a huge earthen snake. It was not a manned defence like Hadrian's Wall, but rather a line of demarcation between the races which was meant to be permanent. On the whole, the line has stood firm until our own day. There are Welsh people who still talk of going to England as going 'dros Clawdd Offa' (crossing Offa's Dyke).

By 800, Wales had clearly resisted the Anglo-Saxon onslaught, but life to the west of Offa's Dyke remained tough, tangled and troubled. The petty kinglets who divided the country quarrelled among themselves. The Vikings ravaged Wales as mercilessly as they looted England. Wales did not have large settlements of the 'black pagans' as there were in the English Danelaw, but they left the mark of their raids in the Norse names of the headlands and islands of South Wales, from Ramsey and Skomer to Worms Head and Flat Holm. But somehow the Welsh survived, and,

Overleaf: Offa's Dyke, near Evanjob, Powys, see p. 159

from time to time, they even united under one ruler. Hywel ap Cadell, who died in 950, was given the title of Hywel Dda – Howel the Good – by his grateful fellow countrymen. He deserved it for his work in first codifying the laws of Wales. Confusion came again after Hywel's death, and although unity was ruthlessly reimposed by Gryffydd ap Llywelyn, he was betrayed by his men and his head sent to his bitter enemy Earl Harold. By 1066 Harold, himself, lay dead on the field of Hastings and his country lay at the feet of William the Conqueror.

For the Welsh 1066 was as fateful a date as for the English. It was not long before the Normans arrived on the Welsh border. William had his hands full in subduing England, and therefore established some of his most trusted barons on the border with instructions to keep the Welsh in check. Being Normans, with the usual Norman appetite for loot and power, these barons soon began to push deep into Wales with the object of carving out for themselves what were virtually independent princedoms. We are in the presence of the Lords Marcher, those bold, bad barons of the borderland who were to play such a prominent part in the history of medieval Wales.

The Normans owed their early success in Wales to their mastery of what for Britain was a new technique of warfare. They were armoured horsemen who could mount a cavalry charge to which the lightly armed Welsh could make no reply. And they could fling up 'motte and bailey' castles – a mound surrounded by a palisade, which gave them a secure base for a further advance. South Wales is covered with these castle mounds which, in the more important strategic spots, were eventually replaced by stone castles of ever-increasing strength and complexity. South Wales is one of the most be-castled areas in Britain. The Normans attained their greatest success in South Wales under Henry I. So powerful were they that they expelled the Welsh completely from south-west Dyfed and Gower, which they then settled with immigrants from Devon and Somerset and, in south-west Dyfed, with a group of Flemings. The Normans had been equally successful in their first assault on North Wales, but they failed to maintain their conquests. The Welsh in North Wales were lucky enough to possess an almost impregnable natural fortress into which they could always retire under pressure – the wilds of Snowdonia and the fertile island of Anglesey, protected by the moat of the Menai Straits. No wonder they called the island 'Môn, mam Cymru' – Anglesey, the Mother of Wales.

South Wales had no such advantage. The coastal plain was wide enough to let in-vaders advance in force. There was a strong Welsh revival after the death of Henry I in 1142. The power of the Lord Rhys, based on his stronghold at Dynefor, near Llandeilo, was acknowledged over most of upland West Wales. But the Normans clung firmly to their castles along the coast. Pembroke never fell into Welsh hands, and by the end of the 12th century, the Lords Marcher and the King were again the dominant power in the South.

How different were matters in the North! Here the Snowdonia-Anglesey combina-tion allowed the Princes of Gwynydd to beat off the Normans. Under Llywelyn the Great Gwynydd expanded vigorously, and when he died in 1240, he had laid the foundations of what was becoming virtually an independent kingdom. The power of Gwynydd was still further increased by his nephew, Llywelyn ap Iorwerth, who was the first native ruler to be acknowledged as Prince of Wales by the English. He was also the last. There was no room in southern Britain for an independent Wales and a powerful England. The final clash came under Edward I. In his two Welsh wars he crushed Llywelyn, who was killed near Builth in South Wales on a dreary December day in 1282. His head was cut off and placed over a gate in the Tower of London.

Wales was now roughly divided into two. The newly conquered principality was placed under English administration as an apanage for the eldest son of the King, who was created Prince of Wales. The rest of the country, including South Wales, was still in the hands of the Lords Marcher, although the King now held a number of these lordships. The Welsh had no option but to make the best they could out of their new situation. Many took the only course of advancement open to them and took service in the King's armies. The longbow had been developed in Gwent in South Wales, and Welsh bowmen played a major part in the great English victories in France at Crécy, Poitiers and Agincourt. Other Welshmen found the new English yoke increasingly irksome, and at last their discontent burst out in the flame and fury of the rebellion of Owain Glyn Dŵr – Shakespeare's Owen Glendower. The rising began in North Wales but soon spread to the south. For a short time, between 1404 and 1408, it seemed that an independent Wales was a possibility, with its own parliament and universities and an archbishopric, independent of Canterbury and in direct touch with Rome. It was a transient dream – killed by the military skill of the future Henry V, who slowly strangled the rebellion. Owain disappeared into the mists, leaving a legend behind him as strong as that of Arthur. The bards kept alive the hope that a new Owain, a new Arthur, would surely come again to restore the Welsh to their lost glory. In a sense, the new Arthur did arrive, but in the unromantic, hard-hearted and practical person of Henry Tudor who, in 1485, landed at Milford Haven and marched through Wales to victory at Bosworth and to his coronation as Henry VII. The event was so improbable that it seemed to justify all the mystical murmurings of the bards. Owain Tudor, an obscure North Wales young squire at the English court, had succeeded in secretly marrying the beautiful widow of Henry V and getting away with it. Their sons were acknowledged by Henry VI. Surely, never did sexual attraction exercise a more potent influence on the destiny of a nation. In that welter of blood-letting and back-stabbing among the aristocracy which history has dignified under the title of the Wars of the Roses, most of the challengers with sound claims to the crown were eliminated. Henry VII was the son of Edmund, Duke of Richmond, who was himself the offspring of that remarkable marriage between Owen Tudor and Katherine of France. He found himself on the throne through the unexpected accidents of fortune. He stayed on it through his own cool courage, diplomatic cunning and financial skill. He became the founder of one of the most successful dynasties ever to rule England and, of course, Wales as well.

The Welsh naturally hailed him as their deliverer, the new Arthur. There was something like a Welsh job rush to London, and Henry was not ungenerous to his supporters. As long as there were Tudors on the throne, they were assured of the total loyalty of the Welsh nation. In return they gave Wales what many modern Welshmen regard as a two-edged gift. Under Henry VIII two Acts of Union were passed, in 1536 and 1542, by which the King decreed, according to the preamble of the 1536 Act, that Wales 'shall, for ever, from henceforth, be united and annexed to and with his realm of England'.

The Acts of Union have had a bad press from many modern Welshmen. They see them as the start of the long and insidious process of the Anglicization of the Welsh gentry which had such a profound effect – disastrous in the opinion of many Welshmen today – on the social structure of the Principality. This was not how

NEAR THIS SPOT
WAS KILLED
OUR PRINCE
LLYWELYN
1282

contemporary Welshmen saw the Acts. The gentry, above all, welcomed them as giving them equality of opportunity with the English in all branches of the public life of the realm – in the church, at court, at the bar and, above all, in local administration. This may account for the ease with which all the violent changes of the Reformation were accepted in Wales. There were no Pilgrimages of Grace here. Alone among the Celtic countries, Wales did not defend the old religion in arms. The monasteries were dissolved without protest and the gentry were only too pleased to take over the monastery lands. They were the foundation of the fortunes of some of the leading South Wales families, like the Mansels and the Herberts.

They were also the rocks that wrecked Queen Mary's attempt to restore the old religion in Wales. Even the fervently Catholic Earl of Worcester, who had got hold of most of the lands of Tintern monastery, refused to disgorge his loot. When Elizabeth came to the throne, the Welsh gentry continued to prosper. And it is worth noting, as we talk of the Anglicization of the ruling gentry of Wales, that the Welsh translation of the Bible was published, with Elizabeth's approval, in the Armada Year of 1588. The Welsh Bible was a vital influence in the preservation of the Welsh language. When Elizabeth died Wales felt no difficulty in transferring its traditional loyalty to the crown to the Stuarts.

Thus, when the Civil War broke out, Wales was predominantly Royalist. There were pro-Parliamentary enclaves in south Pembrokeshire and Flint, but throughout the war the Principality was rightly regarded as 'the nursery of the King's Infantry'. When the New Model Army won the decisive victory of Naseby, it was not only a crushing defeat for the King but a national disaster for Wales. The triumphant troopers cut down the Welsh camp followers under the impression that they were the hated Irish. In the Second Civil War, a section of the New Model smothered the rebellion in the bitter battle of St Fagan's, just outside Cardiff, and Cromwell then marched through South Wales to capture Pembroke Castle and complete the settlement of Wales. The country hardly took kindly to the Commonwealth, and the conduits of Carmarthen ran with wine in joyful celebration for the Restoration of Charles II.

Wales now settled down to what we may call her Supine Century. Nothing disturbed the surface of public life or the political power of the great families. Vaughans from Golden Grove in the Tywi valley represented Carmarthen in Parliament for an unbroken 60 years. The gentry no longer spoke the language of their forefathers and looked to England for their standards in art, education and social behaviour. The gap between them and their Welsh-speaking peasants became ever wider. The Society of Sea Sergeants kept the Jacobite cause alive in South Wales. But when Bonnie Prince Charlie actually landed in Scotland in 1745 and began his march on London, the Sea Sergeants lifted their glasses to his success – but not their swords. The Anglican church in Wales was equally quiescent. Between 1715 and 1871 no bishop was appointed to a Welsh see who was capable of preaching in Welsh. In the general discouragement of the old Welsh culture, the time-honoured method of nomenclature was another victim of the fashionable policy of Anglicization. In the old days a man was proud to trace his ancestry back through many generations with each name linked by *ap* ('the son of'). After the Acts of Union, English lawyers found this practice cumbersome. Henry VIII had urged the nobility

The memorial to Llywelyn, the last native Prince of Wales, Cilmery, Builth Wells, see p. 84

to adopt the names of their estates. The lesser gentry adopted convenient English names and by the beginning of the 18th century, the clergy were giving easy biblical or royal names to the peasantry. Wales became a nation of Williams, Thomas, Jones and the like. It all added to the grey uniformity that now seemed to have spread over Welsh life. No wonder the early editions of the *Encyclopaedia Britannica*, under the heading of Wales, simply printed: 'See England'.

But the appearance of placid conformity was deceptive. There were forces gathering below the surface that were to erupt and violently break the settled pattern of Welsh society. The first to appear was the Methodist Revival. The Revival began in Wales almost independently of the Wesleyan movement in England, although the leaders were in touch with each other. In Wales, Howell Harris was the dynamic organizer, Daniel Rowland the mighty preacher and William Williams (Panycelyn) the moving hymn writer. All were young and all came from South Wales. The Anglican church was totally unprepared for the outbreak of 'enthusiasm'. The Revival leaders spoke and preached in Welsh, and could touch the hearts of the people in a way denied to most of the higher Anglican clergy. By the end of the 18th century the Revival had become an irresistible force, from which the old denominations also drew a new inspiration. By the beginning of the 19th century Wales had become two nations are far as religion was concerned. On one side were the Anglicized ruling families who stayed with the church, on the other were their tenants, who were leaving the church to set up their own independent chapels.

As the Methodists swept through the countryside with ever-increasing fervour, a second revolution was also taking place in the cultural field and the two movements by no means coincided. Scholars and poets had become deeply concerned over the decay of the old Welsh culture. They set about forming societies to revive it and to publish the collections of old Welsh manuscripts. In their enthusiasm for Things Past, they may have tended to see the history of Wales through a romantic haze. One of the central figures of this cultural revival, Iolo Morganwg, was not above adding to the store of medieval Welsh history and poetry on his own account. His fertile imagination created the Gorsedd of the Bards of the Isle of Britain, who now grace the National Eisteddfod with white-robed dignity. If it was a fabrication, it was surely in a good cause.

The French Revolution brought these cultural revolutionaries new hope and inspiration. They toasted Liberty, Equality and Fraternity in eloquent Welsh. A strange incident, however, quenched their early enthusiasm. England went to war with the new French republic, and in 1792 a small French force actually landed on Welsh soil at Fishguard, in the celebrated 'Last Invasion of Britain'. It was a somewhat farcical episode, and the French surrendered in three days, but the Welsh cultural revolution immediately took more respectable paths.

In the meantime, a third revolution was in full swing which, in the end, would remould life in South Wales even more violently than the religious and cultural revivals. Heavy industry had arrived, and all along the northern edge of the coalfield, the great ironworks were being built at formidable speed. Here iron ore had been found in conjunction with coal and limestone. England was now at war with Revolutionary France and the great furnaces roared day and night to supply the guns and cannon balls for Nelson's fleet and Wellington's army. Almost overnight the obscure little village of Merthyr Tydfil grew into the largest town in Wales. Canals were dug in the narrow valleys to bring down the products of the furnaces to ports like Newport, Cardiff and Swansea. The ironmasters experimented in more revolutionary forms of transport, and backed Trevithick when he constructed the first steam train in the world, which in 1806 brought iron bars and a group of daring passengers down through cheering crowds from Penydaren to Abercynon.

The men and women who flooded into these new industrial centres from the Welsh countryside found conditions harsh and strange. Places like Hirwaun, Tredegar and Dowlais were on the edge of wild moorlands, cut off from the old, long-established centres of population. They were bound to become foci of social protest. The revolutionary tradition has a long history in South Wales. In 1831, Merthyr broke out in a three days' riot in which the Red Flag was hoisted for the first time in Britain. The rising was put down by force. In 1839 the Chartists marched down on Newport from the valleys and the soldiers opened fire on them as they attacked the Westgate Hotel, leaving the dead strewn over the pavement.

The countryside was equally disturbed. The birth rate was rising rapidly, and pressure on the land increasing. The farmers vented their anger on the tollgates which were now being placed across the improved roads. The charges were particularly high in the old county of Carmarthenshire. The curiously named Rebecca Riots were aimed at the destruction of these tollgates, and the leaders had read their Bible carefully. In Genesis they found a reference to Rebecca who was urged to 'possess the gates of them that hate thee'. The rioters therefore dressed up in women's clothes and destroyed the gates by night. The whole countryside joined in the conspiracy. The riots were eventually quelled, but the real cure for the woes of the Welsh farmers came with the spread of the railways. In contrast to Ireland, the surplus population of rural South Wales was able to 'emigrate' within the boundaries of the Welsh industrial area.

The second half of the 19th century saw the astonishing expansion of industrial South Wales. This was boom time in the Valleys. The Rhondda became the Black Klondyke and Welsh steam coal supplied power to the whole world. The year 1913 saw the peak of the boom. The Liberals and the Nonconformists were in control, led by the charismatic figure of David Lloyd George. There was a boundless confidence in the perpetual prosperity of South Wales, reflected in the baroque splendours of the Cardiff Civic Centre.

It could not last. Oil displaced the supremacy of coal. Two world wars dismantled the imposing structure of the Empire and the assured markets for the heavy industry of South Wales disappeared. In all this, the South Wales experience was not unique. The same thing was happening throughout industrial Britain. South Wales simply shared in the long succession of depression and recovery and further depression which has been the keynote of the history of Britain in our own time. In one respect only has the political scene in South Wales differed from that in England. After the Second World War, the Welsh Nationalist party – Plaid Cymru – grew in strength and offered a separate solution to the problems of South Wales, based on administrative independence and a strong encouragement for the Welsh language. In 1979, the Labour government then in power proposed a measure of self-government for Wales and held a national referendum on St David's Day. The Welsh Assembly was rejected by a large majority. Did this mean that Wales had ceased to regard itself as a nation? Far from it. South Wales had simply taken the practical view that the economic bonds were too strong to be broken. For the rest, Wales is as passionately conscious of its separate nationhood as ever it was.

SOUTH AND MID WALES

Tylorstown, Rhondda Valleys, see p. 169

Note on Using the Gazetteer

Entries in the Gazetteer are arranged in alphabetical order. Where they differ the English, or Anglicized, names appear first, followed by the Welsh form in parentheses – examples are **Swansea** (Abertawe), *West Glamorgan*, or **Carmarthen** (Caerfyrddin), *Dyfed* – and then the county name is given.

These entry headings are followed by a map reference in parentheses, thus: **Cardiff** (Caerdydd), *South Glamorgan* (5/5C). The figure 5 is the map number; 5C is the grid reference, with 5 indicating the across and C the down reference.

If a place name within the text of an entry is printed in capital letters, this indicates that it has its own entry in the Gazetteer.

Every effort has been made to ensure that information about the opening to the public of buildings, estates, gardens, reserves, museums, galleries, etc., and concerning trails, walks and footpaths, as well as statements about ferries and other boats, were as accurate and up to date as possible at the time of going to press. Such particulars are, of course, subject to alteration and it may be prudent to check them locally, or with the appropriate organizations or authorities.

Previous page: Carreg Cennen Castle, Dyfed, see p. 97

Gazetteer

Abbeycwmhir, *Powys* (2/2C) Even in these days of ever-increasing tourism, Abbeycwmhir has remained off the beaten track. The spread of forestry on the surrounding hills seems to have increased its isolation. The ruins of the great Cistercian abbey lie in the river meadows, and only the outline of the once noble building is visible. The headless body of Llywelyn, the last native Prince of Wales, was brought here after he had been slain near Builth in 1282, and buried before the high altar. The spot is marked by a small memorial tablet, where keen Welsh nationalists lay flowers. They may not altogether approve of the name of the inn, the Happy Union, with a sign showing a Welshman riding a goat.

Aberaeron, *Dyfed* (1/2C) Aberaeron, on the shores of Cardigan Bay, comes as a pleasant surprise to a visitor. Small Welsh towns, on the whole, are not exactly celebrated for their planning. Aberaeron, however, was laid out in the early 19th century, in a good period for British architecture. The place has a Regency charm. Don't, however, expect another Cheltenham. You are in rural Wales, and the squares and terraces are on a modest scale. But Aberaeron now has a Civic Society and is guarding its heritage. The Town Hall, facing the harbour, is pleasing; in fact the whole place has a sort of retired charm. The harbour, once a centre of a busy coastal trade and famous for its boatbuilding, is now entirely given over to yachtsmen. Among them is Sir Geraint Evans, the famous operatic singer, who has made Aberaeron his Welsh home. Luckily, the inevitable caravan parks have been kept on the outskirts.

The Marine Aquarium and the Coastal Centre on the quay on the north side of the harbour depict the local coastline and its history (open summer only). There is also good angling to be found on the river Aeron.

Aberaeron

Above: Statue of Caradog (Griffith Rhys Jones, 1834–97), Aberdare

Aberavon *see* Port Talbot

Aberdare (Aberdâr), *Mid Glamorgan* (5/4B) An industrial town at the head of the Cynon Valley, 9 miles north of PONTYPRIDD. It grew up in the great days of the early Industrial Revolution, with the first ironworks multiplying along the northern edge of the coalfield. It prospered in the mid-19th century but today the area has lost its main industries with the decline of the coal trade. It is, however, doing its gallant best – and with some success – to replace them. The town centre still has the feel of a market town about it. Aberdare has always been proud of its interest in the arts. It was the birthplace of the poet Alun Lewis, and must be the only town in Britain which has the statue of a choir conductor as its main monument. The bronze statue of Caradog (Griffith Rhys Jones) presides over Victoria Square. He led the South Wales Choral Union, 500 strong, to victory in the competitions at the Crystal Palace in 1872 and 1873. Dare Valley Country Park, 1½ miles west of the town centre, has an Industry Trail which follows the development of coalmining here. It follows the old Dare Valley Railway where Brunel's timber viaduct

can be seen. In recent years the head of the Glamorganshire Canal, near the Sports Centre, has been restored and landscaped. At Robertstown, opposite Aberdare Park, is a cast-iron tram bridge built in 1811 which carried horse-drawn trams across the river. Aberdare Park itself has a boating lake and consists of woodland and grass.

The road westwards from Aberdare climbs up onto the higher ground at the foot of a long ridge that guards the RHONDDA VALLEYS to the south. At Hirwaun, a road leads North over the moorlands towards the BRECON BEACONS, and, a mile beyond, a dramatic road climbs over the ridge, past the lake of Llyn Fawr, to the Rhondda Fawr.

Abergavenny (Y Fenni), *Gwent* (5/5B) A busy market town on the Usk, at the point where the river turns south away from the higher hills. A circle of high summits stand guardian over it. The strange Skirrid Mountain (1595 ft) lies to the

east, the pointed Sugar Loaf (1955 ft) to the north and the massive bulk of the Blorenge (1811 ft) to the south-east. Among the summit rocks of the Blorenge are part of the remains of the great horse, Foxhunter, on which Sir Harry Llewelyn led the British team to win the Olympic Gold Medal at Helsinki in 1952. This galaxy of fine hills has led to Abergavenny assuming the proud title of the Gateway to Wales – although it is well inside the Welsh border.

The Romans had a fort here, but the Normans built the first castle, which played a prominent part in the incessant warfare along the Welsh Marches. The few remaining walls are now surrounded by a public park with a museum of local history. The buildings of the main street are a fine mixture of styles reflecting the history of the place, from the Tudor period onwards. The Middle Ages contribute the old tower of St John's Church, the early 19th century the dignified frontage of the Angel Hotel and Victorians the

Town Hall with its green-topped tower and a clock presented by the ironmaster, Crawshay Bailey. The most important architectural monument is the church of St Mary's. Its somewhat over-restored exterior gives no hint of the wealth of interesting tombs inside. Pride of place must be given to the splendid effigy of Jesse, father of the Biblical David. It is carved out of solid oak and was probably part of a complete Jesse tree, set in the old reredos. Sadly, the church has to be kept locked as often as not. Vandalism has spread its ugly hand all too widely over many of the country churches of South Wales. On a happier note – Abergavenny now possesses a small art gallery, a good bookshop and a useful information centre for the Brecon Beacons National Park.

The town is a fine base for exploring the Park on foot, by car or at the leisurely pace of a pony, with major trekking centres in the locality.

Below: The Sugar Loaf, Abergavenny

The road 4 miles north of the town passes the ancient hamlet of Llanfihangel Crucorney, under the slopes of the Skirrid. Here, the Skirrid Inn, the oldest in Wales, has retained its medieval construction.

Nearby is the Tudor mansion of Llanfihangel Court with a beautifully furnished interior. Charles I was entertained here during his unhappy visit to Wales in the final stages of the first Civil War. It is open occasionally during the summer months.

Abergorlech *see* Brechfa

Abergwesyn, *Powys* (4/3A) This tiny hamlet, at the top of the Irfon valley 4 miles north of LLANWRTYD WELLS, gives access to what was once the loneliest country in South Wales – known as the Green Desert, a great, exhilarating expanse of open moorland, sacred to sheep. Today, the Forestry Commission has taken the area over, but it has provided ample well-landscaped picnic sites for the motor tourist and walker. The lonely sheep farms are deserted and a tarred road, once a remote drovers' route, leads you safely through the wilderness into the Teifi valley at TREGARON. The journey is still worth making. The final reach of the Irfon is now kept permanently free from those regimented conifers. The rocks crowd around it and, in a miniature gorge, is the place where, by tradition, the last wolf was slain in Wales. The roads still climb steeply in and out of the valleys in hair-raising zigzags, and, in the valley of the Camddwr, a side road leads down to the mountain chapel of Soar-y-Mynydd. And here, if anywhere, you can sense the moving simplicity of the way of life enjoyed by the folk who once farmed in these hills. To the south, but out of sight from Soar, are the headwaters of the vast reservoir of Llyn Brianne, which was opened in 1973.

Aberporth, *Dyfed* (3/3A) Aberporth, and nearby **Tresaith**, are villages that have remained popular with holidaymakers along Cardigan Bay. The houses look down onto two good, sandy beaches with safe bathing. At Tresaith a small waterfall tumbles into the sea. At the corner of the steep road that drops into Tresaith is the house built by the popular Edwardian novelist, Allen Raine. Her greatest success was *A Welsh Singer*. At low tide Traeth Penbryn can be reached (*see* Llangranog).

The coast immediately south of Aberporth is now not accessible. The high headland of Pen-cribarth has been taken over by the Ministry of Defence as an RAF guided missile range and research centre. The danger zone extends well out to sea in Cardigan Bay on firing days. It is worthwhile, however, driving around by road to reach the sea again, 4 miles south of Aberporth at Mwnt – in Welsh, Traeth y Mwnt meaning the Beach of the Mound (hill). The 250 ft hill has a tiny, whitewashed church on its grassy side and, below, a small, sandy beach guarded by cliffs and reached by a steep path. It is a remote and delightful landscape. Luckily, Mwnt is in the hands of the National Trust, for the price of beauty is eternal vigilance.

Aberystwyth, *Dyfed* (1/3B) The town, almost in the centre of the long curve of Cardigan Bay, happily leads a double life. On one hand, it is a seaside holiday resort, and a very pleasant one at that, and on the other a university town. It first developed in mid-Victorian days with the advent of the railways. Enterprising promoters billed Aberystwyth as 'The Brighton of Wales'. A pardonable exaggeration, perhaps, but the Promenade, with its line of bow-windowed hotels and boarding houses – stretching from the castle ruins to Constitution Hill – has an undoubted air of distinction about it. It has all the amenities you expect in a popular holiday town, including a pier. Constitution Hill is reached by a cliff path or railway. The beach is shingle with a little sand but there are many attractions along the front. Bathing north of the pier is good. On the summit of Constitution Hill is the world's largest camera obscura, which projects over 60 miles of landscape, as far north as the mountains of Snowdonia. A liberal sprinkling of Welsh chapels ensures that Aberystwyth does not tread the path of rakish Brighton. Near the castle, which dates from the reign of Edward I, stands the extraordinary Gothic structure that began life as Aberystwyth's first luxury hotel. It slid into bankruptcy and was sold cheaply to become the first college of the future University of Wales. Behind it, attractive Laura Place adds to the feeling that you are now in academic and not seaside Aberystwyth.

The heart of University College has now been moved away from its original site. Aberystwyth took an enthusiastic part in the university explosion of post-Second World War Britain. The modest structure on the Promenade was rapidly supplemented by a big, new complex on the hill overlooking the town. Here is the bright, modern campus, complete with lecture rooms, assembly halls, laboratories and halls of residence, and a

Aberystwyth with Constitution Hill

thriving arts centre which is open to the general public. In the forefront – and still the dominant building on the hill – is the dignified, classical building of the National Library of Wales. It was placed in Aberystwyth as a compromise between the rival claims of North and South Wales. The first section was opened in 1911 and the whole was completed in 1955. The library contains over 2 million printed books and 35,000 manuscripts. A changing selection of the Library's treasures is always on display in the public galleries. The Cardigan Museum, housed in a former cinema and music hall, vividly depicts the history and rural way of life of the locality.

One mile east of Aberystwyth, and today almost linked to the town by houses, is the ancient religious settlement of Llanbadarn Fawr. The church was regarded as one of the mother churches of Wales. It has a stern and solid appearance, with a powerful, square tower. Within is a collection of Celtic crosses, one of which – with its intricately laced patterns – must be among the finest examples of its kind. Welsh readers will remember Llanbadarn for its association with Dafydd ap Gwilym, the greatest of the medieval poets of Wales.

The Rheidol valley continues eastwards from Llanbadarn into the hills. It increases in charm as it goes. The Vale of Rheidol Railway still runs in summer (Easter–October) from Aberystwyth station to the beauty spot and waterfalls at DEVIL'S BRIDGE. It is the only one of the 'great little trains' of Wales which is managed by British Rail and is the last of its steam operated railways. In a fold between the lower courses of the Rheidol and the Ystwyth 4 miles east of Aberystwyth, is the estate of Nanteos, where the imposing mansion has now been restored. It once held the celebrated wooden cup claimed to be the Holy Grail. The house, which is open to the public, also has demonstrations of rural crafts and traditions.

Due north of Aberystwyth, over Constitution Hill, is the popular sandy bathing beach of Clarach, set between two steep hills. South of the town centre is Pen Dinas, the site of a large prehistoric hill fort.

Ammanford (Rhydaman), *Dyfed* (4/2B) A mining township in the upper section of the Loughor valley 14 miles north-north-east from SWANSEA. The coal here is anthracite, and still in demand

with a big new anthracite mine at Betws. The extensive open-cast excavations are being carefully restored. Ammanford is on the northern edge of the coalfield, and the country north and west of it becomes steadily more rural and attractive after you pass Llandybie and its limestone quarries. The Loughor turns south here after following the line of the north outcrop. The little mining villages here have all lost their mines, but behind them rise the high moorlands of the CARMARTHENSHIRE FANS. At Brynamman a splendid road leads into the BRECON BEACONS National Park up over the Black Mountain – not to be confused with the BLACK MOUNTAINS, far away to the east. This Black Mountain is really the most westerly ridge of the Fans. Old George Borrow, the writer who took to the road, came tramping over it in a thick mist on his journey through Wales as described in his *Wild Wales* (1862). He thus missed the great attraction of the Mynydd Du (Black Mountain) – the magnificent view from the summit. The road reaches 1618 ft. The rich Tywi valley lies at your feet, and beyond are the lonely hills of Mid Wales.

Amroth, *Dyfed* (3/3B) This seaside village, 5 miles north-east of TENBY, marks the east end of the Pembrokeshire Coast Path. It has a fine, sandy beach, but fights a constant battle against its old enemy, the sea. The winter gales can sometimes drive the waters over the long pebble bank that protects the houses. The beach is extensive and stretches from Wiseman's Bridge, north-east of SAUNDERSFOOT, to Telpyn Point. At Wiseman's Bridge the beach is sandy while at Amroth the sand is backed by the pebble bank. East from Telpyn is Marros with its 2-mile stretch of wide sands to PENDINE with a further 6 miles of sandy beach and dunes. At low tide at Amroth the stumps of an old submerged forest appear; a reminder that the sea has been encroaching on the land around Carmarthen Bay since the end of the Ice Age. Amroth Castle, behind a long wall near the seafront, is a 19th-century reconstruction now part of a holiday complex. Lord Nelson and Lady Hamilton were welcomed here by the Pembrokeshire gentry during their South Wales tour of 1802.

Angle, *Dyfed* (3/1B) An attractive fishing village, tucked away at the west of the southern arm of the winding MILFORD HAVEN, it comes as a welcome relief after the industrial installations

Llanbadarn Fawr Church, see p. 73

that now line the shore westwards from PEMBROKE town. Although it now has a background of oil tanks, the church at Rhoscrowther is worth a visit. It has a typical Pembrokeshire type tower, corbelled and steepled, a large porch with a cobbled floor and the figure of Christ on the tomb set over the pointed door. Angle Bay is visible from the churchyard and gives promise of better things to come.

Angle itself consists of a single, delightful street, with the columned front of the old Globe hotel as the centrepiece. Angle churchyard has a small fisherman's chapel built in 1447. Separated from the chapel at high tide is a moated enclosure with a pele tower. There is also a round dovecot close at hand. Continuing through the village westward you come to West Angle Bay, with its sandy beach and small natural harbour, at the road's end. The fort on offshore Thorn Island is now a hotel. The Pembrokeshire Coast Path here gives you a fine cliff walk facing the Atlantic. After 3 miles of exhilarating coastline, you come down onto the wide sands of Freshwater West, a great sweep of a beach backed by dunes. It can also be reached by a roundabout and narrow road. The Atlantic rollers make a glorious display here when the western wind gets behind them. But intending bathers are warned that the beach has a notorious undertow in some states of the tide. The local advice goes: 'Come and build sand castles but keep out of the water.'

The fine prow of Linney Head marks the beginning of the tank range that has sealed off the next stretch of the Dyfed coast. This time it is the Ministry of Defence that gives the warning 'Keep out!'

Baglan, West Glamorgan (4/3C) Situated 2 miles north-west of Port Talbot on the road to SWANSEA, the old village has been overwhelmed by new housing estates which stretch along the foot of the hills. The big petro-chemical works at the mouth of the Neath river dominates the seaward view. Baglan, however, still retains a few traces of its former beauty, which made it a favourite resort of artists in the early 19th century. Baglan House has been pulled down and the grounds, which possess a sycamore tree reputed to be the largest in Wales, are a public park. The poet Gray was a frequent visitor here in the days of its former beauty. The old church, dedicated to St Baglan, is now a ruin. The new church is known as the Alabaster Church, from the lavish use of that material in its construction. It contains stained glass by Burne-Jones.

David Davies, Llandinam, the founder of Barry Docks

Barry (Y Barri), *South Glamorgan* (5/4C) The town is on the shore of the Bristol Channel 8 miles south-west of CARDIFF. It developed as a great coal port at the end of the 19th century when that most formidable coal owner, David Davies, determined to find another export point than Cardiff for the steam coal of the Rhondda. He eventually succeeded and his statue stands at the gates of the docks he created. It may be wondered what David Davies would say about the present state of the docks at Barry – the coal has gone and the only ships that use them import bananas from the West Indies. The wide sidings and marshalling yards became 'Woodham's Graveyard of Steam' and were filled with British Rail's abandoned engines. Industrially, Barry has turned its back on coal and developed other industries. Barry Island became a popular holiday resort. It is still popular with day visitors attracted by the largest funfair in the west of Britain, and, at Cold Knapp, the largest open-air swimming pool in Wales. The best beaches are at The Knapp, Whitmore Bay and Jackson's Bay. To the west runs Pebble Beach, a remarkable geological formation 1 mile long, which falls steeply to the water's edge. The Golden Stairs at the far end of the beach lead up to Porthkerry Country Park, a valley left in its natural state through which runs the Porthkerry viaduct. Further east is Sully with a pebble beach. Barry is expanding inland, and has become increasingly popular as a residential area for Cardiff. The Cardiff-Wales Airport is at Rhoose, 2 miles west, and can now take air traffic of international standard. The Wales Aircraft Museum (open Sundays) is also at the airport.

Beaupre *see* St Hilary

Berriew (Aberriew), *Powys* (2/3B)The name of this delightful village is an Anglicized version of the Welsh – the mouth (*aber*) of the Rhiw. This little river flows down from the lonely country behind it and in the old days this was great sheep country. The sheep and their wool brought prosperity to the weavers of Berriew and gave them the money to build their beautiful black-and-white oak-framed houses which now give such pleasure to visitors. The residents take pride in their heritage and Berriew has repeatedly won the award for the Best Kept Village. There is a waterfall on the Rhiw, and the massive but now slightly dripping aqueduct of the MONTGOMERY branch of the Shropshire Union Canal crosses the stream near the village. Plans are in hand to restore the whole of the canal to full navigable standard. A quarter mile downstream is Berriew Lock. There is a 6 ft monolith of glacial origin, called Maen Beuno, near Dyffryn Lane. Berriew has been lucky in retaining its peace for it is just off the main road to WELSHPOOL.

Bishopston (Llandeilo Ferwallt), *West Glamorgan* (4/2C) A village, tucked into a narrow valley, that has been almost overwhelmed by the housing developments spreading out from SWANSEA, but has not yet lost its character of being the first village of English GOWER. Welsh has not been spoken here by the population at large for 700 years. You approach it from Swansea over the wide, breezy commons which were the line of demarcation formed after the Norman conquest of Gower. The little church, with its dark tower and tiny nave and chancel, is wedged into one of the narrowest parts of the valley. In front of it the Bishopston stream runs over a watersplash and on down a beautifully wooded valley to the sea at Pwlldu. The stream disappears from time to time underground, for this is lime-

Berriew, Powys

stone country. Pwlldu Head is the highest in Gower, touching 300 ft. To the east is Brandy Cove, with a name to remind us that this was great smuggling territory during the Napoleonic Wars. Smugglers Lane still leads out of the Bishopston valley to Southgate. Here the church has a Jacobean pulpit and a memorial to the poet Vernon Watkins, who lived on the cliff top.

Black Mountains of Gwent, *Powys and Gwent* (5/5A) This fine range of mountains – a delightful surprise for anyone in search of lonely, unspoiled hill country – forms the eastern climax to that long escarpment of Old Red Sandstone that runs along the northern border of the South Wales coalfield. At its eastern end, it overlooks the Hereford plain. These hills must be distinguished from the Black Mountain, which lies away to the west at the other end of the great escarpment (*see* Ammanford). With the exception of the Sugar Loaf and Mynydd Troed, the summits all lie on high-sloping ridges which end

with a plunge to the north, and are separated by deep, narrow valleys. The highest top is Waun Fach which reaches 2660 ft and is set between the deep, out-of-the-world valleys of the Grwyne Fawr and the Grwyne Fach. The walking can be boggy in parts and climbers should be properly equipped and carry a compass. The narrow valleys of the Black Mountains also hold ecclesiastic delights in the small, lost churches (*see* Crickhowell and Llanthony). The road in the Vale of Ewyas climbs up to Gospel Pass at 1778 ft over Hay Bluff, with spectacular views to the north across the BRECON BEACONS National Park.

Blaenavon, *see* Pontypool

Borth, *Dyfed* (1/3B) A holiday resort 5 miles north of ABERYSTWYTH, consisting of one long street sheltering behind a high pebble beach, with fine sands that have a habit of blowing in among the houses in a high wind. The sands run for 3 miles

Overleaf: The Vale of Ewyas, Black Mountains of Gwent

Llyfnant Valley, Dyfed

to the dune-covered point of Ynyslas, stretching out into the Dyfi (Dovey) estuary. There is a nature trail through the dunes here. The railway skirts the edge of the estuary and behind it lies the impressive Borth bog of Cors Fochno. A section of it is now a Nature Reserve, together with part of the Ynyslas dunes. The RSPB has also established a reserve at Ynyshir, next to the grounds of the Ynyshir Hall Hotel at Eglwysfach.

The road east of Cors Fochno skirts the foothills of the wilderness of PLYNLIMON, and the villages along it, from Talybont to Glandyfi, are gateways to narrow side roads leading into lonely and beautiful valleys, where motorists will find turning points difficult. Further on Tre-Taliesin is the reputed birthplace of the 6th-century Welsh poet Taliesin, but the ruined buried chamber, now called Bedd Taliesin (Taliesin's Grave) dates from thousands of years before his time. Tre'r-ddôl is the place where the 1859 Revival began – one of several periodic outbursts of religious enthusiasm that occurred at intervals after the Methodist Revival of the 18th century. The chapel at Tre'r-ddôl is a museum devoted to that Revival. At Furnace, the great waterwheel – once part of an important iron-

works beside the falls of the Einion – has been restored. One mile inland the Taliesin Forest Walk starts from the Forest Office on the A487 in Cwm Einion. A few miles west of MACHYN-LLETH, the Llyfnant river comes out of its romantic valley to join the Dyfi. It also forms the boundary between Dyfed and Powys.

Bosherston, *Dyfed* (3/2B) This small village is $5\frac{1}{2}$ miles south-south-west from PEMBROKE town and is the key to a particularly fine section of coastline. A lane beside the interesting church leads down to the great attraction of Bosherston, the Lily Ponds, a group of small lakes beautifully set in deep woods. In late spring and early summer these lakes are bright with waterlilies. The show is over by August. Stackpole Court nearby was demolished in 1967 and its land with coastline and Lily Ponds transferred to the National Trust. The Pembrokeshire Coast Path will take you westwards past the delightful and tiny private harbour of Stackpole Quay, Barafundle Bay with its secluded beach with sand dunes, and unspoiled Broad Haven to an equally delectable part of the coast around St Govan's Head. It can also be reached by road from Bosherston. From the car park on the edge of the cliffs, a flight of steps takes you down through a fissure in the rocks to the small hidden chapel of St Govan. The chapel itself is 13th-century, but set into the rock is the tiny cell of the 5th-century saint, which takes you back to the days of early Celtic Christianity. The rocky prow of St Govan's Head encloses the view to the east but, on days when no warning flags are flying, it is possible to walk westwards into the CASTLEMARTIN firing range – keeping strictly to the path – to view a remarkable cleft in the rocks known as the Huntsman's Leap.

Brechfa and **Abergorlech,** *Dyfed* (4/2A) Although only 9½ miles north-east of CARMAR-THEN, Brechfa, hidden in a bend in the Cothi valley, must be one of the most secluded villages in South Wales. It has been described as 'on the road to nowhere'. Maybe it is all the better for it. With its few inns and houses clustered around its small, bell-coted church, it seems to have the air of being happy in its seclusion. Fishermen, however, know how to find it for the Cothi, a tributary of the bigger river Tywi, is famous for its sewin or sea trout. The Forestry Commission has been active in this area for many years and the great Brechfa Forest is now coming to maturity. The village cobbler's now houses an attractive pottery. Beyond Brechfa, further up the course of the Cothi, is Abergorlech. Its old, three-arched bridge is a delight. The curious, turtle-backed stones, known as Gorlech stones, are a geological curiosity and come from a narrow bed in the Gorlech stream. They have been used as decoration and as parts of the rockeries in some of the houses. In both villages the Forestry Commission has made provision for visitors, with waymarked forest walks and picnic sites.

Brecon (Aberhonddu), *Powys* (5/4A) The site of this ancient and interesting county town and agricultural centre must be one of the most beautiful in South Wales, with the Brecon Beacons rising nearly 3000 ft in the background above the wooded valley of the Usk. Brecon is also rich in history. The Roman fort of Y Gaer – *Gaer* is fort in Welsh – lies 3 miles west of the present town. Excavated in 1920, its massive, grassy ramparts are pierced by well-built gates. The Normans chose a different site for their castle on a bluff overlooking the junction of the Honddu stream and the Usk, and this castle was the origin of Brecon town. The walls still look impressive from below, but there is little substantial left of what was once an important centre of power in these parts. But close at hand is a Norman foundation which has endured for 600 years – the strong, imposing abbey church, which was elevated to the status of a cathedral for the newly formed diocese of Swansea and Brecon in 1923. Most of its structure is 14th-century, but its exterior still has a stern Norman air as you approach it up the hill from the town. The interior is rich with interesting monuments and chapels.

The main street of Brecon is usually crowded; it widens at St Mary's Church, which contains much original Norman work, including the strong, round pillars of the nave. In 1755, the actor Richard Kemble brought his infant daughter to be christened here, for she had been born in the Shoulder of Mutton inn nearby. She became the great tragedienne, Sarah Siddons, and the inn in the High Street has been renamed in her honour. A more recent musical addition to the town is the annual Jazz Festival held in August, which transforms this little market town into a mini New Orleans for three days. It attracts many artists of world renown. The statue of the Duke of Wellington outside the Wellington Hotel reminds us that Brecon has always been a military town. The old barracks of the county regiment, the South Wales Borderers, is not far beyond the main street on the road to ABERGAVENNY. The regiment is now merged into the Royal Regiment of Wales, but the regimental museum (limited opening) in the old headquarters contains notable memorials of the action at Rorke's Drift in the Zulu War, where the regiment won a record number of Victoria Crosses against overwhelming odds. The Breck-nock Society has created another important museum in the centre of the town which well deserves a visit. Exhibits include a prehistoric boat, a reconstructed Welsh kitchen, a collection of love spoons, and Welsh costumes.

The bridge across the Usk is a fine, five-arched structure. Just beyond it, in the river meadows, is Christ's College, the older of the two recognized public schools in Wales. The other is at LLAN-DOVERY, and the annual rugby match between the two is a notable event for followers of the game. Within the town the Promenade Walk along the banks of the river Usk has been restored.

Brecon Beacons (Bannau Brycheiniog), *Powys* (5/4B) This splendid range of mountains forms the central section of that great escarpment of Old Red Sandstone rock that runs north of the coal-field from the Tywi valley to the borders of England. The CARMARTHENSHIRE FANS and the BLACK MOUNTAINS are part of it, but the Beacons deservedly take the centre of the stage. The twin flat-topped summits are unmistakable over a wide area of South Wales. Pen-y-Fan at 2906 ft is the higher but its twin summit, Corn Du, is only 43 ft lower. The sharp-pointed Cribyn keeps them company on the flank, and the whole forms an impressive mountain spectacle. The panorama includes not only the Beacons themselves but a whole series of lesser but still high summits stretching away to the west, and presenting a bold front to the upper Usk valley. These form the Fforest Fawr, the Great Forest, once the hunting domain of the Lords of Brecon.

Three roads cross the massif, which provide convenient access for the walker and give the motorist some taste of the scenic splendours that are concealed in the inner recesses of the range. Two start from Merthyr on the south side of the Beacons. The most easterly one, narrow in parts, follows the valley of the Taff Fechan, past Vaynor and Pontsticill. This was the route followed by

The Brecon Beacons under snow

the old Brecon and Merthyr Railway. The track has long since been pulled up, but a small section of it from Pont to the Pontsticill Reservoir has been converted into a delightful little narrow gauge railway. The road drops down onto the other side past Talybont Reservoir, which supplies NEWPORT (Gwent) with water. The second road – part of the scenic A470 north–south trunk road – leaves Merthyr and goes through the central part of the Beacons range, following the main Taff stream to its source. At the top of the pass is the old Storey Arms inn, now a mountain pursuits centre. The popular track to the summits of the Beacons starts close by. A gently sloping path takes you easily upwards and an hour and a half at the most will land you on the top of Pen-y-Fan. You have climbed the easy side and it is well to remember that there are precipices on the north side, and that the summits are just short of 3000 ft, distinctly dangerous in bad weather. From the Storey Arms the road drops down the Tarell Valley, past the cliffs of the Nature Reserve of Craig Cerrig Gleisiad on the left. A little further down a side road at Libanus leads to the Brecon Beacons National Park Mountain Centre, excellently laid out and a useful start for anyone wishing to explore the range.

A third road crosses the great escarpment from the top of the Neath valley to Sennybridge on the Usk. It has spectacular zigzag bends with a Roman milestone near the top of the pass and the massive prehistoric stone of the Maen Llia just before the drop into the Senni valley.

Breidden Hills, *Powys* (2/3B) These bold, pointed, volcanic hills 7 miles north-east from WELSHPOOL are visible from far out on the plains about Shrewsbury. They mark the point where the Severn flows into England. The highest of the sharp cones is Moel y Golfa (1324 ft), but its sister summits, Middletown Hill and Breidden, are almost equally high. Breidden itself is quarried on the western side and a tall pillar stands on the summit. It was erected in 1782 in honour of Admiral Rodney, who won the Battle of the Saints against the French in the American War of Independence. Another memorial near the Breiddens is the Prince's Oak. Take the road east from Llandrinio; just before you cross into England, the oak – now somewhat decayed – stands on your right. It marks the spot where the Prince of Wales, later George IV, visited the Principality for the first and only time as its prince. He drank a glass with the loyal local gentry and then hurried back to the more appealing

Walkers, near the Brecon Beacons

delights of Brighton.

A final curiosity on the border – at Middletown Hill was the home of Old Parr, said to be the oldest man in Britain. He was born in the reign of Edward IV and died in the reign of Charles I, aged – it was claimed – 153. Charles insisted on seeing the old man who was brought to London. The journey proved too much for him and he died of the shock. He was, however, buried in Westminster Abbey.

Bridgend (Pen-y-Bont ar Ogwr), *Mid-Glamorgan* (4/3C) A busy and successful town about 20 miles west of CARDIFF at the western end of the Vale of Glamorgan. Its position, at the point where a group of mining valleys open out on to the Vale, made it a natural market and administrative centre for a wide area. The Llynfi, Ogmore and Garw rivers unite to flow through the town. The Normans naturally found it a convenient centre to control the mountains to the north which were held by the Welsh. The scanty remains of their castle, known as the Newcastle, still stand on the hill overlooking Bridgend from the west. The real growth of Bridgend began when coal began to be mined in the valleys to the north. Unfortunately the little mining townships of the Ogwr and Garw

are in decline, but Bridgend has successfully survived the Great Depression. A Royal Ordnance Factory, established in the Second World War, has been developed into a big trading estate which continues to attract industry. The Ford Motor company is an important employer here, at its modern new engine plant.

Modern Bridgend has equipped itself with new leisure and shopping centres, but has not lost its old atmosphere of being a market town, not only for the mining valleys, but for the agricultural Vale. Two miles north of the M4 junction at nearby Sarn, the Blaen Garw Country Park has been established.

Broad Haven, *Dyfed* (3/1B) This small seaside resort stands near the centre of the wide sweep of St Brides Bay in west Wales. St Bride or St Brigid of Kildare (*c.* 450–525) was an Irish saint whose cult spread to west Wales and far beyond on to the Continent. This part of the coast is in English-speaking Dyfed. There are a few anchorages in sheltered coves along this strongly cliffed coastline. One is Nolton Haven, busy when the Pembrokeshire coal trade flourished in the 19th century, but now crowded with caravans. The anthracite coal measures are compressed into a remarkably few miles between Newgale and Little Haven. The small collieries are now gone but the coal seams can be distinguished in the cliffs. Broad Haven has fine sands at low tide, and a narrow promenade along the sea front. Just over the hill is Little Haven, with its colour-washed houses and an inn on the rocks overlooking the beach.

The Pembrokeshire Coast National Park Information Centre, located at Kilgetty, near SAUNDERSFOOT, illustrates the mining history of the whole area.

Builth Wells (Llanfair-ym-Muallt), Powys (5/4A) A market town set in a lush and beautiful section of the Wye valley, which added Wells to its name after Lady Hester Stanhope, the niece of the younger Pitt, stayed nearby at the beginning of the 19th century. The waters are no longer drunk, but Builth has gained a new importance by becoming the permanent headquarters of the Royal Welsh Show. Livestock sales are also held regularly at the showground. For one crowded week in summer every year it becomes the agricultural capital of Wales. The grounds lie across the river at Llanelwedd and are joined to the main town by a many-arched bridge across the Wye. The statue of the local poet at the bridge side has aroused controversy. A pleasant tree-lined promenade along the river bank is the framework for the main street. Overlooking the river on the south side is the flourishing Wyeside Arts Centre, which holds a regular programme of concerts, theatre, films and art exhibitions. Builth is mainly 19th-century as far as architecture is concerned. The large church of St Mary's has been extensively rebuilt, and the remains of the once important castle are buried under grassy mounds behind the Lion Hotel. It played a tragic part, as far as the Welsh were concerned, in the final Welsh War of Edward I. Llywelyn, the last native Prince of Wales, had slipped out of Snowdonia in an attempt to get reinforcements from South Wales. He became separated from his men and was run through by an English knight from the castle at Builth. A monument, consisting of a single great stone from Snowdonia, now stands at the roadside at Cilmery, 4 miles west, near the spot where tradition maintains that Llywelyn died.

Builth is a pony-trekking centre with hillsides above the Wye. To the south of Builth, the Wye runs through wooded hills which become romantically rocky at Aberedw. It is popular with fishermen, and downstream it also attracts enthusiastic white-water canoeists. High among the rocks above the village is Llywelyn's Cave,

where the Prince may have spent the night before he died. At Erwood, in a particularly fine section of the stream, a light bridge crosses the Wye. In the old days this was the place where the drovers urged their bellowing cattle through the shallows on their way to the markets of England. There are some good walks on Mynydd Epynt – east of the B4519.

Burry Port and **Pembrey,** Dyfed (4/1B) The little harbour of Burry Port, on the railway line west of LLANELLI, was the creation of the great days of the coal and tinplate trade. Those days are over and the small port, dominated by a big power station, is now only of interest to local yachtsmen, who are familiar with the complex channels of the Burry estuary and the dangerous Cefn Sidan Sands.

The oldest building in the area is Pembrey Church, with the village pound still at the gate. The tall tower is Norman and the timber roof 16th-century. In the churchyard is a monument to a French soldier, Col. Coquilin, and his daughter Adeline. They were drowned when their ship, the Jeanne Emma, struck the Cefn Sidan Sands. The inscription states that Adeline was 'the niece of Josephine, Consort to the renowned individual Napoleon Bonaparte'. Envious neighbours suggested that many of the wrecks were 'assisted' by the people of Pembrey – to their great profit. As a result, the men of Pembrey were known as 'Gwyr y Bwyell Bach', the Men of the Little Hatchets. These were supposed to come in useful when it came to cutting off fingers for their rings. In truth the Cefn Sidan Sands were dangerous enough in an onshore wind in the days of sail without human intervention. Today, they form a splendidly uncluttered stretch of sand, devoted to bass fishing and sand yachting. To the west of Pembrey is a country park with an exhibition and visitor centre, woodland, grassland and an extensive sandy beach which has become one of the top ten visitor attractions in Wales. Nearby the Welsh Motor Sports Centre holds a series of motor racing events throughout the year. Behind the town lies Mynydd Pen-bre – the Pembrey Mountain.

Caerleon, Gwent (5/5C) The City of the Legions lies 4 miles up river from NEWPORT (Gwent) at a point where the fiercely tidal Usk could be safely bridged. The houses of the Newport suburbs creep ever closer, but Caerleon still reminds us, at every turn, of its two great claims to fame – its

The Roman amphitheatre, Caerleon

association with the Romans and with King Arthur.

The Roman advance into South Wales met its fiercest resistance from the tribe of the Silures, and Isca Silurum was established as a base from which this wild country could be subdued. From Isca a network of roads and forts spread through the whole of Wales. Its counterpart in the north was Chester. Isca became the permanent home of the Second Augusta Legion, 5600 strong. The fort covered 5½ acres, and the outline of the ramparts can be clearly traced on the west and south-west, although houses still cover the rest of the site. The parish church stands on the foundations of the old basilica, and a large section of the wall and the legionary barracks can be seen in the Prysg field. The showpiece, however, is the Roman amphitheatre, excavated by Sir Mortimer Wheeler in 1920. In the Middle Ages, it was covered with grass and known as King Arthur's Round Table. That powerful romancer, Geoffrey of Monmouth, cast Caerleon in the role of King Arthur's Camelot and Tennyson, the poet, came here to capture the Arthurian atmosphere when he was writing the 'Idylls of the King'. More recent excavations have exposed the remains of the Roman Baths, which are interpreted in a new exhibition centre at the site which is in the hands of CADW.

The excellent little Legionary Museum near the church, recently rebuilt and now part of the National Museum of Wales, has a comprehensive display of the finds made over many years of careful excavation. Further along the High Street, tall walls hide the castle, with its Norman motte, which, because it stood in Caerleon, gathered legends around it. It was the haunt of Merlin and, from its summit, you can see the Bristol Channel. Even the modern traffic, swirling through the narrow streets, cannot eliminate Caerleon's Roman and Arthurian magic.

Caerphilly (Caerffili), *Mid Glamorgan* (5/5C) Some 7 miles north of CARDIFF, this town is famous for two things – its cheese and its castle. The cheese market, once famous throughout the mining valleys of South Wales, closed in 1910, but the castle remains – a vast fortification, second only to Windsor in size among the castles of Britain, and a magnificent example of what a great medieval stronghold looked like at the peak of castle building. Visitors to Caerphilly often wonder why such a huge and expensive structure should have been built on what may seem a comparatively obscure site. Caerphilly's strategic position becomes clear when you drive to it from Cardiff over the 888 ft high Caerphilly Mountain. In recent years the town has spread out with industrial estates and new housing, but you can still see how Caerphilly controls the exits from all the valleys to the north – all still Welsh strongholds in the Middle Ages. This was the time when the Welsh cause had notably revived under the leadership of Llywelyn ap Gruffydd, the last native Prince of Wales. In 1266 Gilbert de Clare, Lord of Glamorgan, felt that he had to overawe the men of the hills by building the greatest castle ever planned in Wales.

Caerphilly was built when the art of castle construction had reached its climax in Europe. The concentric principle demanded that there should be two rings of defences, one inside the other. The inner ring was higher and could still dominate the outer one, even if the enemy breached the latter. A moat surrounded the whole castle so that siege engines could not get near the fortifications – this was the nearest to an impregnable castle that the Middle Ages could show. Caerphilly is a concentric masterpiece. In addition, it has a vast barbican in front of the main construction, and its moat is on the grand scale. The castle was only taken by the voluntary surrender of the garrison. The 'leaning tower' in the inner ward was created when the castle was 'slighted' after the Civil War. Caerphilly is now under the care of CADW, the Welsh equivalent of the English Heritage Authority. CADW plans to add to the attractions of Caerphilly with boat trips around the moat and special functions in the restored Great Hall.

Finally, cheese-making has returned to Caerphilly. The old Court House has now been imaginatively renovated as an inn and restaurant, and guests can see Caerphilly cheese being made according to the old formula as they look across to the illuminated towers of the castle, mirrored in the moat.

Caersws, *Powys* (2/2B) Caersws lies in the heart of typical Mid Wales country – with the rich meadows of the Severn backed by high hills not far from NEWTOWN. The Romans had a fort here, and the outlines can be traced near the railway station. The popular 19th-century Welsh poet Ceiriog (John Hughes) was general manager

of the little Van railway, which ran from the main line at Caersws up to the rich Van lead mines. It must have been the only railway in the world with a poet as general manager. The passenger traffic never paid but the shareholders got a lot of poetry for their money.

At Caersws, the railway leaves the Severn and follows the Carno valley westwards. Carno itself is a small village with two claims to fame. The first is the inn with the extraordinary sign of the Aleppo Merchant. Some say it celebrates a local man who made a fortune out of Middle East trade. Others, less romantic, claim that the inn derived its name from the special pudding made there, with liberal allowances of Middle East raisins. The second claim to fame is more substantial. Laura Ashley set up her first factory here for those dresses, materials and furnishings with a bright, refreshing country style about them that have won worldwide acceptance. She died in a tragic accident in 1986.

A few miles south from Caersws, along the main Severn valley, is Llandinam the birthplace of David Davies, the railway and coal king, whose statue stands at the roadside (*see also* Barry and Rhondda Valleys). The Davies money has returned to Wales through the numerous contributions made by the family to the world of art and social improvement, including the valuable collection of French Impressionist paintings at the National Museum of Wales, CARDIFF.

Caersws offers a final pleasure. Just before you cross the bridge over the Severn you pass Maesmawr Hall, a fine example of oak-framed Jacobean black-and-white architecture. It is now a hotel. Many black-and-white timbered buildings – most of them farms – can be seen nearby in the upper Severn Valley.

Caerwent, *Gwent* (5/6C) This is an evocative place. The M4 motorway from the SEVERN BRIDGE passes near it, but Caerwent remains a place apart. Its secret lies in its remote past. Some 1500 years ago, Caerwent was Venta Silurum, the biggest Roman city in south-west Britain after Bath. It was the market town of the Silures, after they had submitted at last to Rome. Roman legionaries retired here after their period of service at CAERLEON. It was a peaceful civilian settlement, until the growing troubles of the Empire in the 4th century forced it to equip itself with walls. A long line of the south walls remains intact with its multi-angular towers – one of the

The Carno Valley

most impressive remnants of Roman power remaining above ground in this country. The remains of the shops and houses around the forum have also been excavated, and the main street of the little village still follows the line of the central avenue of the Roman city. Numerous Roman relics are displayed in the porch of the church, but most of the finds are now in Newport Museum.

The church is dedicated to St Stephen, but the founder was the old Celtic saint, Tathan. In 1912 it was claimed that the bones of St Tathan had been discovered. They were reverently reburied in the south aisle under an inscribed slab now covered with a red carpet. The fine carved oak pulpit dates from 1632 and bears the inscription, 'Woe unto me if I preach not the gospel'.

Penhow Castle, which lies 2 miles west, served as a lookout for the great Norman castle at Chepstow. It has a 12th-century keep, a dovecot, and a Tudor wing.

Caldey Island (Ynys Pyr), *Dyfed* (3/3B) All the fascinating islands off the Dyfed coast have their own individual charm and character. Caldey has always been the Isle of the Monks. This small island, $1\frac{1}{2}$ miles long and $\frac{3}{4}$ mile wide, lies about 3

The Roman tower and wall, Caerwent

miles offshore, within sight of the busy holiday resort of TENBY. The day trippers come over during the summer months, but once they are gone the island returns to the peace and seclusion that were such poweful attractions to those early Celtic monks who first settled here. The island takes its Welsh name from their first abbot, Pyr. The first monastic community may have been destroyed by the Vikings, who gave its Norse name of Caldey – the Cold Isle.

The Middle Ages saw the arrival of the Benedictines, and their simple priory and St Illtud's Church, its spire 40 inches out of true and its floor paved with pebbles from the beach, still stand. The church contains a 6th-century Ogham Stone. The monks did not return to Caldey after the Dissolution until the 1900s, when Abbot Aelred came here with his Anglican Benedictines. He had ambitious plans for building an abbey on the scale of the great foundations of the Middle Ages. He completed part of it, but the funds ran out so he and his monks joined the Catholic church and left Caldey. The island monastery is now occupied by monks of a Belgian Cistercian order, who are self-sufficient. They work on the land, and the perfume they make is sold to visitors from their shop on the mainland at Tenby.

The limestone caves of the island are rich in prehistoric remains. The stone was worked extensively on the little islet of St Margaret's, which is joined to the main island at low tide. Caldey is the home of numerous seabirds who have their separate colonies here. Boat trips run regularly from Tenby harbour in the summer months.

Caldicot, *Gwent* (5/6C) Caldicot, near the SEVERN BRIDGE on the Welsh side, looks out over the strange, level fen-like country that borders the Bristol Channel as far as NEWPORT (Gwent). It has a castle which played little part in history, but was well restored in the 19th century and is now well known for its medieval banquets. A country park surrounds the castle. The old pumping station for the Severn Tunnel at Port-skewett, a marvel of Victorian steam engineering, has been dismantled, to the regret of industrial archaeologists. The main line emerges from the tunnel near Severn Tunnel Junction, and the large church at Magor, close to the railway line, is known as the Cathedral of the Moors. It looks out over the Caldicot Levels which, together with the Wentloog Levels between Newport and CARDIFF, are protected from the sea by a high dyke, well seen at Gold Cliff. The protection is needed, for the sea broke through in 1607, and the Drowning of Wentloog Hundred was long remembered by the ballad singers. The height reached by the sea is marked on the walls of the churches of the levels. In the background are the huge and complex structures of the Llanwern Steelworks just outside Newport.

Cardiff (Caerdydd), *South Glamorgan* (5/5C) Cardiff is the capital of Wales. It was only officially designated as the capital in the reign of our present queen, Elizabeth II, in 1955, but it had long been preparing for its premier position. In the 19th century it expanded at an astonishing rate, in response to the great boom in the coal trade. The city fathers wisely used some of their newly acquired wealth to plan an impressive Civic Centre. The government offices and the national institutions were naturally attracted to the biggest centre of population in the Principality, and today Cardiff has over 275,000 inhabitants. Not big as capital cities go, but perhaps all the better for it. Cardiff is still a place where people can get to know each other and not

be overwhelmed in some huge, heartless conurbation. It is also – to the surprise of many visitors who arrive with pictures of coalmines and heavy industry in their minds – a clean, smokeless city, where the nearest mines are 10 miles away to the north, hidden in the valleys. Communications to the city are good – London is a mere 1 hour 40 minutes away by train.

Fervent Welsh nationalists criticized the choice of Cardiff as the capital. They claimed that it was hardly a truly Welsh city. In the days of its expansion it naturally attracted not only Welshmen but people from over the border and even from overseas. Yet somehow the city has succeeded in absorbing all these diverse elements and the Welsh have also played their part. The capital is the centre of Welsh broadcasting and television. Statistically, Cardiff has a remarkable amount of Welsh speakers even though you do not hear the language commonly used in the streets. On the day when Wales play rugby in the National Stadium at Cardiff Arms Park it is another matter!

Cardiff Castle is the heart of the city and the focus of its early history. The Romans built a big fort here in the days when the Empire was girding itself against pressure from the barbarians outside the boundaries. A surprising amount of Roman walling remains above ground and the outlines of the rest have been carefully reconstructed. The east and north walls of Cardiff Castle give an excellent impression of what a great Roman fort looked like in its heyday.

The Normans were the next people to leave their imprint on the castle. By 1091, Robert Fitzhamon, Earl of Gloucester, had begun the conquest of Glamorgan, and a motte and bailey were constructed inside the old, ruined Roman fort. The motte, or mound, is still there – the largest in Wales and crowned with a later shell keep of stone. In the 13th century a new walled circuit and towers enclosed a wider area. The final transformation of Cardiff Castle came in Victorian days, and an astonishing transformation it proved to be. The 3rd Marquess of Bute was one of the richest men in Britain and he had the money, produced from the world of coal and the Cardiff docks created by the 2nd Marquess, to realize his dream of what a medieval castle should look like. He employed an architect of genius, William Burges, and the result is a splendid fantasy in stone. A new clock tower soared from the south curtain wall to become one of Cardiff's most notable landmarks. The interior is even more remarkable. Every room seems to be

Above: The City Hall, Cardiff

a glittering jewel box. The magnificent Banqueting Hall makes a splendid entertaining centre for important visitors to the city, and the castle also houses the Welsh Regiment Museum. It is open to the public for organized tours.

The castle park runs north alongside the River Taff for some miles to Llandaff Cathedral. It has presented Cardiff with the fortunate gift of a magnificent open space right through the heart of the city. On the west side of the Taff lie the Sports Centre, the Glamorgan Cricket Club ground and a long line of football and cricket pitches. A stately avenue of tall trees runs along the edge of this parkland. A cycle path through the park links the three castles of Cardiff, Castell Coch and CAERPHILLY.

The Bute interests gave Cardiff another opportunity for happy expansion when the family sold Cathays Park, the open space immediately to the east of the castle, to the city fathers for £16,000. Here the council took the bold decision to lay out an administrative centre on the largest scale.

Left: The Keep, Cardiff Castle

These were the heady days of the early 20th century, when Cardiff's prosperity, firmly based on coal, seemed destined to last for ever. Along the wide avenues, a whole series of important buildings were grouped into a harmonious whole, with the City Hall in the centre flanked by the Law Courts and the National Museum with its re-created coal mine. This dignified classical building also houses the national picture collection, which is especially strong in French Impressionists and Post-Impressionists. The New Theatre, close at hand, is the home of the Welsh National Opera Company, which has acquired a European reputation.

South of the Civic Centre is the main shopping area of the city. In its middle stands the city church of St John's with its fine 15th-century tower and rich interior. It reminds us that Cardiff grew up as a little town in the shadow of church and castle. They owned the land along the River Taff and space was tight when the great expansion of the city began in the 19th century. The shopkeepers found their solution by building shopping arcades which have always been a convenient and delightful feature of the Cardiff scene. When the rebuilding of the shopping area took place in the 1970s, the arcade principle was adhered to with pleasing success. The occasion was also seized to give Cardiff a much-needed concert complex, and St David's Hall ranks among the finest of modern concert halls in Europe for its acoustics.

The docks, once the very lifeblood of the city, have sadly declined, but again Cardiff has grasped the opportunity of turning what was, on the face of it, a loss to the city into a new asset. As the old docks are filled in, new buildings arise. The South Glamorgan Council will have its new County Hall here, where a steam centre is being established. The new Industrial and Maritime Museum has been established near the old pier head in Bute Street as part of a major dockland development which will include a big trade centre, mooring, housing and other facilities. The opulent Victorian Coal Exchange was hopefully converted to act as the new Assembly for Wales. Alas, the Assembly was rejected. Only 13 per cent of the population voted for it at the referendum. But much of the building is put to good use, housing television studios serving Sianel Pedwar Cymru, the Welsh language fourth channel.

Cardiff's suburbs also hold surprises. Llandaff, at the end of the park lands that run north from the castle, has a cathedral which, like Coventry, was bombed during the Second World

Above: Castell Coch

War, but has risen triumphantly again from the ruin. It is well worth a visit (*see* Llandaff). Some miles further north, at the wooded entrance to the main valley of the Taff and clearly visible to drivers along the M4 motorway, is the fairly-tale castle of Castell Coch, again an architectural fantasy of the 3rd Marquess of Bute and his architect, William Burges – owned by CADW, it is open to the public.

St Fagans, a few miles to the west, can supply a contrasting experience. Here the Welsh Folk Museum, a branch of the National Museum, has been established in an old Jacobean mansion and the surrounding 80 acres. The gardens are a delight, and the galleries display an excellent collection of exhibits illustrating the old social life of Wales. Everything seems to be here from Welsh dressers to love spoons. Perhaps the most imaginative part of the museum's layout is the erection in the grounds of traditional buildings from the 15th to the early 19th century, including

Right: Interior of the Welsh Chapel,
St Fagan's Folk Museum, Cardiff

farmhouses, two working mills, a tannery, chapel, even a country school, all moved stone by stone from various parts of Wales. The whole place is one of Cardiff's greatest attractions for the visitor – a worthy adjunct to a national capital.

Cardiff City Council Parks Department has organized a series of walks and nature trails in the area. Leaflets are available from the City Hall.

Cardigan (Aberteifi), *Dyfed* (3/3A) Cardigan stands at the point where the river Teifi starts to open out into its estuary. The Normans built their castle here, on a knoll looking down on the river. It looks a little woe-begone today, with its outer walls propped up with steel girders, but Welshmen will remember that this was the castle to which the Lord Rhys, who then held it, summoned the bards and musicians of Wales in the 12th century to the first National Eisteddfod. The old bridge below the castle has survived with more success. Its six arches have been strengthened and widened, and the old warehouse around it reminds us of Cardigan's past, in the early 19th century, as one of the busiest ports in Wales. With the advent of the railway, Cardigan

Cardigan Town Hall

lost its sea-going importance and slipped back to its present role as a pleasant market town, much frequented by tourists in the summer.

The main street sweeps up from the bridge past the castle, and is lined with shops and hotels. At the central point stands the most surprising building in Cardigan – a 19th-century Town Hall in a style that can only be described as pseudo-Gothic with a touch of the Middle East. It is crowned by a chirpy little clock tower. The parish church of St Mary's has been extensively rebuilt; next to it, beside the river, is the site of the old Benedictine priory. It was renowned throughout Wales for the wonder-working image of the Virgin and her miraculous taper. Both priory and taper were swept away in Henry VIII's Dissolution of the Monasteries.

The Teifi estuary winds through wooded hills from Cardigan to the sea. One mile from the town, on the south side of the Teifi, is St Dogmaels and its ruined abbey. The road ends at the popular beach of Poppit. Here the Pembrokeshire Coast Path begins with a stiff climb up to the 600 ft high Cemaes Head, with its remarkable, contorted cliffs of Pen-yr-Afr. Across the estuary from Poppit Sands, Gwbert-on-Sea marks the northern exit of the Teifi to the sea.

Cardigan Island

Here there are small bays of shingle but bathing is only safe close to the beach. From the grounds of the hotel, with its small golfcourse, you can look across to Cardigan Island, a reserve of the West Wales Naturalists' Trust which carries a particularly shy variety of the old Norse breed of Soay sheep. The low cliff line continues north, seal-haunted and loud with the clamour of seabirds, to Mwnt (*see* Aberporth).

Cardigan Wildlife Park along the river banks has animals and birds found in the area. The town is also popular as a fishing centre for salmon and sea trout.

Carew, *Dyfed* (3/2B) A small village, strung along the road leading down to an attractive waterway, part of the upper reaches of MILFORD HAVEN. It has three attractions: the castle, the Celtic cross and the church. The castle was first built by Gerald de Windsor, on his marriage to Nest, the daughter of Rhys ap Tewdwr, the last King of South Wales. Her numerous matrimonial adventures gave her the title of 'The Helen of Wales'. The main construction of the castle dates from the 13th century. Its moment of greatest glory

came in 1507, when Sir Rhys ap Thomas, supporter of Henry VII, held a memorable tournament here. The dam at the foot of the castle holds back the waters to work the only tidal mill still functioning in Wales.

The high Celtic cross stands in an enclosure opposite the inn. Like the cross at NEVERN, it is decorated with complex, twisting patterns, including a swastika. The inscription reads: *Margiteut rex Eng. fili* – Maredudd the King, son of Edwin.

Carew Church stands a ½ mile south of the castle across the main road. It has the usual tall defensive Pembrokeshire tower and contains some fine tombs. One depicts a little girl (*c.* 1325) holding a heart. It was formerly claimed to represent a 'boy bishop'.

Carmarthen (Caerfyrddin), *Dyfed* (4/1B) Carmarthen is the administrative centre for the new county of Dyfed, which has swallowed the old Carmarthenshire, Pembrokeshire and Cardiganshire. It stands at the point where the long estuary of the Tywi (Towy) begins to be tidal. The old bridge has been replaced by a new concrete one, and little remains of the castle beyond the gatehouse. The site, once the strong point of royal power in south-west Wales, is now occupied by the County Hall, with its high slate roof. It dominates the view of Carmarthen from the river. Visitors to Carmarthen on a busy market day will be surprised to find that the Welsh name for Carmarthen – Caerfyrddin – invests it with the aura of high romance. It is the town of Myrddin, or Merlin in English, the Great Enchanter of Arthurian Legend fame. For centuries Merlin's Oak stood on the outskirts to the town. The wizard himself prophesied:

> When the oak falls down
> Then falls the town.

The stump of the oak, propped up by concrete, was finally condemned as a traffic hazard and, not without some forebodings, removed to the Carmarthen Museum. Surprisingly, the town still stands and prospers.

Carmarthen's history is more solidly based than on the misty but romantic memories of Merlin. The Romans had a fort here, Moridunum, the capital of the Demetae. The amphitheatre has recently been excavated and partially restored. The parish church of St Peter stands on the site of the fort and has a Roman altar in the porch. It is a dark, austere building and has a memorial to Sir Richard Steele, who retired to quiet Carmarthen after editing *The Tatler* and *The Spectator* in London. His wife had property at Llangunnor, 1 mile south across the river from Carmarthen. In Spilman Street, a stained-glass window in the Ivy Bush inn commemorates the fact that the eccentric genius, Iolo Morganwg (Edward Williams), in 1819 succeeded in wedding the Gorsedd to the National Eisteddfod in a ceremony held in the hotel garden.

Carmarthen had a taste for memorials and statues, especially if they had a military connection. The statue of General Sir William Nott, who played a gallantly obscure part in the Afghan wars, stands before the castle gateway. Nott Square leads down to the Guildhall and Law Courts, with the South African War memorial in front of the classical and dignified Guildhall façade. Carmarthen's longest and widest thoroughfare, Lammas Street, contains the Crimean War memorial to the Royal Welch Fusiliers and, as you leave the town to the west, you pass the obelisk to Sir Thomas Picton, who fell at Waterloo. The top of the monument has been removed giving it a stumpy appearance. Has Carmarthen lost its taste for military commemoration? There has been talk of removing the gate of the old Workhouse, through which the

dragoons charged on the Rebecca rioters on a memorable day in 1849.

The old town has undergone a certain amount of rebuilding behind Guildhall Square. The market has gone, although the attractive old clock tower has been retained. The new market hall, however, has kept the atmosphere of the old one and there is a wonderful variety of stalls ranging from those selling Welsh flannel and laverbread to a maker of love spoons. Even the ancient coracle fishermen are represented. There are still 12 registered practitioners of the craft of salmon fishing in coracles, these strange lightweight turtle-shaped and portable boats, made of wickerwork and tarred canvas, which go back to prehistoric times. Fishmonger Raymond Rees still makes them and has a specimen in his market stall.

It remains to add that every day seems to be market day in Carmarthen. A charter of Henry VIII gave the innkeepers the right to open all day on the five market days – a practice which has made Carmarthen a relaxed and happy town.

The Tywi flows in from the east here, and a mile or so upstream is Abergwili, with the Bishop's Palace for the diocese of St David's. Part of it now forms the excellent Carmarthen Museum which displays many local finds. Three miles north of Carmarthen at Bronwydd Arms is the Gwili Railway, a standard-gauge steam-operated railway which runs during summer.

Carmarthenshire Fans (Bannau Sir Gar), *Dyfed and Powys* (4/3B) This fine range – part of the Old Red Sandstone escarpment that makes such an impressive barrier across South Wales – rivals the BRECON BEACONS in its attraction for walkers, although it is not quite so high. Still, Ban Brycheiniog, the highest point, reaches the respectable level of 2642 ft, and looks every inch of it. The Fans have one advantage over the Beacons – they are far less frequented. Strong walkers will have no difficulty in reaching the summits, but again, bad weather can present dangers for the inexperienced. Map, compass and proper equipment are wise (*see also* Black Mountains and Ammanford).

One of the best points of entry for the motorist is the attractive limestone region at the top end of the SWANSEA valley. Once past CRAIG-Y-NOS the road starts its climb over the main range. At Tavern-y-Garreg there is a choice of routes. The road to the east runs under the high prow of Fan Gihirych then down past the Cray Reservoir and Defynnog, with its interesting church, to reach the Usk valley at Sennybridge. The western road from the fork at Tavern-y-Garreg takes you deeper into the mountains. It climbs under the layered cliffs of Fan Hir to the summmit of the pass over to Trecastle. Near the top of the pass a boggy track leads up the steep mountainside which brings you to the dark and sinister lake of Llyn-y-Fan Fawr – the Lake of the Big Fan. A steep pull up an impressive and narrow path places you on the highest summit. Strong walkers can continue westwards along the edge of the steep slopes and cliffs that takes them on to the choicest part of the range, the mysterious lake of Llyn-y-Fan Fach, cradled by dark precipices. This is the scene of the well-known legend of the Lady of the Lake, and can be reached by an easier route from the north up the wide track from the Llanelli waterworks in the Sawdde valley. This walk among the two lakes is one of the best mountain expeditions South Wales has to offer.

Carreg Cennen Castle, *Dyfed* (4/2B) It is hard to avoid superlatives when you start describing this small but astonishing castle 3 miles south-east of LLANDEILO. Its site is its fortune, for it is perched on the summit of a 300 ft limestone crag which leaps up from the secret valley of the Cennen, with the dark ridge of the Black Mountain in the background. Its history is tangled and obscure. It was in Welsh hands in the 12th century under the Lord Rhys. Thereafter, it was

in English hands. It looks impregnable, but Owain Glyndwr captured it – no doubt he had sympathizers inside the walls. It was demolished after the Wars of the Roses, when Sir Richard Herbert of Raglan got rid of what he described 'a nest of robbers, living by robbery and despoiling our people'. It remained in quiet obscurity, until the car made it easier of access to visitors.

It has an inner ward and an outer one, defended by a barbican with a deep rock-cut ditch, but its most remarkable feature is the passage, cut along the face of the rock, with dizzy views down the precipice, which suddenly turns and drives deep into the heart of the cliff. It supplies an adventurous trip for tourists, groping their way in the darkness to the wishing well. The castle is now in the hands of CADW, and the farm at its foot adds to the attractions by showing rare breeds of animals and sheep-shearing demonstrations among other things.

Castlemartin, *Dyfed* (3/2B) This village is $4\frac{1}{2}$ miles south-west of PEMBROKE town by road, but most visitors will come to it perforce, for at the breezy bay of Freshwater West, the Pembrokeshire Coast Path is compelled to make a wide detour to avoid the firing range at Linney

The Green Bridge of Wales, near Castlemartin, see
pp. 42 and 106   *(Martin Dohrn)*

Head. The headquarters of the range is at Warren, just outside Castlemartin. Castlemartin has a fine church with a tall, defensive tower that dominates the country around. The village pound still stands, and has been converted into a pleasant shelter with seats. The village gave its name to a famous breed of cattle, which has now been merged, in the herd book, with the Welsh Blacks.

From Castlemartin the road cuts back to the coastline through the ranges to reach the Eligug or Stack Rocks. There is a car park on the cliff top. In early summer, the Stacks are an astonishing sight, with breeding birds clinging to every nook and crack in the cliffs. Nor far beyond is the fine natural limestone arch known as the Green Bridge of Wales.

Ceibwr *see* Moylegrove

Cenarth *see* Cilgerran

Chepstow (Cas Gwent), *Gwent* (5/6B) Perched on its steep hillside, with its impressive castle set above the winding river Wye, Chepstow is a splendid point of entry into South Wales. Before the construction of the great SEVERN BRIDGE nearby, the steep winding streets of the town presented a traffic problem, which has certainly been eased by the bridge. The name is derived from the Old English *ceap* (market) and *stow* (place or town). The Romans probably forded the Wye here, and there are traces of OFFA'S DYKE on the English side to the east of the town. The Normans built the first castle, and a powerful ·one it is. The great square keep is particularly notable. The round tower to the left of the gatehouse is the Martin Tower, named after Henry Martin, the regicide, who was imprisoned here for 20 years. He was that rarity among Parliamentarians, a wit and a lover of the ladies. He is buried in the much-restored church and his gravestone is inscribed with his own ironic epitaph:

> My time was spent in serving you and you
> And death's the pay, it seems, and welcome, too.

In the centre of the town is Beaufort Square, laid out, like everything in Chepstow, on a slope. The Town Gate stands at the top of High Street and the town still possesses its medieval defences known as the Port Walls. Chepstow is also a town of bridges. The road bridge across the Wye,

Previous page: Chepstow Castle

constructed by John Rennie in 1816, was one of the earliest iron bridges in Britain. Brunel built the original railway bridge – a tubular suspension bridge.

To the north of the town is the well-known Chepstow Racecourse, laid out on one of the finest sites in the country, Piercefield Park. Proud lions still guard the entrance gates. Racing men will have a fellow feeling for Valentine Morris, the 18th-century grandee who laid out the park in its present splendour. He had to leave hastily for the West Indies to restore his falling fortunes. The tradesmen of Chepstow rang a special peal on the church bells as he drove through the town for the last time. The park is surrounded by a long stone wall. Once past it you approach the splendours of TINTERN and the lower reaches of the Wye. The Wyndcliff Nature Trail gives fine views of the Wye and starts at the car park $\frac{1}{2}$ mile from St Arvans.

Chepstow today is also well-known for its golf courses at St Pierre, the venue for many championship events. The town's museum recalls its seafaring and shipbuilding traditions.

Cilgerran, *Dyfed* (3/3A) This large village is a single long street, 2 miles south of CARDIGAN. Here the river Teifi cuts its way through a gorge of great beauty, and the old quarry workings have now mellowed into a green landscape. Although it is so close at hand, the gorge is hidden from the village street and comes as a pleasant surprise to visitors. In the heart of the defile stands the small but striking Cilgerran Castle, on a steep bluff overlooking the dark river – a scene that inspired memorable paintings by both Richard Wilson and Turner. The main buildings of the castle, including the two prominent drum towers, date from the 13th century.

The coracle men, who were once such a feature of Cilgerran, are slowly disappearing. They were masters of the craft of fishing from the curious lightweight turtle-shaped boats which go back to the days of remote prehistory (*see also* Carmarthen). The coracle men have age-old rights of fishing on certain stretches of the river, which are passed down from father to son; but now unfortunately the younger generation does not seem keen to continue the tradition. To record the village's history a coracle centre is now being developed. The best chance of seeing coracles in action is now at **Cenarth**, where some have been kept as tourist attractions. There is also a Coracle Regatta in August. The river runs upstream to Cenarth past the old church of Manordeilo and

Above: Bridge over the Teifi, Cenarth

the fine bridge at Llechryd. The river Cyrch joins the main stream at Abercyrch. Wales' only Fishing Museum is located here in Cenarth. Its displays include a unique collection of rods and coracles, as well as an art gallery. Cenarth has become a bit of a tourist trap in high summer, but the bridge is still graceful as it crosses the river which tumbles down in a series of cataracts to a deep salmon pool. The gleaming fish can occasionally be seen jumping the falls on their way upstream to the distant spawning grounds in the wilds south of PLYNLIMON.

Cilycwm, *Dyfed* (4/3A) A quiet village, 3½ miles north of LLANDOVERY, with an interesting church, and the gateway to one of the most lonely and romantic regions in all southern Britain. Perhaps not as lonely as it used to be, for the Forestry Commission has been over-busy in these parts, and roads now run where once you had to ride or walk if you wanted to get into the heart of the hills. The upper waters of the Tywi have also been dammed to form the vast new reservoir of Llyn Brianne. The dam is not exactly an architec-

Right: Llyn Brianne Reservoir

tural masterpiece and may seem a disappointment to those who have already visited the older dams in the Elan Valley or Lake Vyrnwy, but it must be admitted that the lake behind it now has its own impressive attraction. The wild gorge of the Tywi at its junction with the Camddwr has fortunately been left untouched. A delightful Nature Trail now takes you under the tumbled crags, which hide Twm Shon Catti's cave. Twm was a real personage, who lived in the late Elizabethan period and acquired a reputation as a Welsh Robin Hood and a practical joker. They called him 'The Wild Wag of Wales'.

Near Rhandirmwyn, a road turns off left up the fine, craggy valley which skirts Mynydd Mallaen to climb over the pass into the upper waters of the Cothi (*see also* Pumsaint). The valley now has a farmhouse which has become the local headquarters of the NSPB, for here we are on one of the classic grounds where British ornithology is concerned. That magnificent bird, the red kite, still soars over the hills, with its forked tail and thrilling whistle. The breeding grounds are best left undesignated, for there are still misguided fools who collect rare birds' eggs. The preservation of the kite in the upper Tywi valley is the story of the loyalty of the whole community to the protection of the last few breeding pairs. The reward of their devoted work is the sight of these noble birds still increasing in numbers among the fastnesses of the hills.

Clyro (Cleirwy), *Powys* (5/5A) This peaceful village just across the river from HAY-ON-WYE, took an honoured place on the map of English literature with the publication in 1939 of the diary of the Reverend Francis Kilvert, who was a curate at Clyro for seven happy years. Critics have compared his diary to that of Dorothy Wordsworth in its vivid picture of life in the rural peace of a Welsh border village in the days of Queen Victoria. This lush landscape of the winding Wye, with the ramparts of the BLACK MOUNTAINS in the background, is Kilvert's Country as surely as Wessex belongs to Thomas Hardy. The little village has hardly altered since his day. You can still see the house where he lodged opposite the Swan Inn – now the Baskerville Arms. Conan Doyle may have heard of the local legends of a wicked member of the Baskerville family being chased to death by a gigantic hound and neatly transferred it, for the use of Sherlock Holmes, to the better-known Dartmoor. But then, Kilvert's Diary was unknown to him.

Kilvert was a tremendous walker, and pious Kilvertian pilgrims usually try to follow in his footsteps, diary in hand. The hills behind the village hold many of the farms he mentioned, and stretch past Painscastle, with its high castle mounds, to the open moor of Llanbedr Hill. Few countrysides in Wales have remained quite as unchanged in charm and atmosphere as this warm, lovely country that Kilvert loved so well.

Coety, *Mid Glamorgan* (5/4C) A village, 2 miles north-east from BRIDGEND, that is worth a visit for its church and castle. The ruins are extensive and are now in the hands of CADW. The castle was founded by Payn de Turberville, and the traditional story relates that when Morgan, the last Welsh ruler of Coety, was confronted by Payn's men-at-arms, he appeared leading his daughter in one hand and carrying a naked sword in the other. 'I am old,' he said to Payn, 'if you marry my daughter you shall have all my lands when I die. If you refuse, we will fight you to the last drop of our blood.' Payn accepted. A pretty story, which one must hope is true.

The cruciform church has been little altered since the early 14th century. The embattled tower, with its remarkable gargoyles, is of a slightly later date. In the north transept is an oak chest carved with emblems of the Passion. This is quite probably one of the few surviving examples of a portable Easter altar. On either side of the main altar are two small effigies of members of the de Turberville family.

Corris *see* Machynlleth

Cowbridge (Y Bont Faen), *South Glamorgan* (5/4C) This pleasant little town, 12 miles from CARDIFF on the road to the west, has always been regarded as the prosperous capital of the Vale of Glamorgan. It has also been described as Cardiff's 'Cranford'. It certainly has an air of being quietly pleased with itself – and with justification. It has been bypassed and a certain amount of peace has returned to its one long, main street with its old inns and shops. In the centre of this street stands the old Town Hall and Market House, a classical building which was also the House of Correction for most of the county and still contains the cells. An earlier part of Cowbridge's history is concentrated around the South Gate (the Mill gate) just off the main street. The old gate and a section of the south wall still stand. Next to the gate is the Grammar School, an early Victorian building although the foundation goes

Above: Clyro Church   *Below: The river Tawe near Craig-y-Nos*

back to Stuart times. Sir Leoline Jenkins (1623–85) Judge, Privy Councillor and Secretary of State – described by Pepys as 'a very learned, rational and uncorrupt man' – was one of its most notable supporters. The church stands next to the school, with an entrance tucked away by the churchyard among the school buildings. The church of the Holy Rood has a 13th-century embattled tower and is a complicated structure of buttresses and outer stairways.

South of Cowbridge is the town's twin settlement of Llanblethian, which also has a fine church and the gateway and remains of St Quintin's Castle. The monument on Stalling Down, just outside Cowbridge, commemorates the service of the men of the Glamorgan Yeomanry in the First World War.

Coychurch, *Mid Glamorgan* (5/4C) Coychurch is 2 miles east of BRIDGEND, close to the end of the big trading estate. The church has interest and atmosphere, being one of the largest in the Vale of Glamorgan. It is dedicated to St Crallo, and is mostly 13th-century in style. The arcading in the nave is especially fine and the roof of the nave has intricately carved angels. The Ebissar Cross is preserved at the west end of the nave. It must have been one of the tallest crosses in the county. A second stone records that 'Ebissar, the founder of this church, rests here'. In the churchyard is the grave of Thomas Richards, who was a curate at Coychurch for 40 years and compiled an important Welsh–English dictionary which was published in 1753.

Craig-y-Nos, *Powys* (4/3B) At the top end of the SWANSEA valley, at the point where the river Tawe has not yet entered the coal measures and thus runs clear and trout-filled, and where the great singer Adelina Patti sought seclusion from the world in 1878. She was the world's most famous and richest 'diva', but she needed a retreat to which she could retire with her lover, the tenor Ernest Nicolini, whom she subsequently married. Under the limestone crags of Craig-y-Nos – the Cliff of Night – she built her baronial castle, complete with a small private theatre. It still stands, with a curtain carrying a painting of Patti in her favourite role of Semiramide in Rossini's opera, driving a pair of spirited horses in a chariot. A preservation order has been placed on the theatre, although, at this moment (1986) the future of the rest of the building is uncertain. Patti died at Craig-y-Nos in 1919, and there are many people in the upper

Swansea valley who still cherish the memory of the 'Queen of Song'. On the edge of the present estate of Craig-y-nos, a lovely country park has been established, where many countryside activities are staged every summer.

Beyond Craig-y-nos are the well-known tourist caves of Dan-yr-Ogof which rival those of Cheddar in their stalactites and stalagmites and underground lakes. They are considered Europe's largest cave complex. A recently developed ski slope – green to blend into the landscape – brings visitors to the area all year round. The nearby Gwyn Arms has become a centre of cave exploration. *See also* Carmarthenshire Fans.

At Abercraf, a sign points to the by-road to Glyn Neath and Henrhyd Falls. These are now 90 ft high and give a foretaste of the glories of the waterfalls around PONT-NEATH-VAUGHAN, some miles to the east. They have the advantage of a car park and an easy, if steep, path down into the deeply wooded valley.

Crickhowell (Crucywel) *Powys* (5/5B) This pleasant little town, on the main road between ABERGAVENNY and BRECON, is happily placed in one of the most beautiful sections of the valley of the Usk. The river winds through rich parklands to flow under the old, multi-arched bridge which is the chief architectural glory of Crickhowell. For the rest, there are the scanty remains of a Norman castle; a fine old coaching inn – the Bear – in the centre of the town; the high walls that once surrounded the old Tudor mansion of Porth Mawr, built by the powerful Herbert family but long since replaced; and, on the western outskirts the house of Gwernvale, the birthplace of Sir George Everest, whose name is attached to the world's highest mountain. Gwernvale is now a hotel, with fine views across the valley to the hills on the south side of the Usk. They are far below Everest in height, but contain remarkable caves in the limestone crags, including Agon Allwed, one of the longest caverns in Wales. The Monmouthshire and Brecon Canal runs along the foot of the hills: one of the most delightful holiday waterways in the whole of Britain and navigable from PONTYPOOL to Brecon itself. It offers an unrivalled series of locks, towpaths, tunnels and swing bridges in splendid scenery all the way along the Usk valley.

Narrow roads twist northwards from Crickhowell into the narrow valley of the Grwyne Fechan, which curves around the back of the Sugar Loaf. Here is the little village of Llanbedr Ystrad Yw, with its ancient church and air of

The bridge at Crickhowell

complete withdrawal from the busy world. The Grwyne Fechan is walking or riding country, for it is a dead end for motorists and all the better for it. The Grwyne Fawr and the smaller stream join at Llanbedr: again a valley with no drivable road out of it at the top end, which is guarded by a small reservoir. The two Grwyne valleys show the BLACK MOUNTAINS at their lonely best, and the Grwyne Fawr has an added charm – the tiny church of Patrishow. Patrishow is lost among the hills and so escaped desecration in the Reformation. It has an early Tudor rood screen, decorated with Welsh dragons, wall murals with the figure of Death, and an oaken roof. The view from the churchyard is soul consoling.

From Llanbedr, the united Grwyne streams flow down to join the Usk near Cwrt-y-Gollen, originally the centre for the Royal Regiment of Wales but, under new arrangements, shortly to be a Territorial Army training centre.

Cwmbran, *Gwent* (5/5C) Situated between NEWPORT (Gwent) and PONTYPOOL on the edge of the eastern mining valleys of Gwent, is the biggest example in Wales of a New Town created after the Second World War, as a solution to the nation's housing problem. This idea was criticized at the time, both for its concept and its architecture. Cwmbran has mellowed over the past 30 years and developed its own community feeling. It is also the administrative centre of Gwent. The Llandegfedd Reservoir, with its attractions of boating and fishing, lies a few miles north-east in unspoiled country.

Cwmystwyth, *Dyfed* (2/1C) The river Ystwyth enters the sea at ABERYSTWYTH, but it rises in the lonely moorlands south of PLYMLIMON. Near Pontrhydygroes – the Bridge of the Ford of the Cross – a few miles west of the present scattered village of Cwmystwyth, that rich, romantic idealist Thomas Johnes lived between 1783 and 1815. Here he poured out his wealth in creating his own private Xanadu among the hills. He planted thousands of trees, many of them rare and exotic. Wordsworth and Coleridge admired the result. Turner painted his mansion named Hafod, which was filled with rare manuscripts and books from his private printing press. He and his wife were 'Peacocks in Paradise' – the title of a book about Hafod. Alas, little remains of these glories. Hafod was burned down and the Forestry Commission has commercialized Johnes' exotic

plantations. Yet much beauty still tantalizes the visitor with memories of what once has been.

From Cwmystwyth a spectacular mountain road runs across remote countryside to the lakelands of the Elan Valley and the market town of RHAYADER.

Cynwyl Elfed, *Dyfed* (4/1A) A village in the Gwili valley, which runs up from Abergwili in the Tywi valley near CARMARTHEN. The Gwili Railway – one of the 'great little trains' of Wales – puffs its way up the deeply wooded almost gorge-like valley, from Bronwydd Arms to almost within sight of Cynwyl. An enchanting holiday trip for the family. On the hillside above Cwmduad, 2 miles north of Cynwyl Elfed, the dyke marks the boundary of the old kingdom of Dyfed in the Dark Ages. The well-known Welsh hymn writer, Dr Elvet Lewis, took his name from Cynwyl. His birthplace, Y Gangell Farm, in the hills west of the village, has been preserved for the nation.

Dale, *Dyfed* (3/1B) Dale is the most westerly village on the north shores of MILFORD HAVEN. South of it is St Ann's Head, with its lighthouse and coastguard station, marking the entrance to this magnificent haven. Dale is tucked away in the shelter of the headland, and thus provides good anchorage for yachtsmen in the sandy Dale Roads. In 1485, Henry VII landed at Mill Bay near St Ann's Head to begin his march through Wales, which led him to the victory of Bosworth Field and the throne. North of Dale is the interesting village of Marloes, overlooking a fine, sandy beach. The curious rock formations of the Three Chimneys are notable on the cliffs. It is also possible to cross over to the little island of Gateholm at low tide. The group of irregular huts on Gateholm may be the remains of an early monastic settlement. Beyond lies the bird island of SKOMER, separated from the mainland by the fierce currents of Jack Sound.

There are many good sandy beaches near Dale. A 7-mile nature trail extends round the Dale Peninsula.

Devil's Bridge (Pont-ar-Fynach), *Dyfed* (2/1C) This spectacular and therefore highly frequented beauty spot is 12 miles inland from ABERYS-TWYTH, at the point where the Mynach stream meets the Rheidol in a series of spectacular water-

Devil's Bridge (Martin Dohrn)

falls, set in deep woods with the wilds of PLYNLIMON in the background. To add to its attraction, during summer months you can reach Devil's Bridge by way of the narrow-gauge Rheidol Railway from Aberystwyth – the only one of the 'great little trains' of Wales run by British Rail. The Mynach Falls are hidden in a deep gorge below the Hafod Hotel and, as you might expect, you must pay to see them. They are well worth the money, especially after rain. There are three bridges, piled on top of each other. The lowest one is ascribed, on doubtful evidence, to the monks of Strata Florida (*see* Pontrhydfendigaid). The old legend tells that it was thrown across the ravine by the Devil, on condition that he should possess the first living creature who crossed it. He was outwitted by an old lady who rolled a loaf across it – which was immediately followed by her little dog. The Evil One disappeared, frustrated, in a puff of sulphurous smoke! The circuit of the falls takes about $1\frac{1}{2}$ hours and can be strenuous for the elderly.

Previous spread: left: On the Dale Peninsula, see p. 108 (Martin Dohrn); right: The great waterfall at Dylife, see p. 109

A few miles north along the PONTERWYD road, you reach the little church of Ysbyty Cynfyn, set in a churchyard surrounded by great stones which could be the remains of a prehistoric circle. The churchyard contains a touching little gravestone to the first quads recorded in Wales. A path near the church takes you over the brow of the hill to drop steeply down into the Rheidol gorge at Parson's Bridge. The whole of this secret, wooded defile is filled with the music of falling waters – a delectable place, where you can recapture the atmosphere of Devil's Bridge before it was turned into an official 'beauty spot'.

There are many forest and nature trails in the area. Leaflets are available at the start of the walks and the Forestry Commission has a Visitor Centre 2 miles east of Ponterwyd at Nant-yr-arian.

Dylife, *Powys* (2/1B) Dylife, high up on the eastern flank of the PLYMLIMON wilderness, is reached by the mountain road that winds up from LLANIDLOES, past Llyn Clywedog (the 6-mile long reservoir) and Staylittle – a journey which emphasizes its remoteness. When you arrive there, you find no village – just a lonely inn, some scattered houses and the remains of what was once one of the richest lead mines in Wales. The free-traders Cobden and Bright both took a close interest in this Welsh El Dorado. The stories still gather around the abandoned spoil heaps and the dripping mine tunnels. Back in the 18th century, the blacksmith at the mine, Sion y Gof, had taken to living with a woman in Dylife although he had a wife and child at Llanidloes. His suspicious wife followed him one night, but he turned on her, murdered her and the child and threw their bodies into a disused mine shaft. They were discovered and Sion was duly hanged on the hill behind the mine, still known as Gallows Hill in Welsh. Not very long ago, excavations were carried out on the gallows site and the skull of Sion y Gof was recovered, still encased in an iron cage. This gruesome exhibit is now at the Welsh Folk Museum in CARDIFF.

But Dylife can offer better attractions today than this macabre story. The Dylife stream drops into a spectacular gorge in one of the highest waterfalls in Wales, the Ffrwd Fawr. North of the mine area, a road leads off past the lonely lakes of Glaslyn and Bugeilyn into the heart of Plynlimon. Steep if shaly cliffs drop to the east near Glaslyn to disprove the legend in certain climbing circles that Plynlimon offers an easy stroll over an uninteresting bog! The view to the north is inspiring.

Ebbw Vale (Glyn Ebwy) and the **Eastern Valleys of Gwent,** *Gwent* (5/5B) Ebbw Vale, at the top of the valley of the Ebbw Fawr, and its closely associated townships of Brynmawr at the top of the Ebbw Fach and Tredegar in the Sirhowey valley, are all products of the early days of the Industrial Revolution. Here coal and iron ore were found with limestone nearby. The great ironworks that grew to strength here had an international reputation. The coalfield developed at breakneck speed in the 19th century and immigrants poured in, with the result that these Eastern Valleys of Gwent became Anglicized earlier than the mining valleys further West. Even in the Depression years, industry in Ebbw Vale was strong enough to attract the first big strip mill in Wales. This is an area with a strong tradition of organized Labour, the home of Aneurin Bevan and with Michael Foot as the MP for Ebbw Vale. In common with every part of the South Wales coalfield, the local authorities are now deeply committed to the search for additional industry. Some 6 miles south is Pen-y-Fan Pond Country Park with recreational facilities.

The history of Gwent's Eastern Valleys can be followed by car from the 18th-century ironworks at BLAENAVON, to the extraction of coal at Big Pit, along the canal which transported the products through to NEWPORT (Gwent). At PONTYPOOL, the Valleys Inheritance centre describes the trail in greater detail.

Eglwyswrw, *Dyfed* (3/3A) This compact little village, north of the PRESELI HILLS in what was the old county of Pembrokeshire, is the proud possessor of a name which is a perpetual puzzlement to the English visitor. Tourists photograph the road sign as a souvenir. The puzzle is solved if you remember that the 'W' in Welsh orthography represents a double 'o', and that 'Y' is a vowel – in this case representing 'i'. *Eglwys* is a church in Welsh, and the village is thus the place of the church of St Wrw. A somewhat cantankerous saint by all accounts, who was said to be so jealous of his privacy in his own church that bodies would be found thrown out after burial. This may account for the font at Eglwyswrw being exceptionally massive.

Sergeant Inn stands next to the small court house, and the name may be derived from the serjeants-at-law who attended the Court Leet of the Barony of Cemaes here.

See also Newport (Dyfed).

Elan Valley (Cwm Elan), *Powys* (2/2C) This extensive series of man-made lakes in the heart of the moorlands behind RHAYADER has deservedly become the major tourist attraction of Mid Wales. These reservoirs were built to supply Birmingham with water, but the city fathers were not afraid to spend extra money in making their dams, all faced with fine stonework, things of architectural beauty. The middle dam at Caban Coch is especially notable and is a magnificent sight when the waters overflow in winter. One story goes that a fox succeeded in running clean up it when it was dark, to escape the hounds. He would have been hard put to it to repeat the feat on some of the sheer concrete slabs of most modern dams. After the Second World War, the system was further extended by the construction of the vast Claerwen Dam, in a side valley of the Elan. Today there are plans on the drawing board for a new and monster dam – 300 ft has been mentioned as its possible height – to enlarge the upper lake. A civil engineer's dream, no doubt, but a conservationist's nightmare. Perhaps tourists will be wise to see the Elan reservoirs while they can, as a reminder that man-made construc-

Craig Coch dam, Elan Valley

tions can sometimes increase the natural beauty of the landscape. The history of the present dams is vividly told at the recently opened Visitor Centre, which also houses a Tourist Information Centre.

Ewenny (Ewenni), *Mid Glamorgan* (4/3C) Ewenny offers a notable reminder of the Norman past of South Wales and is 2 miles south of BRIDGEND, on a side road off the A48. William de Londres, the Norman knight who built Ogmore Castle to hold down his share of conquered Glamorgan, presented a church at Ewenny to the abbey of Gloucester. In 1141 his son, Maurice, confirmed the gift with a proviso that a convent of monks should be established on the site. The present church, with its embattled tower, its windows set high in the walls of the nave, its massive pillars and strong arches, has the air of being a fortress as well as a religious building. The monks, as well as the knights, came as conquerors in the eyes of the Welsh, for the Normans always believed that prayers were more efficacious if made with sword in hand. The impression is confirmed by the high walls and fortified gatehouse that surrounded the conventual structure. The modern mansion occupies part of this site behind the walls. The

The fortified gatehouse, Ewenny Priory

tombs in the church include a finely carved memorial to Maurice de Londres, the son of the founder. The young Turner, on one of his tours through South Wales painted a memorable picture of Ewenny as it was around 1800.

Apart from the priory, Ewenny is also well known for its potteries, and the fine clay has probably been worked here since the days of the Normans.

Farmers, *Dyfed* (4/2A) This village, in isolated country between the valleys of the Teifi and the Cothi, is presumably named after a public house – one of the very few Welsh villages so designated. The present local inn, however, is called the Drovers Arms, and the mystery is increased by the inn sign, which depicts – or did until recently – not a tough Welsh Black but a large Hereford, which would not have lasted a few yards if it had been driven by the drovers over the wild hills around Farmers! The road over to LLANDDEWI BREFI is narrow and complicated, but it takes you into lonely and beautiful country – a combination of forests and bird-haunted moorlands.

Ferryside (Glan-y-feri), *Dyfed* (4/1B) The village stands on the east side of the Tywi (Towy) where the river goes out to the sea through a vast expanse of sandbanks at low tide. The main railway line to CARMARTHEN curves along the foreshore, and gives passengers a fine view of Llanstephan Castle on the opposite western bank. One mile to the south of Ferryside is the old 13th-century church of St Ismael's, perched on a high bluff above the railway and the sands. The nearby, off-the-beaten-track village of **Llansaint** was once the centre of a thriving cockle-gathering industry. The sturdy village women used to drive their donkeys the long distance out onto the sands to rake up the cockles in all sorts of weather. This picturesque industry has unfortunately died at Llansaint, although the tradition still survives at PENCLAWDD, on the northern shore of the Gower Peninsula.

Fishguard (Abergwaun), *Dyfed* (3/2A) Fishguard, overlooking a wide bay on the west coast of South Wales, is divided into three distinct parts. The first is Fishguard Harbour, with its rail terminus, quay and huge breakwater. Behind this port installation lies the village of Goodwick. The Harbour is a modern creation, dating from

1907 and, in its earliest days, had high hopes of becoming a port of call for the Atlantic liners, landing passengers in search of a quick route to London. This service never materialized, but Fishguard Harbour is now an important ferry port for the Irish Republic. The crossing takes about 3 hours in good weather and the big, modern ferries cope with an increasing amount of drive-on/drive-off traffic. The Irish landing point is Rosslare.

A good mile away, on a hill looking across to the Harbour, is the old town of Fishguard itself. It is grouped around a central square, dominated by the pleasant classical façade of the Town Hall. After leaving the square, the road north makes a sharp turn and dives down a steep hill into the separate village of Lower Town. Here the river Gwaun comes out to the sea into a delightful little harbour, protected by an old pier and crowded with holiday yachts. A little further along the Gwaun valley is the 18th-century house of Glynymel, built by Richard Fenton, author of the *Historical Tour of Pembrokeshire* (1811). Close at hand is the art gallery and craft centre which has added to the interest of Lower Town (*see also*

Lower Town harbour, Fishguard

Gwaun Valley).

Fishguard had two moments when it was suddenly propelled into the spotlight of history. The first came in the American War of Independence, when Paul Jones appeared off Lower Town, bombarded the port and extracted a ransom from the frightened inhabitants before sailing away. As a result of this episode, the gentry of Pembrokeshire subscribed to build a small fort on the point near Lower Town. It went into action on one occasion only. In February 1797, two French warships appeared in the bay and the guns opened fire. The French ships withdrew around Pen Anglas Point and then landed a motley force of French soldiers on the cliffs of Carreg Wastad on the rocky Strumble peninsula. The whole of Pembrokeshire was aroused. Lord Cawdor came racing up with the local militia and shots were exchanged. But the proceedings ended in farce, for the French got drunk on the liquor found in the Strumble farmhouses, and General Tate, the French commander, had no option but to surrender. The terms were signed in the present Royal Oak inn in the square at Fishguard, which bears the proud inscription 'The Last Invasion of Britain'. The church nearby has a memorial in the churchyard to Jemima Nicholas, the

formidable female cobbler who rounded up 12 Frenchmen with a pitchfork and earned herself the title of the 'Pembrokeshire Heroine'.

There is an interesting coastal walk called Dinas 'Island' Walk – 3 miles around the promontory, north-east of Fishguard.

Flat Holm, *South Glamorgan* (5/5C) Flat Holm and Steep Holm are two small islands in the centre of the Bristol Channel, clearly visible from the Welsh coast and the hills behind CARDIFF. Their names exactly describe their nature. Steep Holm is a high rock on which landing is difficult: it is now a bird sanctuary, and administratively part of Somerset. Flat Holm is low, round and rocky and, in the past, was always regarded as part of the parish of St Mary's in Cardiff. It has now been acquired by South Glamorgan County Council on a 99-year lease. The Council plans to develop the island in the best interests of the public. It is already a local nature reserve.

Flat Holm has played many roles throughout its history. The Celtic St Cadoc visited it seeking peace and meditation. The Vikings gave it its name of 'holm', from the Scandinavian word for a river island. It was a farm in the Middle Ages especially valued for its conies or rabbits. Trinity House built the first lighthouse here in 1825. Marconi made history on Flat Holm in May 1897 when he succeeded in transmitting the first radio messages ever sent across the sea, to a receiver mast on the mainland at Lavernock Point. In late Victorian times it acted as an isolation hospital for seamen suffering from tropical diseases. But its strangest role came in 1865, when the island was heavily fortified against the French. Huge muzzle-loaded cannon were mounted in deep circular pits and large sums were spent on guarding the coastline against a most improbable attack. Today, the great guns – known as Palmerston's Follies, after the Prime Minister of the day – lie quietly rusting among the nests of the thousands of gulls that come to the island in the breeding season.

Glasbury (Y Clas-ar-Wy), *Powys* (5/5A) Situated 3 miles upstream from Hay, Glasbury is in the centre of a particularly attractive section of the Wye valley. Here the river begins to curve north against the impressive background of the BLACK MOUNTAINS. The village is also in Kilvert country, and the diarist made frequent visits here (*see* Clyro). In his day, the Wye was a notable salmon river, but in our own time a sad change has taken place, not only on the Wye, but on most of the famous Welsh rivers. Up to the Second World War, poaching could almost be regarded as a secret local sport. Not today. The rivers are now raided by tough, ruthless gangs from the cities, and the bailiffs and police are hard put to it to keep them out. It would be tragic if we can no longer spend a lazy morning looking down into the clear waters of the Wye on Glasbury new bridge and spot the bright fish on their way up to their distant spawning grounds under PLYNLIMON. Three Cocks, on the road southwest to BRECON, is a fine, ancient angling and coaching inn, and the Jacobean mansion of Gweruyfed played a prominent part in local history.

Gogerddan, *Dyfed* (1/3C) The old mansion of Gogerddan, once the home of the powerful Pryse family, lies in a pleasant valley near the curiously named village of Bow Street, a few miles northeast of ABERYSTWYTH. It is now the Plant Breeding Station, associated with University College, and won an international reputation with the work of the late Sir George Stapleton on mountain grasslands, although it is now threatened with closure due to Government cutbacks. There was a time, in the 18th century, when Gogerddan controlled the political life of the whole of this wide countryside, and the mayors of Aberystwyth were supposed to take their oath with the formula, 'I swear to be faithful to the King and to the House of Gogerddan'. The Pryses were one of the last of the old Welsh houses to keep their own private harper. Much of their wealth came from the lead mines which once flourished in the hills behind Cwm Symlog and Goginan. The mines have long gone, leaving a strange landscape of old workings and small lakes behind them.

Gower (Gwyr), *West Glamorgan* (4/1+2C) This delectable peninsula, running out between the Bristol Channel and the Loughor estuary for 16 miles west of SWANSEA, is a delightful surprise to find in the middle of what is, after all, part of the South Wales coalfield. Geologically, however, Gower is formed out of bright limestone, with a central ridge of Old Red Sandstone. It has thus escaped industry and remained a farming community. With its sandy beaches, high cliffs, open downs and wide commons, it was rightly chosen to become one of Britain's first Areas of Outstanding Natural Beauty. Inevitably there has been much tourist development of recent years, but mercifully much is still unspoiled. Tribute

must be paid to the devoted work of the members of the Gower Society, who have been strong and successful defenders of 'The Land of the Setting Sun'.

The greatest part of Gower has been English-speaking for the last 700 years. Like that part of Dyfed which forms the southern section of the old county of Pembrokeshire, it became a 'Little England beyond Wales' after its conquest by the Normans in the 12th century. The old Gower dialect, rarely heard these days, was related to that of Devon and Somerset. The Normans covered Gower with castles, and their ruins at Oystermouth (near Swansea), Pennard, Oxwich, Penrice and Weobley are all impressively picturesque. Two main roads enter the peninsula, running on either side of the central ridge of Cefn Bryn. Motorists are warned that they can become extremely crowded on warm summer weekends. The south road crosses the breezy Fairwood Common to dip down into the wide dingle of Parkmill. The water mill here still works, and a track leads up through the hidden valley of the aptly named Green Cwm to the remarkable prehistoric tomb of the Giant's Grave. The Green

Left: The river Wye, near Glasbury, see p. 113
Below: Flat Holm, see p. 113

Three Cliffs Bay, Gower   *(Martin Dohrn)*

Cwm marks the beginning of the central ridge of Cefn Bryn which offers a splendid walk, lifted high over the peninsula with great views northwards towards the mountains of the CARMARTHENSHIRE FANS. The giant cromlech called Arthur's Stone stands in the centre of the ridge, and the road across the middle of Cefn Bryn leads down to Renoldston, with the King Arthur Inn facing the village green on which the sheep and ponies wander down from Cefn Bryn.

But it is the coast of Gower that offers the greatest delight to the rambler. A path runs the whole way along the south coast, over the cliff tops and down into the bays, from the Mumbles headland at the entrance of Swansea Bay to the remarkable Worms Head at Rhosili. A good 20 miles walk of pure delight.

The cliffs become steadily higher the further west you walk. The bays nearest to Swansea – Langland and Caswell – are naturally the most frequented, and you begin to get the real feel of the Gower coast as you reach Pwlldu (*see* Bishopston). The strange caves of Bacon Hole and Michin Hole are excellent examples of the Gower bone caves, rich in prehistoric remains. Three Cliffs Bay is especially attractive with its view of

Pennard castle, perched on its rock above the valley. The sandy beach is accessible from Parkmill and Pennard, but you have to walk. The wide sweep of Oxwich Bay follows, backed by sand dunes behind which lie the picturesque lakes of the Oxwich marshes. They are overlooked by the 18th-century mansion of Penrice, backed by the ruins of the 13th-century castle. Oxwich village lies under the bluff headland of Oxwich Point, with its charming little church nestling in the shelter of the headland on the very edge of the sea. Oxwich is crowded in summer, as, indeed, are the next villages of Horton and Port Eynon. The fine sands of all these places have made them tourist 'honeypots'. The Oxwich Sand Trail is an interesting walk, demonstrating the influence of sand on flora and fauna.

Beyond Port Eynon, the Gower coast reaches its most impressive development. On Port Eynon Head you come across one of the strangest places along the whole coast of Wales. Culver Hole is a giant fissure in the rock which has been mysteriously blocked up with a thick wall, pierced by open windows. No one has yet given a satisfactory explanation of this curious structure. At Paviland, you reach Gower's most famous bone cave. You have to wait for low tide to visit it if you are not a rock climber. The cliffs are particularly splendid around Mewslade Bay, which you can reach by walking down from Middleton or Pitton. The cliffs reach their exciting climax at Worms Head. There is no stranger headland in the whole of southern Britain. It really does look like some huge serpent, rearing up its head from the sea. It guards the wide stretch of the sands of Rhosili Bay, with the high Rhosili Downs in the background – perhaps the finest seascape composition Gower can offer and with few rivals in Wales. Llangemith, with its ancient church, lies behind the sand dunes in the centre of Rhosili Bay, with the island of Burry Holms marking the northern arm of the magnificent sweep of the sands.

Whitford Point is the long, low sand spit that pushes out into the swirling currents of Carmarthen Bay and is the beginning of the northern coastline of the Gower peninsula, which is totally different in character from the south. It looks out over the wide salt marshes and sands of the Loughor Estuary, but offers a compensation in the richness of its bird life. The villages stand back a little from the marshes and all have the typical Gower churches with their strong defensive towers. The tiny Llanmadoc church has a Norman font and a Romano-British tombstone. Cheriton church can claim to be the largest in Gower, but there is not much competition for the title. Gower churches rely on charm, not size. Llanrhidian church has the strangest relic of all: the so-called Leper Stone, carved with curious animal shapes, and human figures which could be either Christian or pagan symbols. The villages hold a further mystery in the two massive stones that stand on the village green opposite the pleasantly named Welcome to Town pub. Llanrhidian is the last village of English-speaking Gower. Weobley Castle, overlooking the marshes, is an excellent example of a fortified 13th-century manor house. It is open to the public.

For the rest, Gower is rich in prehistoric tombs, Iron Age forts and underground caverns that are a challenge to the caver. Only try to avoid it on Bank Holidays. The traffic jams along the south road are not recommended. A last lament: old Gowerians are distinctly vexed by the new practice of calling their beloved peninsula 'The' Gower. Even the Ordnance Survey is now guilty of this unpleasing misnomer. The place has been known as Gower throughout history, from the Welsh 'Gwyr'. Let it remain so!

Grassholm, *Dyfed* (3/1B) This rocky hummock of an island, 12 miles out in the Atlantic off the west coast of Dyfed, has become one of the largest breeding colonies of gannets in Britain. At the beginning of the century, the puffins were masters of Grassholm. They have retreated to SKOMER, and these noble birds have taken their place. There are now 20,000 pairs breeding on the islet in the season. They are a thrilling sight, flying over Grassholm in a white cloud, or folding their wings and plummeting straight down into the sea. The gannet colony is carefully protected by the West Wales Naturalist Trust and makes one of the finest natural bird spectaculars in Wales. Beyond Grassholm lie the treacherous rocks known as the Barrels and Hats. Further out still – 20 miles offshore and forming the most westerly patch of Welsh rock – are the Smalls, crowned by the tall tower of the lighthouse. In 1891, one of the keepers died. There had been bad blood between him and his fellow keeper, and the single man made a rough coffin and lashed the body to the lantern rail. He was finally relieved after weeks of bad weather, almost demented. Since then, there have always been three keepers in those lonely lighthouses of Britain that are still manned.

Grosmont, *Gwent* (5/6A) Grosmont, with its castle now in the care of CADW, and a surprisingly large church, is right on the border between Gwent and Hereford and Worcester, where the winding river Monnow forms the boundary – an unspoiled landscape of hills and woods well worth exploring if you are in search of quiet places off the beaten track. The single street of the village runs between the castle and the church. The castle still has its mound or motte, but it is crowned with towers. Grosmont also has a deep ditch around it, with groves of old trees to keep it company. Not a big castle, but most attractive. It formed part of the defensive plan of the Trilateral fortifications, and together with Skenfrith Castle and White Castle held down this part of Gwent against the Welsh. Grosmont was an important little town in the Middle Ages. The church, with its ample proportions and fine arcading, was designed for a large population. But the town was burned by Owain Glyndwr in 1405 and never recovered.

Guilsfield (Cegidfa), *Powys* (2/3B) Guilsfield, 2 miles north of WELSHPOOL, was once the starting point of a branch of the Montgomery Canal, which was itself linked with the important Shropshire Union canal system. Canal lovers will probably lament the activities of the road engineers,

Grosmont Castle

whose new bridges have made any re-opening of the waterway more than difficult. Other visitors, however, will come to Guilsfield for the pleasure of seeing its church. The ceiling is especially notable for its finely carved and decorated wood. The yew trees in the churchyard make a fine setting for the building. On a gravestone near the gate, an inscription records that one of the trees was planted in memory of Richard Jones, Gent:

> Under this yew tree
> Buried would he be,
> For his father and he
> Planted this yew tree,
> December ye 10th 1707 aged 90.

The yew must therefore be nearly 300 years old.

Gwaun Valley (Cwmgwaun), *Dyfed* (3/2A) The deeply wooded Gwaun valley runs inland from Lower Town, FISHGUARD, to its source high on the slopes of Foel Eryr in the PRESELI HILLS. It has always been a well-known beauty spot, and walkers can get a first taste of its quality along the path that has now been cleared through the woods from Lower Town to the first village in the valley, Llanychaer. The Gwaun has always

regarded itself as a place apart. When the change to the Julian calendar was made legal in 1752, the people of the Gwaun indignantly ignored it. They still celebrate the New Year on the old date – 13 January – and the warmth of their celebration rivals Hogmanay in Scotland.

There is a string of small churches along the valley, many with inscriptions from the Dark Ages. The church at Pontfaen fell into ruin but it was restored by the Arden family of nearby Pontfaen House, who turned it into an ecclesiastical jewel box, with rare velvet vestments. In contrast, Nonconformity is represented by Jabez Chapel in the valley below Pontfaen, which has an outside baptismal tank and a hall presented by William Evans, a successful son of the valley, who made a fortune out of soft drinks. The Gwaun is a famous trout stream, but the fish are reputed to possess exceptional cunning.

Gwendraeth Valleys, *Dyfed* (4/1B) The two Gwendraeth rivers unite just below KIDWELLY to join the Tywi flowing out to sea through wide salt marshes and sand banks. They rise in the hills behind Cross Hands, and contrast in character.

Overleaf: Worms Head, Rhosili Bay, Gower, see p. 116

The Gwendraeth Fach flows through pastoral country. The church at Llandefaelog has the grave of Peter Williams, one of the leaders in the development of the Methodist movement, and a plaque commemorating Dr David Davies, who attended the Duchess of Kent at the birth of Queen Victoria. The Gwendraeth Fawr is industrial, and has a string of colliery villages from Trimsaran to Pontyberem and Tumble. The coal is anthracite and the worst consequences of the Depression were ameliorated with the sinking of the big modern pit at Cynheidre. The last section of the motorway to be completed will take the M4 clear of Cross Hands and of the pleasant little village of Llanddarog. Llanddarog still deserves a visit for its delightful thatched roofed inn.

Haverfordwest (Hwlffordd), *Dyfed* (3/2B) Haverfordwest, at the limit of navigation on the western arm of MILFORD HAVEN, still keeps its air of being the county town, although the old Pembrokeshire has been merged into the new, outsized county of Dyfed. (In an attempt to re-create Pembrokeshire a flag of the old county has recently been designed and can even be seen flying on a number of public buildings in the area.) It is a handsome town, with its main street rising steeply from the bridge over the Western Cleddau river towards the parish church of St Mary's. The church is worthy of the town, and is one of the finest parish churches in Wales. The nave arcades are early English in style, and the capitals of the columns are crowned with delightful and imaginative carvings, which alone make St Mary's worth a visit. The castle, on its high hill, looms impressively over the town, but it is a mere shell. Oliver Cromwell insisted on its being 'slighted' during his campaign in South Wales, and when the city fathers tried delaying tactics, threatened to come and pull their castle down about their ears. They obeyed. The interior was eventually occupied by the jail, which has now been converted into the county museum. Another recent improvement has been the damming of the Cleddau river between the two town bridges. This has created a still pool which mirrors the castle and a riverside walk to a new shopping centre. Immediately behind it, in the shadow of Castle Hill, is the small but busy Castle Square.

Haverfordwest has a profusion of early 19th-century houses, many of them built in the days when travel was difficult and the county families felt the need to have a house in the county town.

The Mariners Hotel has a good Regency façade, while the Palladian Shire Hall in the High Street has distinction, both in its interior and exterior. The old warehouses along Quay Street remind us that Haverfordwest was once a busy port. The town is well within the limits of the English-speaking area of old Pembrokeshire, but it has always been the place where both the English and Welsh sections of the county met to do business. This tradition happily continues.

In the grounds of Picton Castle, at Rhos on the eastern approach to the town, the Graham Sutherland Art Gallery is located. The artist found much of his inspiration in this south-western corner of Wales. It was in recognition of this that he left a large bequest of paintings in trust to establish this gallery.

Hay-on-Wye (Y Gelli), *Powys* (5/5A) Hay is the gateway town to the Welsh section of the Wye valley, and is a typical border town. Hereford and Worcester are a bare mile down the road to the east. This was the way the Normans entered Mid Wales, and the castle stands in the centre of the town. The Elizabethans converted it into a more comfortable manor house, and it has since undergone many reconstructions. It has also been heavily damaged by fire, but it still remains as a reminder of the past turbulent history of the border. All is peaceful now. Hay is the market town for a wide area of farming country, where sheep are a main preoccupation. The Hay Smithfield is exceptionally large, and the sheep sales bring an excitement to the normally placid little township. In the 1960s and 1970s, Hay underwent a surprising transformation. An enterprising if eccentric entrepreneur – a self-proclaimed King of Hay – turned it into the world's largest centre for second-hand books. Every shop in the town seemed to burst with old and rare volumes. The boom seems to have passed its peak but Hay still remains an important centre of the second-hand book trade.

The name of the town has always puzzled visitors. It comes from the Norman-French *haier*, a word of Germanic origin meaning to enclose. The Hague, in Holland, shares the same ultimate derivation. Finally, Hay is also very much part of the Kilvert country: the diarist was curate at CLYRO, just across the high level bridge over the Wye, and Hay features continually in his diary. It gives a wonderful picture of what life was like in this little border town over 100 years ago.

Hay-on-Wye, Powys

Kenfig, *Mid-Glamorgan* (4/2C) There was a time when this rather straggling settlement of modern bungalows and old farmhouses carried an air of mystery and even romance. It lies a few miles north of PORTHCAWL, confronting the largest wilderness of sand dunes in South Wales. The M4 motorway now roars through it, and the nearby housing estates of Pyle are ever expanding. Yet the dunes are still there, and they still cover what was once the thriving small town of Kenfig, clustered around the castle built by Robert of Gloucester in the 12th century. But by the beginning of the 14th century, the sand was becoming a serious menace, steadily encroaching on the fertile land. This was happening all along the South Wales coast, especially in GOWER. The end came with the great storms of the early 16th century, when the castle and the remaining houses were buried under vast mounds of sand during a storm. The 'borough', complete with its portreeves and officials, survived as an independent corporation until 1886. The mace is now in the Nationl Museum at CARDIFF. Hidden among the dunes is Kenfig Pool, the largest naturally formed body of water in Glamorgan. It remains fresh, in spite of its proximity to the sea. Legend declares it to be bottomless, but when sounded recently it was found to be 12 ft at its deepest. The dunes stretch westwards for miles beyond Kenfig, but industry has begun to encroach on them, as the traveller can observe from the railway. Eventually his train runs into PORT TALBOT, where the dunes have been buried under the largest steel plant in Europe.

There is a 3-mile nature walk through Kenfig Burrows organized by the Glamorgan County Naturalists' Trust.

Kerry (Ceri), *Powys* (2/2B) A quiet village on the edge of the Kerry Forest 3 miles east of NEWTOWN in Mid Wales. It has an ancient church with powerful Romanesque arcading. Kerry must be unique among the small churches of Wales, for there is a complete description of its consecration in 1170. The ever-travelling churchman, Geraldus Cambrensis, was present and has left us a vivid description of the scene. Was he Wales's first 'special correspondent'? Little Kerry has another claim to fame. It is one of the few villages in Wales that has given its name to a breed of sheep. This large, sturdy, broad-bodied type of sheep originated on the steep, grassy, close-cropped Kerry Hills to the south of the village. This is great grazing country, and great walking country as well. An ancient trackway runs the whole length of the hills; it is lifted high above the tumbled landscape, with great views to the north. A glance at the large-scale map shows you that the Kerry Hills are in the 'waist of Wales'. Only about 32 miles separate the highest tidal point on the Dovey estuary to the west from the English border to the east. Several organizations have an annual walk over the course – it is tough going and usually ends up at the Anchor Inn, just over the English boundary at the top of the valley of the Teme.

Kidwelly (Cydweli), *Dyfed* (4/1B) A little town full of history which marks the point where the Gwendraeth rivers unite to pour out into the wide estuary of the Tywi. Its pride is its castle, now in the care of CADU. It was a one of a string of fortresses constructed by the Normans to safeguard the river crossings along their route to the West. In its early years it was repeatedly captured by the Welsh, but by the end of the 13th century, the castle had been immensely strengthened by the modern method of concentric defence. It played no part in the Civil Wars and thus escaped being 'slighted' by Cromwell. As a result, it still presents an excellent idea of what a great medieval castle looked like in its heyday. The gatehouse of the little town that grew up at the castle's foot also survived. There is a 14th-century bridge across the river and beyond is the impressive parish church of St Mary the Virgin with its tall spire. It was once the church of the Benedictine Priory, which accounts for its spacious air.

Kidwelly is proud of its castle and church, but South Walians also remember it for a celebrated court case of the 1920s. Harold Greenwood, the local solicitor, was accused of poisoning his wife, and was cleared of the charge by the eloquence of the celebrated advocate, Sir Edwin Marshall Hall, at the Carmarthen Assizes. Greenwood's house is the large house beside the bridge as you leave the main town for the castle.

Industrial archaeologists will be relieved that Llanelli Borough Council has retained the remains of the old tinplate works to create a museum which will form part of a more ambitious project to interpret this once important industry in the area.

Knighton (Tref y Clawdd), *Powys* (3/3C) Knighton is the perfect border town, if ever there was one. Not only does it straddle the present border between England and Wales along the river Teme, but its Welsh name, Tref y Clawdd –

St David's College, Lampeter

the Town of the Dyke – indicates that it is firmly planted astride the oldest of all the demarcation lines between the Welsh and the English, that of the great earthwork built by the Mercian king, Offa, in the 8th century. Knighton is the only town on OFFA'S DYKE. It is also a good centre for exploring the Dyke and information is available at the Offa's Dyke Heritage Centre and the Maes Offa Riverside Park in the town.

Knighton is officially in Wales but it is hardly a typically Welsh town. The Welsh language has steadily retreated westwards over the last few centuries, and the only proof that this countryside was once Welsh lies in the names of the rivers. The Lugg comes from Llugwy, the Arrow from the Welsh Arwy while the Teme, Knighton's river, is the Anglicized form of Tefeidiad. Knighton is now a quiet and pleasant market town, which still has the luck to possess a railway station. The line runs south-west through the heart of rural South Wales – a leisurely trip through times past, crossing the splendid Knucklas viaduct only a few miles from the town.

Lake Vyrnwy *see* Llanwddyn

Lampeter (Llanbedr Pont Steffan), *Dyfed* (4/2A) Lampeter is the 'capital' of the upper Teifi valley – an important market town and administrative centre. Its Welsh name means the church of St Peter near Stephen's bridge. The present bridge across the Teifi is 19th-century, but Giraldus Cambrensis certainly knew the old bridge as 'Stephen's Bridge'. Who exactly Stephen was remains a mystery. The town developed around the Norman castle. The motte or mound of the castle still stands in the grounds of Lampeter's most important building, St David's College. Built in 1827 under the inspiration of Bishop Burgess, St David's came under the wing of Oxford University and its design reflected that of a typical quadrangle in an Oxford College. In 1965 it was greatly expanded as part of the University of Wales, with new halls of residence and lecture rooms and the admission of women students. The chapel is a fine example of early Victorian neo-Gothic.

The Teifi valley north of Lampeter is green and wooded, enclosed by ever-rising hills. The river runs under a succession of attractive bridges and trout-filled pools. The great house at Derry Ormond has been demolished but the viewpoint tower still looks down on the valley. The little local railway line, which once went over the hills here into the Aeron valley, has sadly been pulled up.

Lamphey (Llanfydd), *Dyfed* (3/2B) Situated 2 miles east of PEMBROKE town, Lamphey has the impressive ruins of one of the old palaces of the Bishops of St David's. In the Middle Ages St David's was the largest and the only wealthy see in Wales, and Lamphey gives a good idea of the princely scale on which a medieval bishop could live. The bishops enjoyed their rural retreat at Lamphey from the 12th century, but it was Bishop Gower, in the 13th century, who gave the palace its present form. He was also responsible for the splendid palace at St David's, and many of the architectural features it embodied reappear at Lamphey. In 1507 Bishop Sherborne lavishly entertained Sir Rhys ap Thomas and his guests

here after the celebrated tournament at CAREW. The manor of Lamphey passed to the Devereux family on the Dissolution and Robert, the Earl of Essex and favourite of Queen Elizabeth I, passed his youth here. On his execution after his unhappy rebellion, Lamphey fell into ruins. However, these are now carefully cared for and are open to the public. The fine Georgian house of nearby Lamphey Court is now a country hotel.

Laugharne (Talacharn), *Dyfed* (4/1B) This charming and out-of-the-main-run little town, at the point where the Carmarthen Taf comes out to the Tywi estuary, has a long history which it has carefully guarded. It is on the eastern boundary of the 'Little England beyond Wales', conquered by the Normans 700 years ago. The castle stands near the reedy foreshore, and was greatly altered by Sir John Perrott in Elizabethan days. It has recently been tidied and the walls cleared of age-old ivy. It is not opened to the public. Laugharne

Laugharne Castle   *(Martin Dohrn)*

has succeeded in retaining its status as a borough, and the portreeve is installed with due ceremony at a formal breakfast, which must be the longest and most cheerful breakfast in Wales. The small but intriguing Town hall is graced by a tower crowned with a belfry. There is a plentiful supply of pleasant Georgian houses, and the main street, partly lined with trees, leads to the big 15th-century church on the outskirts of the town. The grave of the poet, Dylan Thomas, is in the churchyard, marked – as the poet would have wished – by a simple wooden cross. The memories of Dylan Thomas have now become the main attraction for visitors to Laugharne, and much of the atmosphere of the town is evident in Dylan's radio play *Under Milk Wood*. The Boathouse, where the poet lived for the later stages of his life, is now a museum dedicated to Dylan and draws enthusiasts from all over the world, including ex-US President Jimmy Carter. It was recently threatened by a rock fall from the narrow Cliff Walk, now known as Dylan's Walk, that leads to the house, but this has been cleared. No poet could have wished for a more romantic residence, looking out over the sands and winding waterways of what he described with deep affection as his 'heron priested shore'.

Llanarthney (Llanarthnau), *Dyfed* (4/2B) A small village in one of the most fertile parts of the valley of the Tywi. There is an ancient towered church, with a cross dating from the Dark Ages, a spacious inn and, on the wooded heights over-looking the Tywi, a splendid architectural folly known as Paxton's Tower. It was built by the enormously rich Sir William Paxton in honour of Lord Nelson. Paxton's great house of Middleton Hall was burned down in 1931, but the grandiose stables remain. Paxton's Tower has, however, been rescued from ruin, and gives a splendid viewpoint over the Tywi, winding far below. Two miles east at Dryslwyn the castle stands on a steep bluff overlooking the river. The ruins are scanty but make a fine impression in their dramatic setting.

Llanboidy, *Dyfed* (3/3B) Situated 5 miles north of WHITLAND, in the heart of a green, rolling countryside, off the obvious tourist route. The village shows signs of the influence of the local 'great house' of Maesgwynne, and the village hall was built with money won by a member of the Powell family of Maesgwynne in backing a horse called Hermit. Maesgwynne House has fallen from its high estate and part of it is a farmhouse.

The church has been heavily restored, and the family vault of the Powells has a figure of Grief carved by Sir William Goscombe John. A few years ago, little Llanboidy hit the headlines through the prowess of its tug-of-war team, which beat all comers. Today it is noted for its farmhouse cheese.

Llanbrynmair, *Powys* (2/1B) A village, in the heart of the high country immediately north of the PLYNLIMON range, divided into two parts. Old Llanbrynmair, with its few houses grouped around the ancient church, lies in the deep, beautiful valley of the river Twymyn, which flows down from DYLIFE over the spectacular waterfall of the Ffrwd Fawr. The church has massive oak beams supporting the roof and, unfortunately, these days generally has to be kept locked. The second part of Llanbrynmair is a few miles down the valley, where the Twymyn meets the Afon Taen and the Afon Cam, and the united streams turn towards the Dovey. This was the way the railway came, after driving over from the Carno valley through a deep cutting at Talerddig. This cutting is almost a linguistic barrier against the ever-spreading English language coming up from the Severn valley. Llanbrynmair is still an intensely Welsh place, and Welsh Nonconformists remember it as the birthplace of S. R. Roberts (1800–85), the Independent minister, publicist and patriot known to all Wales as 'S.R.'. Hen Capel, the Old Chapel, has a memorial to S.R's father.

The country is wild and lonely immediately north of Llanbrynmair – a curlew-haunted moorland, with small, lost but attractive lakes like Llyn Coch Hywel.

Llancarfan, *South Glamorgan* (5/4A) This village is 2 miles south of the main COWBRIDGE–CARDIFF road in the Vale of Glamorgan. It is very much a residential area for Cardiff commuters, but its ancient church reminds us of its early fame as a centre of Celtic Christianity. Here St Cattwg set up his monastery in the 6th century, and the Carfan brook, which was there in his time, still runs down the side of the road near the church. The church is mainly 13th-century work, and contains a chapel that has been most successfully modernized. Apart from the church, set in its grassy hollow, modern Llancarfan with its comfortable villas may not carry the mind back into the past. But the surrounding countryside is full of fascinating survivals if you seek them out. Back on the main road, both the villages of

Bonvilston and St Nicholas have old thatched houses once characteristic of the Vale of Glamorgan, and close to St Nicholas is the oldest memorial of them all – the great cromlech of Tinkinswood, with its giant capstone. The contrast is striking between this age-old prehistoric relic lying in the shadow of the tall television transmitters of Wenvoe, with the super-modern studios of HTV not far away over the brow of the hill towards Cardiff.

Llandaff, *South Glamorgan* (5/5C) Llandaff is officially part of CARDIFF. Busy motorways surround it and new suburbs expand to enclose it, but somehow it has succeeded in remaining a place apart, a little community set around a cathedral close which has the friendly air of a village green. The medieval gateway of the old bishops' palace stands at the south end, although the palace was burned down by Owain Glyndwr. The cathedral itself is set in a little valley at a lower level from the Green, and this adds to its special atmosphere of being withdrawn from the world. The buildings have suffered strangely from the misfortunes of time. Nothing remains of the early Celtic monastic settlement founded by St Teilo. The Normans began a new church, and the work went steadily on through the 12th and 13th centuries. The early construction period closed with the great dedication ceremony of 1266, although Jasper Tudor added the elegant north-west tower. The Reformation ushered in centuries of appalling neglect. By the early 19th century, James Wood, the architect of Bath, built what was described as a classical temple among the ruined arches. The 19th century saw a splendid transformation and the cathedral was restored to its 13th-century splendour. The restoration was only temporary. In 1941 the cathedral was all but wrecked by a German landmine. Among British cathedrals only Coventry received worse damage. Once again Llandaff was renovated and rose from the dead. A thanksgiving service celebrated its return to life in 1958.

A visit to the renewed cathedral is inspiring. A bold arch now spans the nave, carrying Epstein's figure of 'Christ in Majesty'. There are John Piper stained-glass windows and the new chapel to the memory of the men of the Royal Welsh Regiment fits perfectly into the scheme. Some old treasures survived the blitz, including Rosetti's triptych 'The Seed of David'. Not far away the

The Jacob Epstein statue 'Christ in Majesty', Llandaff Cathedral

river Taff, now much cleansed, runs under the shadow of tall trees. Llandaff is a precious oasis of peace in an unquiet world.

Llanddeusant, *Dyfed* (4/3B) This small village, high in the hills, is the nearest point to the easiest route to Llyn y Fan Fach, in the impressive mountain range of the CARMARTHENSHIRE FANS. There is an old church with cross beams supporting the roof of the nave. The thirsty should note that the inn is now a youth hostel. The mountain road to the north-east gives fine views over the range. The narrow road to the north descends towards the Tywi valley through the village of Myddfai, which has a good church. It is chiefly famous in Wales for its physicians – supposed to have descended from the magical Lady of the Lake who rose from Llyn y Fan Fach. A fascinating medieval manuscript, now at the National Library of Wales, Aberystwyth, gives a list of their remedies, some of them well in advance of their time. The last physician of Myddfai was doctor to Queen Victoria.

Llanddewi Brefi, Dyfed (2/1C) A little township with a big church, halfway between LAMPETER and TREGARON in the upper Teifi Valley. Llanddewi has a special place in the story of St David. One of the most cherished legends of the saint relates that he attended a conference of bishops here to combat the Pelagian heresy. The crowd was so dense that the voices of the bishops could not be heard. St David was equal to the occasion. He was a small man, but he placed his handkerchief on the ground. The earth underneath it immediately rose into a small hill. St David stood upon it, and his clear voice carried to the far corners of the crowd. The True Faith was saved. The pious medieval pilgrims noted that the church of Llanddewi Brefi does indeed stand on a high bluff overlooking a charming little square, now surrounded with neat, whitewashed houses. It must have been an impressive shrine in the Middle Ages, with its tall tower, but it has now lost its transepts and has been much restored. In the south-west corner of the nave is a large statue of St David by Frederick Mancini, placed here in 1960. There are, however, five Celtic crosses which take you back in spirit to the sixth century and the age of the saint.

A half mile to the west, near the bridge over the Teifi, is the site of the Roman fort at Llanio, which could be the Bremia of the Antonine Itinerary. An exciting road goes south-east behind Llanddewi Brefi to emerge at FARMERS.

Llanddewi Brefi

Llandeilo, *Dyfed* (4/2B) Llandeilo, in the rich, central section of the Tywi valley, stands on a hill above the river. From the noble bridge, which crosses the stream in a great arch claimed to be the biggest stone arch in Wales, the houses climb up to the little square around the church of St Teilo, almost rebuilt by Sir George Gilbert Scott. The main street has some dignified frontages including the colonnaded Cawdor Hotel. The bluff, on which most of the town is built, is crowned with two magnificent groves of trees, which allows you to distinguish the site of Llandeilo from a long way off as you approach the town. These trees mark the beginning of the extensive and beautifully wooded park of Dinefwr (Dynevor) Castle. The great house is rather sadly neglected, but the old medieval castle still looks impressive on its crag above the Tywi. It was the proud seat of the Lord Rhys, in the 12th century, when he was Lord of most of South Wales.

The scenery along the Tywi, as it flows beyond Llandeilo towards CARMARTHEN, is richly pastoral, with the brooding presence of the high hills in the background. It was celebrated by John Dyer, a Carmarthenshire man, in his celebrated poem, 'Grongar Hill' – a forerunner of Wordsworth and the Romantics. Wooded Grongar Hill rises behind Llangathen, and the track up it is tangled, and slightly baffling to those literary pilgrims who might wish to stand in the exact spot where Dyer found the inspiration for his poem. There is easy access to Golden Grove (Gelli Aur), a few miles beyond on the south side of the

Tywi. This was once the seat of the powerful Vaughan family, and here the celebrated Anglican divine, Jeremy Taylor, took refuge during the turmoil of the Civil Wars to write his spiritual masterpiece *Holy Living, Holy Dying*. The house was rebuilt in 1832, and the mansion eventually became an Agricultural College. It is now expanding its scope as the Gelli Aur Country Park in its 90 acres of parkland with deer herd, nature trails and arboretum. The park is 3 miles west of Llandeilo.

Llandovery (Llanymddyfri), *Dyfed* (4/3A) The market town at the top of the Tywi valley, surrounded by hills and unspoiled country. The main street has a small square with the Market House in the centre and next to it, a curious structure with a clock tower. Nearby is the Black Ox Inn with memories of the days, in the late 18th and early 19th centuries, when Llandovery was an important centre of the droving trade. The great herds of black cattle were collected here, to be driven over long routes on the hills to the cattle markets of England. The drovers were the first bankers of rural Wales, and the Bank of the Black Ox issued its own notes. Llandovery is still very much a drovers' town on market days, with the busy stockyards crowded by farmers in the shadow of the castle ruins. The town also has one of the two recognized Welsh public schools. Llandovery College was a 19th-century foundation, and, besides a good scholastic record, has also produced some of Wales's finest rugby players. There are two notable churches in the town, both, curiously enough, outside the centre. The parish church of Llandingat, south of the town, was restored by W. D. Caröe in 1913. In the churchyard is the unmarked grave of old Vicar Prichard, who wrote the homely verses of religious exhortation which became famous in Wales as *Canwyll y Cymry* (The Welshman's Candle). He was a strong churchman, but his verses may have prepared the ground for the coming Methodist Revival in the 18th century. The church of Llanfair, about 1 mile north of the town stands on a high, tree-clad bluff and was also restored by Caröe. It may stand on the site of the old Roman fort, and the thick walls and strong tower give it almost a Roman air. The grave of William Williams, Pantycelyn, the great hymn writer of the Methodist Revival, is in the churchyard.

Llandovery stands at the junction of several roads. The road to the east, towards BRECON and the Usk valley, runs through a deep, wooded defile, which contains a curious roadside monument to the victims of a coach accident, and a warning against drunken coach driving. In a side valley is the farm of Pantycelyn, William Williams' birthplace. The road to the south follows the fertile Tywi valley to Llanwrda and Llangadog, from which the route goes over the Black Mountain (*see* Ammanford). The road due north follows the Tywi to its source in the wild country around Llyn Brianne (*see* Cilycwm). The north-east road takes the same course as the railway into central Wales. The railway crosses a high viaduct at Cynghordy and then tunnels under the pointed hill of the Sugar Loaf. In fact, whatever road you take in or out of Llandovery, you find yourself in delectable country.

Llandrindod Wells, *Powys* (2/2C) This is the chief spa town of Wales. The curative properties of the sulphurous mineral springs were discovered in the 18th century, but 'The Wells' really took off with the advent of the railway. At the beginning of the 20th century Llandrindod was the fashionable place, where – in between taking the waters – political careers could be advanced, promotions to better churches or

Edwardian architecture, Llandrindod Wells

chapels tactfully solicited, and satisfactory and lucrative marriages arranged. These glories have long since departed, with the band that played in the decorative bandstand in the Pump House gardens. But Llandrindod still has a defiantly attractive Edwardian air about it, with its large redbrick hotels, its marine lake and golf course, 1000 ft up on the breezy moorlands behind the town. Llandrindod has bravely set out to create a new role for itself. It has become an important conference centre and has attracted many of the administrative bodies of the new county of Powys. The old Pump House has been refurbished and you can still 'take the waters' here at Rock Park Gardens if you are brave enough. There is a local museum, a Welsh Crafts Centre and an interesting collection of bicycles in the Automobile Palace, in Temple Street. A drama festival is held in the grandly named Albert Hall, at the beginning of May, each year, and the atmosphere of yesteryear is re-created in the town every September for the week-long Victorian Festival, when everyone from the butcher to the baker dons the traditional costume of the period. It is also a good touring centre for the attractive countryside around. The important Roman camp at Castell Collen, near Llanyre on the west bank of the Ithon, has been excavated, although there is not much to see above ground. The lover of old and out-of-the-ordinary churches will find some unexpected delights awaiting him. South of Llandrindod, near Howey, the church at Disserth still retains its old box pews, each with the family name on it. There are two surprises on the long road that leads north from Llandrindod to the Kerry Hills and NEWTOWN. The church at Llanbister still has its 18th-century singing loft, where psalms were led by the village band. But the greatest treasure is preserved in the little church of Llananno, at the roadside a few miles beyond Llanbister. The church was rebuilt in the 19th century, and the magnificent carved rood screen was carefully re-erected in the new church – a medieval masterpiece in a lost corner of Wales.

Llandysul, *Dyfed* (4/1A) A little town in the central section of the Teifi valley in West Wales. Its two main and parallel streets are set on a slope down to the river, where the ancient church looks down on the rushing stream. The west tower is unusual in being tapered all the way to the top. It contains a relic which takes you back to the Dark Ages, a stone inscribed *Velvor filia Bromio* – Velvor, daughter of Bromio. Like so many of

Bridge of the Teifi, Llandysul

these small townships in the Teifi valley, Llandysul developed in the early 19th century as a weaving centre. Now it is a market town, and also the home of one of the leading Welsh publishers, Gomer Press. There are numerous Iron Age forts in the hills that encircle Llandysul. The best of them is Carn Wen which has a wall of loose rock 12 ft high in parts.

The river itself is one of the attractions of Llandysul. At points it runs through racing narrows, which are now a well-kown test for canoeing enthusiasts. The banks of the Teifi to the west are richly wooded, and there is a fine bridge, leaping the stream in a high arch at Allt-y-Cafn with an old woollen mill at its side. The valley even gains in beauty as it continues down to Henllan. The road comes near the river bank and allows the motorist to appreciate the tumbling stream under its canopy of tall trees, as it races under the Henllan Bridge, built in 1774. The river here is famous for its salmon.

Llanelli, *Dyfed* (4/1B) Llanelli, on the main railway line from SWANSEA to West Wales, was once the tinplate capital of the world. A forest of tall chimneys flung a pall of lucrative smoke over the town, as the gleaming tinplates were passed through the rollers and into the tinning pot of a host of small individual works, manned by craftsmen to whom tinplate making was almost a fine art. The boisterous song of 'Sospan Fach' (The Little Saucepan) was Llanelli's trademark, until it was annexed by the crowds at the international rugby matches at Cardiff Arms Park. The advent of mass production of tinplate in the great new strip mills at PORT TALBOT and Llanwern put paid to Llanelli's speciality, and closed the works in a number of the surrounding villages like Gorseinon, Gowerton and PENCLAWDD. Llanelli managed to get a small part of the Port Talbot complex transferred to Trostre, but the great days are now over. As with so many other once-busy centres in South Wales, Llanelli is bravely hunting for new industry – and with success. Anyone who doubts the sturdy spirit of the town has only to attend a rugby match at the famous Stradey Park ground to know that Llanelli is still very much alive. Today the town has a large shopping centre serving West Wales. It has a neo-Jacobean Town Hall and nearby in the People's Park is the Jubilee Swimming Pool. The mansion house in Park Howard to the north has an interesting museum demonstrating the history of the tinplate industry. At nearby Machynys a wildfowl centre, established in 1985, is now attracting a wide variety of nesting birds.

Llanerfyl, *Powys* (2/2B) A small village, 15 miles west of WELSHPOOL, in the heart of a still unfrequented part of Mid Wales. The river Banwy, which rises in the high moorlands that border the Dovey valley, has here grown into a fine stream, particularly beautiful as it winds past Llanerfyl. Llanerfyl Church stands in a circular churchyard and, like a similar one at Ysbyty Cynfyn, near DEVIL'S BRIDGE, has given rise to speculation that the church was originally deliberately planted in the middle of a prehistoric stone circle. It also has a gravestone from the Dark Ages commemorating the 13-year-old daughter of a man called Paterninus. In the graveyard stands an impressive yew tree, claimed to be the largest in Wales. South of Llanerfyl the land rises to sparse moorland and lonely country.

Llanfair Caereinion, *Powys* (2/2B) A small and pleasant market town on a hill above the river Banwy 8 miles from WELSHPOOL. The main street runs up the hill from the bridge over the river to what amounts to a small, sloping square. The church has been extensively restored and the tower does not quite harmonize with the older part of the edifice.

The Methodist chapel, in the centre of the town, is perhaps more prominent than the church – a symbol, maybe, of the great 19th-century rivalry between church and chapel. No great architectural sensations here, but you do not expect that from most of the small market towns in Wales. However, the houses all have a friendly, lived-together look.

On the low ground to the north of the bridge is the terminus of the Welshpool and Llanfair Light Railway, one of the 'great little trains' of Wales. The line was built in the early years of the 20th century, in the days when the light railway seemed the answer to communication problems in remote country areas. The Earls of Powys took a great interest in its development and two of the remaining steam engines are appropriately named 'The Earl' and 'The Countess'. The line was taken over by a group of railway enthusiasts in 1956 and, after the restoration of the track had

The Llanfair Light Railway

been completed from Llanfair through Castle Caereinion to Sylfaen, the railway proudly returned to Welshpool in 1981. The line, with a 2 ft 6 in gauge, runs through pastoral country.

After Llanfair Caereinion, the Banwy swings north to join the Vyrnwy in the lush and secluded Vale of MEIFOD.

Llanfyllin, *Powys* (2/2A) This little market town, on the northern edge of Powys, comes as a pleasant architectural surprise. It seems to have decided to stay firmly in the late 18th century. Do not expect a miniature Bath, but little Llanfyllin, with its one main street, has retained its charm. The houses are mostly of warm red brick, mellowed by time. Even the church is 18th century red brick, and so is the chapel at the opposite end of town, which bears the inscription: 'This Protestant Chapel was rebuilt in the Year of our Lord 1717 Being the 172 year after the Reformation, the XXIX Since the Revolution And the IV year of the reign of King George'.

The great house of Bodfach Hall stands amid

Llangorse Lake from Llangasty-Talyllyn

the woodlands that line the Afon Cain, which is also Llynfyllin's river. Bodfach is now a country hotel. The Cain, and its sister rivers, the Vyrnwy and Tanat, flow through fertile land rich in the oaks for which this countryside in the old county of Montgomeryshire was famous in the past. The countryside thus has a plentiful supply of attractive, half-timbered houses. All the rivers twist and turn making the landscape complicated. The roads wander happily up and down among the small hills. This is a land to loiter through and enjoy.

Llangammarch Wells, *Powys* (5/4A) A compact little village on the river Irfon some 7 miles west of BUILTH WELLS. The railway line that still wanders happily through central and south-west Wales passes it, and was the reason for this quiet little village giving itself the airs of a fashionable spa. Visitors could come to the mineral springs, which according to the doctors contained the rare element of barium chloride, supposed to be specially effective in curing heart disease, chronic rheumatism and the gout. The new Lake Hotel flourished, but the glory of the Mid Wales spas started to fade after the First World War, and

Llangammarch was no exception. It still has its hotel and lake but those cure-all mineral waters now well up unheeded. Llangammarch is now more valued as a fishing centre on the trout-filled Irfon than for its barium chloride. It lies, however, in lonely, unspoiled country. To the south lie the high ranges of the Epynt which rise to over 1500 ft. A fine road crosses them from near Llangammarch, south through Upper Chapel to BRECON; but motorists are warned that the whole of the western Epynt is a firing range under the control of the MoD. A red warning flag is flown when firing is in progress. The headquarters of the range is at Sennybridge, in the Usk valley on the south side of the Epynt. The gaunt outline of the Drover's Arms still stands on the skyline as a reminder of the days when the Epynt was one of the great drovers' routes out of Wales.

Llangeitho, *Dyfed* (1/3C) A village at the top end of the valley of the river Aeron, which reaches the sea at ABERAERON on Cardigan Bay. The centre of Llangeitho is built around a square which has a certain architectural charm, but for Welshmen the village is inseparably associated with Daniel Rowland, one of the three great leaders of the 18th-century Methodist Revival in Wales. Howell

Harris was the organizer, William Williams (Pantycelyn) the hymn writer, and Daniel Rowland was the Voice – the great preacher whose fiery oratory had a hypnotic effect on his listeners. He did not travel. Rather the crowds came to him, camping out at times in their hundreds around his first chapel, built in 1760. The present building dates from around 1806, but it has retained one of the unique features of the earlier building – the outside staircase to the pulpit, which allowed the preacher to appear suddenly high above the expectant congregation, with powerful dramatic effect. A memorial to Daniel Rowlands stands in front of the chapel.

Llangeitho today is noted for its pony trekking.

The Aeron rises in the bleak moorland of Mynydd Bach to the north-west of Llangeitho. The land here reaches over 1000 ft and holds the unfrequented and windswept small lakes of Llyn Eiddwen and Llyn Fanod.

Llangorse Lake (Llyn Syfaddan), *Powys* (5/5A) The largest natural lake in Wales after Bala, in North Wales, lies 5 miles east of BRECON town. It is also a mere 1¾ miles from the river Usk, but between the lake and the river rises the narrow ridge of Allt yr Esgair, over 1000 ft high, which offers a splendid walk along the ancient trackway that runs on the summit of the ridge. There are great views south over the BRECON BEACONS. The ridge also sends the lake waters north and the Afon Llynfi thus flows out of the lake to enter not the Usk but the Wye, near GLASBURY. Legends have naturally gathered around Llyn Syfaddan. As at Bala there is supposed to be a drowned city under its waters, but even stranger is the long-held local belief that there is a connection between Llangorse and the tiny tarn of Llyn Cwm Llwch, under the summit of the Brecon Beacons. Any attempt to drain the larger lake will lead to Llyn Cwm Llwch bursting its banks and sweeping down to drown Brecon town. The legend was put to a severe test at the beginning of the 20th century, when London proposed a scheme for raising the level of the lake by 100 ft. Luckily it was abandoned before the anger of Llyn Cwm Llwch was aroused.

The village of Llangorse lies back from the lake on the north side, but a narrow road brings you, on the south side, to the lake edge at Llangasty-Talyllyn, with its church and school set among the trees. Llangorse Lake is somewhat of a battleground between the conservationists and those who want to exploit it for pleasure. One section has been protected as a nature reserve but water skiers have the freedom of the other half and here watersports are actively pursued. Peace descends in the winter and leaves the lake to the pike fisher. Llangorse is famous for the size of these ferocious fish. To the east is the high, shapely peak of Mynydd Troed, an outlier of the BLACK MOUNTAINS.

Llangranog, *Dyfed* (4/1A) A seaside village between NEW QUAY and CARDIGAN on the coast of Cardigan Bay. The hills come close to the sea here, and the houses are almost wedged between the high ground and the waves. Narrow roads lead down to it, with some hairpin bends, but the holidaymakers crowd here in midsummer, for the sands under the high cliffs are firm, yellow and attractive. The Welsh League of Youth (Urdd Gobaith Cymru) has an important youth holiday centre here. The coastal scenery is impressive. Apart from the main sands at Llangrannog itself, there are several sandy and secluded coves reached only by cliff paths which adds to their attraction. Just north of the main beach is the rounded hill of Pendinaslochtyn, with the summit surrounded by the entrenchments of a fine Iron Age fort. From the hill, the strange headland of Ynys-Lochtyn projects thrillingly into the sea. It is a great viewpoint along this impressive coastline and is now in the safe hands of the National Trust. There are two sandy coves here. Just south of Llangranog is Traeth Penbryn with a sandy beach and low dunes. It lies at the end of a wooded valley and is owned by the National Trust.

Llangurig, *Powys* (2/1C) This village, high up in the upper reaches of the Wye valley, is somewhat of a road junction. The main road from BRECON via BUILTH WELLS and RHAYADER, much used by motorists from south-east Wales on their way up to the north, swings away here towards LLANIDLOES and NEWTOWN, while a western road runs from Llangurig along the Wye valley and then climbs over the high pass at Eisteddfa Curig on the slopes of PLYNLIMON, to come down eventually at ABERYSTWYTH. The little village is neat, well built, with two attractive inns and a church surprisingly large for the size of the place. This is basically sheep country and the well-known sheep farmer, the late Captain Bennett, had a vast sheep ranch covering the upper course of the infant Wye to its source almost on the summit ridge of Plynlimon. Once again, the Forestry Commission has moved in on a big scale.

There are large plantations on the hills to the south of the Wye and west of Llangurig, but a small clearing has been left for the little Roman fortlet of Cae Gaer 5 miles west of Llangurig. To the north of the tumbling Wye the moors are covered with the conifers that are part of the big Hafren Forest. The course of the Wye, however, is still clear and strong walkers can follow it up to the source by taking the old mine road that leaves the A44 at Pont Rhydgaled.

The road north from the village to Llanidloes rises over open country to run down into the Severn valley. This was the country that finally defeated the optimistic promoters of the Manchester to Milford railway and still has traces of the trackway that foundered in the bogs.

Llangyfelach, *West Glamorgan* (4/2B) A village, on the northern outskirts of SWANSEA, that is administratively part of the borough; the lines of houses continually expand towards it, but it still has the feeling of a separate place. The church is curious, with a tower some distance from the rest of the building. This gave rise to the legend that the Devil had tried to make off with the tower while St Cyfelach was building his church, but the powerful curses of the good saint forced him to drop it. The old church, however, was demolished for structural reasons, and the new one built some distance away. It contains a Celtic wheel cross, and a painting by the artist Evan Walters, presented in memory of his parents. The tall, semi-skyscraper of an office block just east of Llangyfelach is the DVLC Motor Licence registration centre, only too familiar to British motorists.

Across the M4 motorway is the big Velindre works, part of the steel and strip mill complex of PORT TALBOT, placed here for social reasons when the new methods displaced the small local tinplate works. The hills to the north are a surprise – lonely moorlands with no trace of industry. The mountain road runs from Llangyfelach over Mynydd y Gwair to the earthworks of Pen-lle-castell at 1000 ft – a splendid viewpoint.

Llangynog, *Powys* (2/2A) The river Tanat joins the Vyrnwy near LLANYMYNECH on the English border, but if you follow its course back to its point of origin you find yourself, within 15 miles of the border, in the heart of the Berwyn mountains. The contrast is striking between the rich Shropshire plains and the wild Welsh moorland so close to England. The Tanat gains in beauty the closer you get to the high hills. At Llangynog the mountains close in. The village grew up in the shadow of a great crag of the Berwyns, which was extensively quarried. These workings are now closed, and little Llangynog, with its houses closely pressed together, is glad to see tourists to replace the money once obtained from the quarries. The place has retained a secluded charm. A spectacular road, now greatly improved, climbs out of the valley over the main ridge of the Berwyns. At Milltir Cerrig it reaches 1500 ft, and also crosses the Powys border. Away to your right the heather-clad moorlands roll on to Moel Sych and Cadair Fronwen, the highest summit of the Berwyns at over 2800 ft. No question but that you are now in North Wales.

Llangynog can offer a secret pleasure on the Powys side of the Berwyn ridge. A secluded valley runs up to the little church of Pennant Melangell, lost in the hills. Melangell, or Marcella, according to one legend, was an Irish princess who fled to this secluded spot to avoid an odious marriage. She had extraordinary power over the wild creatures of the wilderness. When a Welsh prince was pursuing a hare, the animal took refuge in her robe, and the dogs drew back in terror. The prince was so impressed that he gave her the land to found a religious settlement here. Part of the structure of the little church may be pre-Norman and there are also some interesting 18th-century candleholders. The key to the church has to be obtained at Llangynog. Walkers will be rewarded if they follow the stream to the top of the valley. They will find themselves in an untouched mountain hollow, with a waterfall singing among the rocks – a rare island of peace among the hills.

Llangynwyd, *Mid Glamorgan* (4/3C) Situated a few miles south of MAESTEG, in the hills bordering the Llynfi valley, Llangynwyd has acquired an aura of romance, which still persists even in our present prosaic days. The place itself is tiny – a row of houses set around the churchyard, two attractive pubs and an ancient church with a high, 13th-century tower. But the visitors come to look at the grave, near the church porch, which is claimed to be that of the poet, Wil Hopcyn, the hero of a love story that captured the heart of South Wales in the 19th century. Wil, so the story goes, was a poor 18th-century thatcher who was also a fine poet. He fell in love with Ann Thomas, daughter of the landowner of the rich estate of Cefn Ydfa, and far above him in social status. She

Llanrhaeadr-Ym-Mochnant, see p. 137

returned his love but her father forced her to marry the son of a wealthy neighbour, Antony Maddock. Ann died of a broken heart a year later, and Wil was allowed to shed his tears at her deathbed. The story was made more touching by the ascription to Wil of the lovely Welsh folk song 'Bugeilio's Gwenith Gwyn' – Watching the Wheat.

Alas, those dreary spoilsports, the professional historians, have cast their baleful eyes on this moving romance. There was, indeed, an Ann Thomas of Cefn Ydfa who married an Antony Maddock in 1725, and, according to the parish registers, died a few years later. Unfortunately, there are three possible Wil Hopcyns noted in the same register, and there is no evidence that Ann ever met any of them. No matter. We are all free to believe in a story that can still move people to come in droves to the quiet hamlet of Llangynwyd, lost among the hills. We can stand before Wil Hopcyn's grave and afterwards retire to the friendly nearby pub – no doubt frequented by the poet – and lift our glass to the memory of the tragic Maid of Cefn Ydfa.

The Market Hall, Llanidloes

Llanidloes, *Powys* (2/2C) An attractive market town in Mid Wales at the junction of the Severn and Clywedog rivers which has developed as a tourist centre in recent years. It owed its early prosperity to the lead mining in the surrounding hills and to the woollen trade. In the heart of the town stands the late 16th-century Market Hall. It is timbered, with an open space beneath for the stalls. A museum of local history is housed in the upper part. Such halls were common in the wool towns of Mid Wales but Llanidloes has the only surviving example. A tablet records the visit of John Wesley, who preached in the open air here at the hall. Llanidloes Church is impressive, and the nave contains the graceful arches which were brought here from ABBEYCWMHIR, when the monastery there was dissolved in 1536. The town contains other half-timbered houses. The wide main street leads down from the market hall to the bridge over the Severn. The left-hand road, immediately across the bridge, leads you into the hills to the north of the Clywedog and gives exciting glimpses of the great new lake that has been formed by the damming of the river. The Llyn Clywedog Scenic Trail is 2½ miles long and starts above the car park on the Staylittle road. It

is possible to make a circuit of the lake if you turn off this road just past Staylittle. The route takes you through the vast Hafren Forest, which spreads over from the Clywedog valley into that of the infant Severn – Hafren is the Welsh name for the Severn. The forest stretches far up the eastern slopes of PLYNLIMON, and the Forestry Commission has designated some attractive trails including the Source of the Severn Walk, the Cascades Forest Trail and the Blaenhafren Falls Walk. Details are available from the Forestry Commission's office in LLANDRINDOD WELLS. The circuit of the lake eventually brings the motorist back into the Clywedog valley and to the area around the dam itself. Here is the headquarters of the Llyn Clywedog Sailing Club. Good fishing, enjoyed by a former US President during his holiday in the region, is available in the lake, under the auspices of the local angling club. The small Bryn Tail Lead Mine site near the dam has been cleared for a well-signed industrial archaeology trail. To the east of Bryn Tail are the remains of the Van Lead Mine – once the most profitable in the region.

Glyndwr's Way, part of a 121-mile walk across Powys from KNIGHTON to MACHYNLLETH also crosses here.

Llanon *see* Llansantffraid

Llanrhaeadr-Ym-Mochnant, *Powys* (2/2A) This village is on the border between Powys and Clwyd and thus just scrapes into our guide. In fact the church and the houses around it are on the north side of the Afon Rhaeadr – the River of the Waterfall – which marks the boundary. But Llanrhaeadr demands inclusion for two reasons. Here William Morgan, the rector and later Bishop of St Asaph's, laboured to perfect the final form of the Welsh translation of the Bible, which was published by order of Queen Elizabeth I in the year of the Armada, 1588. It has the same standing as far as the Welsh language is concerned as the Authorized Version of the English Bible. The second reason lies in the name of the place – the Church of the Waterfall. This magnificent cascade lies 4 miles north-west of the village on the slopes of the Berwyn mountains. The falls are 240 ft high and plunge down in two sections. The lower section passes under a natural arch. A delightful late Victorian chalet of a tea-room gives a good viewpoint.

Llanrhaeadr is a good pony-trekking centre into the Berwyn mountains. But these high hills already belong in spirit to North Wales.

Llanrhian, *Dyfed* (3/1A) The village lies about 1 mile inland from the coast of North Dyfed and 6 miles north-east from ST DAVID'S. The church stands in a grove of trees and has a tower that dates from the 13th century, and though the rest of the edifice looks ancient it was almost entirely rebuilt in the 19th century. The font is 15th-century and bears the arms of Sir Rhys ap Thomas. The road goes down to the sea at Porthgain but before you reach this little harbour you pass a track which takes you to the secluded beach of Traeth Llywn. A narrow cliff path descends to the golden sands. The road inland brings you to the main road between St David's and FISHGUARD at Croesgoch. The Altramont Inn owes its curious name to an Irish noble family that had property in this district. Two miles further along the road to Fishguard is the hill-top village of Mathry, with views northwards towards the PRESELI HILLS over the fields which were regarded as so fruitful in the old days that Mathry was thought of by churchmen as 'The Golden Prebend'. The church, somewhat square looking, was largely rebuilt in the 19th century. The porch has a stone with a Latin inscription, and another stone, built into the wall, has faint outlines of Ogham writing.

Llanrhystyd, *Dyfed* (1/3C) Here the little river Wyre runs down into the sea at Cardigan Bay 7 miles to the south of ABERYSTWYTH. The village stands back from the coast, from which it is separated by low meadows, and the beach is mainly pebble and shingle, although there is some sand at low tide. The church is Victorian, but its spire stands out over a landscape of green, tumbled hills. Sir John Rees, the great Celtic scholar, maintained that the Wyre marked the linguistic separation between the Welsh dialects of North and South Wales. The road north to Aberystwyth from Llanrhystyd climbs over a steep hill, crowned with the Blaen Plwyf TV transmitter, and comes down into the lower Ystwyth valley at Llanfarian. The Ystwyth runs west from the high moorlands south of the main massif of PLYNLIMON past Pont-rhydygroes, the entrance to the once beautiful but now decayed Hafod estate. Ysbyty Ystwyth is perched high above the valley which is deeply wooded. The river flows past Trawscoed, where the Romans had a fort. At Llanilar, where the houses cluster around the rebuilt and restored church, a large stone stands near the churchyard gate, which tradition maintains was used by Henry VII as a mounting-block when

Llanrhian Parish Church, see p. 137

he was riding to the battle of Bosworth in 1485. *See also* Cwmystwyth.

Llansaint *see* Ferryside

Llansantffraid, *Dyfed* (1/3C) This village is set back from the sea and just off the road between ABERAERON and ABERYSTWYTH. It is almost joined to **Llanon,** on the road itself. Llanon takes its name from St Non, the mother of St David, who legend claims was brought up here. A small stream runs down to the sea and breaks into a series of little waterfalls at Llansantffraid. A high shingle bank dams it back on the shore to form a still pool, from which the waters seep through the pebbles on to a shingly, rocky beach. Definitely not one of the popular beaches of Cardigan Bay!

Llansawel, *Dyfed* (4/2A) Built on the Marlais river which joins the bigger river Cothi 1 mile south-east of the village. Like so many Welsh village churches, Llansawel's was heavily restored in the 19th century. The west tower looks as if it were designed for a fortress rather than a church. The square font is built into the west wall. A well-built chapel, not the church, dominates the village, which can also boast of a pleasant fishing inn. Immediately to the south is a strange little hill, Pen Dinas, which is being intensively quarried. It is thus liable to change shape over the years. In 1986 it looked like a miniature Matterhorn from the Llansawel side. The road north from the village turns at the chapel and climbs steadily towards Rhyd-cymerau. The area is heavily forested with conifers. At Rhydcymerau the road straight ahead takes you down into the Teifi valley at LLANYBYTHER. A road to the left climbs still higher on to the moors of Mynydd Llanybyther through the plantations. The trees clear, however, over the high ground to the west to give fine views down into the lush and green woods and fields of the Teifi.

Llanstephan (Llansteffan), *Dyfed* (4/1B) The castle is the main showpiece of this attractive village at the end of the peninsula formed by the rivers Taf and the Tywi, as they approach the sea in Carmarthen Bay. The castle and the village at its foot can easily be seen from the train as it runs through FERRYSIDE on the eastern bank of the Tywi estuary. The ruins are perched on a steep hill overlooking the ever-widening river, and date from the 13th century. As the Normans pushed their way along the coast of South Wales they were forced to guard the crossings of the many estuaries that lay in their path. Hence the string of castles built along Carmarthen Bay, from LOUGHOR and KIDWELLY to Laugharne. The first defences at Llanstephan were earthworks, but the site was soon regarded as important enough to deserve a stone castle. This was completed in the 13th century when the fortress was owned by the de Camvilles. What remains consists of an inner and outer ward. The Great Gatehouse of the outer ward is the most prominent feature, flanked by its two supporting towers, but there is also a gatehouse to the second ward. The ruins were placed by the owners in the care of the then Ministry of Works in 1958, and restoration work has proceeded steadily since then.

The little township at the castle foot has charm and the fine Georgian mansion of the Plas looks across to the ruins. There are also good Georgian houses in Llanstephan itself. St Stephen's church has been extensively restored, but it has a strong defensive tower and some interesting monuments to local families. The sands at Llanstephan can be capricious and obey the whims of the ever-changing river. At their best they are golden and hold cockles. The peninsula ends beyond the castle in the high bluff overlooking the wide estuary and the woodlands behind it are known as the Sticks, from a Welsh mistranslation into English of the word for woods – *coed*. The Llanstephan peninsula is, of course, a dead end – and perhaps all the better for being so.

Llanthony (Llanddewi Nant Hodni), *Gwent* (5/5A) Llanthony is 9 miles due north from ABERGAVENNY, and close to the Herefordshire border. Llanthony Priory lies in the heart of the Hodni valley, also known as the Vale of Ewyas and justly regarded as the most beautiful and fascinating in the BLACK MOUNTAINS of Gwent. The gateway to the Vale is Llanfihangel Crucorney, with its remarkable Skirrid Inn and the Tudor mansion of Llanfihangel Court (limited summer opening) where King Charles I stayed during the Civil War. The road up the valley is narrow, twisting but ever varied; 1½ miles from Llanfihangel you come to the little church of Cwmyoy – the most twisted church in Britain. Hardly a wall is at a right angle to another one, the

Llanthony Priory

tower leans and the roof buckles. A landslip occurred in the Middle Ages not long after the church was built, and the builders did their best to prop it up again. The result is delightful. Cwmyoy also contains one of the most moving of epitaphs – to Thomas Price:

> Thomas Price he takes his nap
> In our common mother's lap,
> Waiting to hear the Bridegroom say,
> 'Wake, my dear, and come away.'

The valley gets narrower, the surrounding hills higher as you come to Llanthony Priory. No wonder the poet Walter Savage Landor bought it in the early 19th century, although his temper eventually alienated him from the local farmers. The arches and tower of St David's Church, the first Augustine foundation in Wales, rise from the green turf, and a hotel now occupies the monastic buildings. The road and the valley both grow narrower and more twisting as they go north from Llanthony. At the head of the valley is the tiny little whitewashed church of Capel-y-ffin, which the diarist Francis Kilvert said reminded him of a 'brooding owl'. An enchanted place, set among ancient yew trees. On the hillside above, the Reverend J. L. Lyte, an Anglican clergyman, decided to build his own monastery. He took the title of Father Ignatius, and strove to revive the monastic spirit in this wild hollow among the hills. He never completed the building, and his grave lies among the foundations. The sculptor Eric Gill came to the monastery in 1924, with perhaps rather different aims. Since his day it has even become a guest house, but the Father Ignatius Memorial Trust still takes care of the founder's grave. Everything seems to have a special atmosphere in Capel-y-ffin. The Baptist Chapel here was established in 1737. High summer may not be the best time to appreciate the remote charm of this refuge, for there is much traffic about. But for the rest of the year, the whole valley is as Walter Savage Landor, Father Ignatius, Francis Kilvert and Eric Gill once knew it. A passable road has now replaced the rough track that led out of the valley to the north over the main ridge of the Black Mountains, down to the Wye valley at HAY. It is known as the Gospel Pass, from the legend that a daughter of Caractacus, the leader of the Silures in their revolt against the Romans, invited St Peter and St Paul to preach the Gospel to her fellow countrymen and women. This was the way they travelled.

Llanthony is also a good pony-trekking centre.

Llantrisant, *Mid Glamorgan* (5/4C) A small township, perched in the centre of a high, narrow ridge 12 miles north-west of CARDIFF. The site is spectacular, with wide views over the Vale of Glamorgan. The ridge was the natural place for the old Welsh ruler of the Vale to have his court. The Normans displaced him, and Llantrisant grew into a small borough, with its towered church devoted to three saints. Llantrisant is the Welsh for the Church of the Three Saints – Illtud, Tyfodwg and Gwynno. The castle, now represented by a single tower, once housed the unhappy Edward II, after his capture in a dingle near Tonyr-efail, still called 'Pant y Brad' – the Valley of Treachery. Little Llantrisant sent a contingent of a 100 archers to fight at Crécy, and the exploits of the 'Black Hundred' are still celebrated. The Corporation was dissolved under the Municipal Corporations Act of 1883, but the Court Leet is still held and new Freemen are presented. Llantrisant's most famous resident in recent times was the remarkable eccentric Dr William Price – ex-Chartist, heir to the Druids, defiant radical and a pioneer of the Permissive Society.

As a protagonist of free love he lived with his young consort at Llantrisant, and begot several children when he was over 80. When his young son, Iesu Grist – Jesus Christ – died, he cremated him on Llantrisant Common at dawn. The townsmen were horrified and Price's consort, Gwenllian, held them off with a gun. Price was arrested, but his brilliant defence of his cause in court in 1884 established the legal right of cremation in Britain. There is a tablet in Llantrisant to his memory, placed there by the Cremation Society.

Llantrisant remains isolated on its hilltop, but industry has spread on the low land all around. Prominent among the newcomers is the Royal Mint, which was moved from its old site near the Tower of London in the 1960s to a new home in the Ely valley behind the Llantrisant ridge. Security here is unobtrusive but highly efficient.

On the edge of the town in the forest are waymarked walks, picnic sites, and for the more enthusiastic, a tough orienteering course.

Llantwit Major (Llanilltud Fawr), *South Glamorgan* (5/4C) A small but historic township a mile inland from the sea along the coast of South Glamorgan. Here, safe from the dangers from the Irish raiders in the Bristol Channel, St Illtud, one of the greatest of the Celtic saints, set up his monastery in the 6th century. It became a centre of learning, famous throughout Northern Europe. Illtud may have settled here because of the presence of a large Roman villa. This was excavated in the 19th century, when a fine mosaic was discovered. The excavations have since been covered.

The narrow streets cluster around the small central square, where the ancient inn of the Old Swan confronts the modern market cross. The Town Hall has two storeys and an outside staircase. It dates, with considerable alterations, from the 17th century. Town Hall is a misnomer, for Llantwit was never a borough. The church of St Illtud is the most remarkable monument in Llantwit Major. It is extraordinarily long, for it consists of two parts. One section was built as the chapel of the old monastery, the other as the parish church. The monastic section is now a museum, containing an important collection of Celtic stones and medieval carvings. The elaborate 14th-century reredos has been preserved, together with a splendid carving of the Tree of Jesse. There is also an ancient stone font and painted frescos. Altogether, a place rich in the early history of South Wales. Nearby is the

St Illtud's Church, Llantwit Major

ruined gatehouse of the monastery and a round columbarium, similar to the one at Ewenny.

The tiny Llantwit stream flows down to the sea in a narrow valley, with the entrenchments known as the Castle Ditches crowning the promontory. They could be Iron Age, or even Norman in origin. The small Col-Hugh Beach, with its shingle bank and many rock pools, has a car park and caravan site. It is popular with Malibu board riders. East of Llantwit is the big St Athan's station, one of the chief training centres of the RAF.

Llanwrtyd Wells, *Powys* (4/3A) One of the central Wales spa towns, at the western end of the Epynt range, and with a station still functioning on the Central Wales line. In the great days of the spas, LLANDRINDOD WELLS was, perhaps, the most fashionable place and the scene of church conferences. Llanwrtyd was less pretentious, more friendly and patronized by the chapel supporters. How things have changed here! The chalybeate waters now flow untasted from the abandoned pump rooms. But Llanwrtyd has turned bravely to other things. It was one of the

first places in Wales to develop pony trekking. An annual race is staged between man and horse, and the horse does not always win over the wild mountain tracks. Other popular pursuits in this area include walking, birdwatching and what is considered a new sport – mountain bike riding, from the recently established specialist centre in Llanwrtyd. Llanwrtyd also has craft centres for the tourists and the British Legion Cambrian Woollen Mills, employing many war veterans, make Welsh tweed with attractive patterns. But Llanwrytyd has a final trump card. It is the gateway to the unspoiled scenery of the Cambrian mountains, the great wilderness in the heart of Wales. The river Irfon gives fine trout fishing and it rises in the wilds beyond ABERGWESYN. The drive across the hills from Abergwesyn is a drive through the lonely heart of South Wales (*see* Llandovery).

Llanwddyn and **Lake Vyrnwy,** *Powys* (2/2A) When Liverpool Corporation decided in 1880 to implement their plan for turning the upper reaches of the river Vyrnwy into a great new reservoir, the waters inevitably drowned the old village of Llanwddyn. By 1883, the high stone-faced dam was completed, and a new village had been built in its shadow. Lake Vyrnwy is now over 100 years old, and has mellowed with the passage of time to become a place of unexpected beauty among the hills. The water spilling over the dam in winter is a memorable sight, and even the Gothic water-gauge tower offshore in the lake has acquired a romantic charm. All in pleasant contrast to the concrete slabs and rubble tips of some of the more recent dams built in Wales. Liverpool Corporation also built a solidly furnished hotel looking down on the lake, now frequented by tourists as well as the fishermen for whom it was first designed.

The extensive woods around the lake have also mellowed and Vyrnwy has become a bird sanctuary. The Severn–Trent Water Authority, which now controls the lake, and the RSPB have set up an excellent information centre in the disused Bethel Chapel on the south side of the dam, where the car park commands the best views.

Lake Vyrnwy is over 4 miles long. Two steep and narrow roads lead out over the mountains at the far end from the dam. One goes due north to the Dee valley, the other west to the exciting pass of Bwlch y Groes under the summits of the Arans. Neither route is easy driving for those unaccustomed to the Welsh mountains, but the road to Bwlch y Groes has been improved.

Llanybyther, *Dyfed* (4/2A) A small market centre in a great loop of the river Teifi with the moorland of Llanybyther Mountain in the background. In the old days this district was crowded with small woollen mills, worked by the swift-flowing streams from the hills. The great days of weaving are now over, although there are still a few mills left in the locality which produce attractively patterned cloth, much appreciated by the tourists. Llanybyther's present fame, not only in Wales but in England as well, rests on its horse fair, which is now the largest in Britain. On the last Thursday of every month, Llanybyther gives itself over to the horse – and the scene can only be matched in some of the country towns of Ireland, where horse fairs still flourish.

If you are not a devotee of the horse and find yourself in Llanybyther on horse fair Thursday, drive west along the Teifi valley to Llanwenog, where the church has many carvings by the Belgian sculptor, Joseph Reubens, commissioned by the owners of nearby Highmead House. They may not be of local craftsmanship, but they are a surprise to find in a church in Dyfed.

Above: The hills around Llanymynech
Right: Near Llanymynech

Llanymynech, *Powys* (2/3A) If there ever was a perfect border settlement the little town of Llanymynech would surely qualify for first prize. There is only one main street and the border with Shropshire runs immediately behind the houses that line it. Indeed one hotel is divided into half by the border line. This was of vital importance in the days when Wales had its sternly teetotal Sunday. The knowledgeable inhabitants simply picked up their glasses and moved to the next room – into England! OFFA'S DYKE also ran through Llanymynech on exactly the same line, but its earthworks disappeared when the houses were built. The river Vyrnwy runs immediately south of the town on its way to join the Severn and, in its turn, marks the border. The high limestone hills behind Llanymynech have been extensively quarried in the past, but the quarries have now mellowed into white cliffs, and the golf course lies on the edge of the cliff line. There must be few golf courses with such a dramatic view from the tees. You look across the level valleys of the Vyrnwy and the Severn, which again unite on the border, up to the pointed BREIDDEN HILLS. Between them, the crags of Llanymynech and the Breiddens form an imposing gateway to Wales.

Llawhaden, *Dyfed* (3/2B) Situated 7 miles due east from HAVERFORDWEST, on the banks of the Eastern Cleddau, Llawhaden has a castle on a hill, and a church and a mill in a deep valley below. The castle belonged to the bishops of St David's, who had three impressive residences besides Llawhaden. One was at TREVINE, of which no trace now remains, a second at LAMPHEY and, of course, their main palace at ST DAVID'S itself. But then, St David's was the richest see in medieval Wales. The first castle at Llawhaden was built by Bishop Bernard. This fell into the hands of the Lord Rhys. The present structure was completed by Bishop David Martin in the 13th century. Bishop Barlow, after the Reformation, stripped it of its lead and allowed it to fall into decay. Llawhaden is now in charge of CADW, and the ruins rise from carefully tended green lawns. The Great Gatehouse placed above the deep, dry moat, is the most impressive section of the castle still standing. A steep lane drops down to the church in the valley, a dark edifice set among trees on the river bank, with some interesting medieval carvings still remaining and a curious double tower. The mill is now a trout farm, which well repays a visit.

Loughor (Lwchwr), *West Glamorgan* (4/2B) This is the lowest crossing place on the river Loughor, at the point where it turns west and widens into its estuary. The Romans built their fort of Leucarum here, on their road to CARMARTHEN. The Norman castle, of which only a tower remains, guarded the crossing and the modern road and railway bridges cross side by side. The pressure of traffic has led to a new road being built between the two existing bridges. It goes through the site of the Roman fort, and a 'rescue dig' in 1985 ahead of the bulldozers revealed fascinating details of the life of the Roman garrison. The amount of shells unearthed around the commandant's house showed that the Romans deeply appreciated the Mumbles oysters from the Bristol Channel.

In front of Moriah Chapel, on the main road between Loughor and Gorseinon, is a memorial to Evan Roberts, who led the remarkable religious revival that swept Wales in 1904.

Machynlleth, *Powys* (2/1B) A small, busy town and tourist centre on the Dyfi (Dovey), where the river begins to widen towards its estuary. The county of Powys here makes a curious extension westwards, a legacy of the way the old Welsh kingdom of Powys extended itself to the sea. The

The clock tower, Machynlleth (*Martin Dohrn*)

two main streets of the town meet at a crossroads, marked by a clock tower put up in 1873 to replace the old market cross. It has had its critics, but a recent proposal to remove it as a traffic hazard saw the whole town rallying to its defence. From the clock tower Maengwyn Street, the main shopping centre, runs east past the oldest building in the town, the house where, it is claimed, Owain Glyndwr held his Parliament in 1404. It has been much restored, and now houses the Tourist Information Centre, with an exhibition illustrating the career of Owain Glyndwr and other aspects of Welsh history and the wildlife of the Dyfi Valley. The great house of Plas Machynlleth, once the home of the Marquess of Londonderry, now houses the District Council offices, while the wide parkland around it gives ample space for playing fields and children's playgrounds. It also has a good selection of craft shops and restaurants. Machynlleth is lucky in still possessing a railway station, on the line between Shrewsbury and ABERYSTWYTH.

Some 2 miles north of the town, a fine bridge crosses the Dyfi on the boundary of Snowdonia National Park – a great place for fishermen. The boundary of Powys now runs north along the east bank of the river Dulas, which flows down from Corris to join the Dyfi not far from the bridge. It runs through a narrow, wooded and beautiful valley, and about half way to Corris a sign at Pantperthog indicates the way to the interesting Centre of Alternative Technology, where there is a permanent exhibition, open to the public daily, demonstrating methods that the average man can use to generate energy, from solar sources to wind and water.

Corris is a small quarrying village, where nearly all quarry working has long ceased. It has a small museum holding relics of the light railway which once brought the slates from the Corris quarries down to the main line at Machynlleth. A recent addition in the village is the purpose-built Corris Craft Centre where artists and craftsmen and women demonstrate a whole variety of skills, from candlemaking to carving. Beyond Aber-llefenni the hills are buried under the ranks of conifers of the Dovey Forest.

The river Dyfi, north-east of Machynlleth, flows past Penygoes, the birthplace of Richard Wilson, the great Welsh 18th-century landscape painter so much admired by Turner. At Cemmaes Road the railway comes down through LLANBRYNMAIR to enter the Dyfi valley. The village of Cemmaes stands near a common, useful for pasturing the sheep at sheep sales. The road follows the river but turns away to the east before it reaches the junction at Mallwyd to climb over the pass that leads down to LLANERFYL and LLANFAIR CAEREINION. The high mountains of the Arans close the view northwards and again bring a feel of wild North Wales to the landscape.

Four miles north of Machynlleth is the Cwm Cadian Forest Walk – starting at the picnic site on the A487. Leaflets are available locally.

Maenclochog, *Dyfed* (3/2A) A rather sprawling village on the south slopes of the PRESELI HILLS, with a Victorian church in the centre of the slightly unkempt village green. In the old days it was a great centre for hiring fairs. A couple of miles to the south-west is the Llys-y-Fran Reservoir, officially opened in 1972. It is well stocked with trout, and has facilities for boating and sailing.

Maesteg, *Mid Glamorgan* (4/3C) Maesteg means 'Fair Meadow'. There was a time when the name was justified, but the 19th century saw the rapid growth of bituminous coal mining in the Llynfi valley north of BRIDGEND. Maesteg, like so many of the Welsh mining towns, grew rapidly. The valley saw a massive increase in the number of surrounding coal pits. In sad contrast, coal mining has almost ceased in the valley, and once again we find a town bravely in search of new industries. Until recent years, Maesteg could regard itself as an intensely Welsh place. It was in a Maesteg chapel that 'Hen Wlad Fy Nhadau' – 'Land of My Fathers' – was first sung in public. It subsequently became the Welsh national anthem. The hills are high around the town and the road north has to climb up through Nantyfyllon to drop steeply into the narrow Afan Valley, birthplace of the late Richard Burton.

See also Llangynwyd.

Manorbier (Maenor Pyr), *Dyfed* (3/2B) Situated 6 miles west of TENBY on the south Dyfed coast, Manorbier stands a little back from the sea. The castle looks impressive on its rocky knoll, but it is now a shell within, with a small private dwelling inside the gatehouse. It is famous, however, as the birthplace of Giraldus Cambrensis, that vigorous but combative cleric to whom we owe so much of our knowledge of Wales in the 12th century. The castle was originally built by Gerald de Barri, who married Nest, daughter of Rhys ap Tewdwr, known, from her surpassing beauty and amorous adventures, as the Helen of Wales. Giraldus was proud of his joint Welsh-Norman parentage. The parish church of St James the Great stands across a little valley from the castle. It has the usual tall, fortress-like Pembrokeshire tower, and is a little cavernous within. It has a 14th-century oak loft and, among other monuments, a tomb of a knight who may have been Sir John de Barri. A lane leads down from the church to a sandy and shallow beach, popular with holidaymakers in summer time.

Margam, *West Glamorgan* (4/3C) Margam is a surprise packet, a remarkable place to find on the outskirts of industrial PORT TALBOT and close to the largest steelworks in Europe. Yet you can turn off the M4 motorway as you approach Port Talbot and find yourself in a wide, secluded park, set among wooded hills which show no sign of industry, and also surrounded by fascinating memorials from the past. Margam Abbey was one of the great Cistercian houses of Wales. After the Dissolution of the Monasteries it passed into the hands of the powerful Mansel family, typical of the 'new men' on whom the Tudors relied. The big abbey church contains an impressive array of Mansel tombs. Of the other abbey buildings,

The Orangery, Margam

only the graceful ruins of the chapter house remain.

Towards the end of the 18th century, the Mansel heritage passed, by marriage, to the Talbots, and it was the art-loving Thomas Mansel Talbot who built the splendid orangery which is the pride of Margam. It is the most important 18th-century building in South Wales, with almost an air of Versailles about it. The orangery is now used for public functions, and the whole wide estate has become a country park with miles of walks, ornamental lakes etc. The mansion itself, a Victorian reconstruction, was severely damaged by fire but is now being refurbished. A herd of deer roam romantically past the ruin. Margam country park is noted for its sculptures, which are displayed under the auspices of the Welsh Sculpture Trust. It also has its own small viewing theatre.

The school alongside the abbey church houses an impressive collection of early inscribed stones and Celtic crosses. Margam was on the Roman road between CARDIFF and NEATH, and Roman milestones are plentiful. The finest of the early Christian monuments is the Great Cross of Cunbelin, with its delightful carving of two horsemen with their dog pursuing a deer. The hills behind Margam are now covered with Forestry Commission plantations, but the planters have left a space for the Bulwarks on the summit, a large Iron Age earthwork. A replica of the Bodvoc stone stands near it on the roadside. The original is in the Margam Museum.

Mathern, *Gwent* (5/6C) This village is not easy to get at. The M4 motorway from the SEVERN BRIDGE at NEWPORT (Gwent) passes close to it, but the place can only be reached by a dead-end road 3 miles west of CHEPSTOW. Mathern was once the chief country residence of the Bishops of Llandaff. The 15th-century palace has a low tower and some charming oriel windows. It was carefully restored in 1890. It has a fine garden, but is in private hands. The nearby church of St Tewdric is richly decorated.

Meifod, *Powys* (2/2B) Meifod is a small village in a delightful pastoral setting, in the heart of northern Powys. Not far away, the river Vyrnwy joins the Cain at Llansantffraid-ym-Mechain, and the united streams flow north-east to join the distant Severn. Sleepy Meifod once played an important part in medieval Welsh history. It was then the residence and power centre of the Princes of Powys. Today, the only reminder at Meifod of the existence of the modern world is the large radio telescope in the hills behind the village, connected to the well-known establishment of Jodrell Bank.

Merthyr Mawr, *Mid-Glamorgan* (4/3C) A little village, famous for its thatched cottages, 2 miles south of BRIDGEND. The place retains the air of a typical Glamorgan village at the end of the 18th century, with the Manor House in the background. Immediately beyond the village is an area of impressive sand dunes, some of which are among the highest in Europe. There are important archaeological sites among the dunes. There were early Welsh inhabitants here in the Early Iron Age, from 500 BC. Many valuable finds are now on display at the National Museum of Wales in CARDIFF. Here also are the sparse ruins of Candleston Castle. A track leads from Merthyr Mawr to the Ogmore river, which approaches the sea past Ogmore Castle, with the well-known stepping stones across the stream. The Ogmore

A thatched cottage at Merthyr Mawr

reaches the coast at the bungalows of Ogmore-on-Sea (bathing is dangerous here), but the road goes on to Southerndown with its sands and surfing bay. The Victorian Dunraven Castle has been demolished, but a recent community project has reserved some parts of the estate to create a peaceful haven just a few minutes from the beach.

Merthyr Tydfil, *Mid Glamorgan* (5/4B) An industrial town on the northern edge of the South Wales coalfield, 25 miles due north of CARDIFF. It takes its name from a 5th-century British princess who was martyred here, and it remained an obscure hamlet until the early days of the Industrial Revolution in Wales. Merthyr then rapidly expanded and, at one moment, was easily the largest town in Wales. The secret of its growth lay in the juxtaposition of coal, limestone and easily worked iron ore on the coalfield's rim. The ironworks became internationally famous, supplying the cannon for the British army in the Napoleonic wars and, later, the rails for the expansion of the railways around the world. The powerful ironmasters, the Crawshays, the Homfrays and the Guests of Dowlais, controlled the town, and industrial unrest culminated in 1831, when a rising took place which was only put down

by military force. Merthyr has always taken pride in being in the forefront of radical movements throughout the 19th and early 20th centuries. The Crawshays made their home in the neo-Gothic Cyfarthfa Castle, right opposite their own Cyfarthfa ironworks. The Castle is now a fascinating museum of Merthyr's industrial past. Dowlais is virtually a suburb of Merthyr, stretching up into the hills to a height of over 1000 ft. The Dowlais works were as famous as those of Cyfarthfa, and the big library built by the Guests is still a dominant feature of the area. Their stables have also been rescued from demolition by Merthyr's Heritage Trust. The ironworks had passed their prime by the late 19th century, and the new steelworks moved down to the coast.

Merthyr has changed profoundly in recent years. A modern civic centre has been built, and new bypass roads encircle the town. A trading estate has also played an important part in reviving Merthyr's fortunes. The air, once so dense with the smoke of the ironworks, is now crisp and clear, and the surrounding hills again show the original beauty of Merthyr's hill setting. The A470 trunk road sweeps up from Cardiff, improv-

Colliery head-gear, Abercynon

ing communication. It passes through the completely flattened tip above Aberfan, which in 1966 slid down to bury the school below it, in a disaster that shook the world. The children were buried in a special line of graves on the hillside. The old road, on the opposite side of the valley through Quaker's Yard, follows the river Taff, and so does the railway line. Railway enthusiasts can still walk along the old grass-grown track laid for the world's first passenger train. In 1804, Richard Trevithick drove his steam engine, drawing a line of trucks carrying passengers from Merthyr to Abercynon amid scenes of great excitement, and heralded the dawn of the world's Railway Age.

There are several walks in the BRECON BEACONS nearby. At Talybont Forest Walks there are both woodland and waterfall walks starting from the car park at Blaenyglyn 5 miles north of Pontsticill. The Forestry Commission has more trails in the Garwnant Forest starting at the Forest Centre off the A470, just north of the town. From Pont, just north of Dulais, the scenic Brecon Mountain Railway, another of the 'great little trains' of Wales, trundles its way along the relaid track to its present terminus at the Pontsticill Reservoir. Plans are in hand to take the

Milford Haven

railway eventually through to BRECON. A narrow mountain road also runs past Pontsticill from Cefn-Coed-y-Cymer, just above Merthyr Tydfil, through forest areas to the pretty village of Talybont-on-Usk within the Brecon Beacons National Park.

Milford Haven and **Town,** *Dyfed* (3/2B) The magnificent waterway of Milford Haven is the outstanding feature of the West Wales coast. The main channel runs for over 25 miles inland and throws off numerous branches, all with their own charm for the yachtsman. Geologically, the Haven is a ria – a drowned river valley. The lower 10 miles, from the entrance at St Ann's Head to beyond Neyland, has the deepest water, and was therefore developed as an oil port in the 1960s. For a time, the area knew an unexpected prosperity. Unfortunately the oil boom has faltered in recent years. By 1985, the big new refineries that had been established around Milford and across the water west of PEMBROKE town had drastically cut production, and some of the long jetties built out into the Haven were waiting in vain for incoming tankers. The future is uncertain but the

fine waters of the Haven are still there – a perpetual challenge to the authorities to find the right use to which one of the finest harbours in southern Britain can be put. The tantalizing problem remains of the Haven's distance from the main industrial areas of the country (*see also* Angle and Dale). Already, it is being developed for serious yachting, with the first phase of a marina now complete at Neyland.

The town of Milford Haven represents one of the first attempts to develop the Haven. Charles Greville, the nephew of Sir William Hamilton and a man of wide interests and enterprise, had been appointed by Sir William to develop his property around Milford, which he had inherited from his first wife. Sir William was Britain's representative at the Court of Naples during the Napoleonic Wars. By a convenient arrangement with his nephew, he took Greville's mistress, the fascinating Emma Hart, as his second wife. Emma, by an equally convenient arrangement with Sir William, became Nelson's mistress after the Battle of the Nile. All four of them descended on Milford in 1802 in a memorable visit commemorated by the name of the Lord Nelson Hotel on the biggest inn in Greville's new town.

Milford has always had to struggle for prosperity. It obtained a naval dockyard, but this was soon transferred to Pembroke Dock. Milford then developed as a fishing centre, and in 1946 landed a record tonnage of fish. But the number of trawlers has steadily declined. Milford, however, seems to remain a brisk little town, and has retained the pattern of its 18th-century layout. From the promenade, there is a fine view out over the Haven.

The next township up the Haven is NEYLAND, where the new bridge crosses the waterway. The Haven now alters its direction and turns from east to north. At Lawrenny, a wide branch of the waterway runs westwards and divides into two. One section goes to CAREW, the other to the pleasant little hamlet of Cresswell Quay. Yachtsmen sailing here must remember that there is a considerable rise and fall of the tide throughout the Haven, but they can find compensation for becoming stranded at Cresswell in the friendly pub that overlooks the water. Lawrenny has become a major yachting centre, but it also possesses a fine church and a viewpoint on the site of the old demolished Victorian castle, with fine vistas over the Haven.

The main channel runs up past the romantic-looking and well-restored Benton Castle and past Garron Pill where local enterprise has re-established the oyster industry, to Llangwm. Llangwm was the great fishing village on the Haven in the old days. The small Llangwm oysters were famous and the cockle women trudged into market at HAVERFORDWEST carrying their pails balanced on their heads. Llangwm folk also had a reputation for their fierce independence. Things have changed. Llangwm has become popular with visitors and has an interesting church with medieval monuments. Some miles further on the Haven splits into two widespread arms. The western arm runs up past the site of the Hook colliery to Haverfordwest, where the Western Cleddau river flows into the Haven. The eastern arm swings away at Landshipping where there is an inn at the end of a road that leads nowhere except to a delightful view of the upper course of the Haven. Landshipping – the name contains a corruption of the English 'shippon', an old term for a cowshed – also had a colliery where, in 1845, water broke into the workings below the Haven and 45 colliers were drowned. The eastern branch, winding up between deep woodland to the Eastern Cleddau, passes Slebech Hall on the north bank, once a Commandery of the Knights Hospitallers of Jerusalem. The church is now ruined but contains the grave of Sir William Hamilton and his first wife. A new church was built on the main road to Haverfordwest. On the south bank lies the big Slebech Forest, where the Forestry Commission has marked out an attractive $1\frac{1}{2}$-mile forest walk. The branch ends at Blackpool Mill, where the well-built mill has been restored to working order. A museum is also housed here.

Between the Eastern and Western Cleddau branches is the promontory that contains **Picton Castle**. Here Sir John Wogan, Justiciary of Ireland, built the first fortress in 1302, and although often altered and modernized, it has been continually inhabited ever since: a record, it is claimed, for Britain. Among the buildings north of the castle in the well-wooded grounds, is the gallery housing the collection of paintings presented by Graham Sutherland in recognition of the influence that what he described as the 'excellent strangeness' of the Pembrokeshire landscape had exercised over his painting. The gallery has become an art centre in its own right and puts on frequent exhibitions by other artists. It can be easily reached from the main road to Haverfordwest at Rhos, where a signpost indicates the turn-off.

Monmouth, *Gwent* (5/6B) Monmouth, originally the county town before Monmouthshire disappeared into Gwent, is rich in history. The Romans had a fort here, Blestium, and the Normans made Monmouth a springboard for their penetration of Breconshire and West Wales. The castle, in which Henry V was born in 1387, no longer remains. Before the victory of Agincourt Henry got his sobriquet of Harry of Monmouth from the Castle. Monmouth was built between the rivers Monnow and Wye which join just below the town. The bridge across the Monnow has, at its centre, a tall medieval fortified gatehouse which is most picturesque and impressive. The town centre has a fine classical Town Hall before which is the statue of C. S. Rolls, of Rolls-Royce fame. He was born here, the third son of Lord Llangattock, and was able to back the engineering genius of Royce with money. He was a pioneer in aviation, ballooning, motoring and aerial photography. He was also the first Briton to be killed in a flying accident, in 1910. Another son of Monmouth was hardly so practical a man. Geoffrey of Monmouth was the 12th-century bestselling writer; his History of Britain, full of marvellous stories that often had no relation to fact but passed into national tradition and from which they are still not eradicated. A window in the ruins of Monmouth Priory is still known as

'Geoffrey's window'. Next to the castle ruins stands Great Castle House, a fine mansion of the late Stuart period (1673), open to the public in summer. The buildings of Monmouth School are close to the Wye, near the park known as Chippenham Meads. The main road from NEWPORT (Gwent) now reaches Monmouth by a dual tunnel near Chippenham Meads and then runs along the river bank, giving fine views of the Wye. Opposite the School a handsome bridge crosses the river, and takes you across to that curious little patch of Gwent which lies on what you can regard as predominantly the English side of the river. Here the Kymin Hill, now in the hands of the National Trust, and accessible only on foot, gives an excellent view. On the top of the hill is the folly tower, built by a group of admirers after Nelson's visit to the town with Lady Hamilton in 1802. The town's museum depicts local history and there is also a collection of Nelson memorabilia.

Montgomery (Trefaldwyn), *Powys* (2/3B) Little Montgomery, on its hill within a mile of the Shropshire border, is a delight. It has a small square with an 18th-century town hall, Georgian houses of warm red brick, old inns, and half-timbered Elizabethan and Jacobean frontages.

Ceibwr Bay, see p. 152

Only recently was a concrete pathway laid over a section of the wide cobblestone pavements of the square. It must be admitted, however, that Montgomery's charm owes more to English than to Welsh architectural features. This is a small-scale Ludlow slipped over the Welsh border.

Behind the square rises the castle hill, on which Roger de Montgomery built his first stronghold in the 13th century, and from which he launched his attack on the lands of the Welsh to the west. The position of Montgomery on its high ridge ending with a crag to the north made it a key point in the politics of the border. In Tudor times it passed into the possession of the Herbert family and it was Lord Herbert of Charbury, brother of the poet George Herbert, who occupied the castle at the time of the Civil War. He made a controversial surrender of the fortress to the Parliamentary forces, and it was heavily 'slighted' in 1647. The ruins have now been much restored.

Montgomery Church is worthy of the town. It is mainly 15th-century, with a splendid rood screen and richly carved tombs of the Herbert family. In the graveyard is the Robber's Grave – John Davies was convicted of murder in 1821 and was buried in this corner. He swore that he was innocent, and declared that, in proof of it, nothing would grow on his grave for over a 100 years.

C. S. Rolls, Monmouth, see p. 150

Beyond the church there are traces of the old walls, with a view out towards England and the east. OFFA'S DYKE ran close to the town and its course can be traced from Montgomery to the Long Mountain behind WELSHPOOL. Remains of the Dyke are preserved in Lymore Park, east of the town. The local civic society has collected a wealth of exhibits relating to the town's history and traditions, which are now displayed in a small but fascinating museum. Local buildings of note are also featured in the town rail leaflet.

Mountain Ash (Aberpennar), *Mid Glamorgan* (5/4A) The name of this mining township, in the Cynon valley north of PONTYPRIDD, is comparatively modern. The Welsh know it as Aberpennar. But the very title of Mountain Ash reminds us there was a time, even after the Industrial Revolution had begun in South Wales, when the Cynon valley was famous for its wooded beauty. The woods disappeared as the collieries multiplied, and now the collieries themselves have closed one by one. Mountain Ash, in common with every other valley town, desperately needs new industries. Today the mountain to

the west of the town is covered once again with conifers planted by the Forestry Commission. In the heart of these new woodlands, on the mountain top, is the little church of Llanwonno. In the churchyard is the grave of Gruffydd Morgan, known as Guto Nyth-Bran, the 18th-century runner whose speed became legendary in South Wales. His backers boasted that Guto could run after a fox on the mountains before the hounds and catch it with ease. He won against all comers, and died, aged 37, in 1737. After the Second World War a race through the valleys was initiated in his honour.

Moylegrove (Trewyddel) *Dyfed* (3/3A) This small village lies 4 miles south of CARDIGAN. It is wedged in the narrow valley of the Awen stream and is approached by steep roads with hairpin bends from either side. It owes its English name to Matilda, the wife of Robert Fitzmartin, the first Norman lord of the Barony of Cemaes. It has no pub, thanks to the teetotal zeal of the Independent minister, William Jones, in 1871. From Moylegrove the Awen runs down to enter the sea at Ceibwr, a romantic inlet, with a splendid coast view. **Ceibwr** was a busy landing place in the days of the coastal sailing trade, and

Montgomery, see p. 151

had a reputation for gambling and other undesirable activities at the little alehouses that once occupied the shore. William Jones cleaned up Ceibwr as effectively as he reformed Moylegrove. Only the abandoned lime kiln remains to bear witness to the village's trading past. The coast path southwards leads to the remarkable inlet of Pwll-y-wrach (The Witch's Cauldron). The south side of Ceibwr Bay has been presented to the National Trust. Seals are common here in late August and September.

Not far off the road that leads from Moylegrove to NEWPORT (Dyfed) lie the two fine cromlechs of Llechydrybedd and Trellyffant.

Narberth, *Dyfed* (3/3B) A small market town in the east of the old county of Pembrokeshire. It is just over the English side of that curious line, known as the Landsker, which separates the English-speaking from the Welsh-speaking people of Dyfed. Narberth is thus in the 'Little England beyond Wales'. In the Dark Ages, however, it was one of the residences of the Welsh

princes of Dyfed and features in the story of Pwyll, Prince of Dyfed, in the great collection of early Welsh stories of the Mabinogion. The Normans built a castle here, which was repeatedly captured by the Welsh. It was finally ruined in the Civil War. The ivy-clad ruins stand on the outskirts of the town. The parish church was rebuilt in 1879, with the exception of the tower. There are some pleasant Georgian houses grouped around the market place, where the market hall stands in the middle of the street with the royal arms on the walls and an outside staircase to the upper floor. The road eastwards passes through places with delightful names, such as Tavernspite and Red Roses.

Nash Point *see* St Donat's Castle

Neath (Castell-nedd), *West Glamorgan* (4/3B) Neath is a busy town, 8 miles east of SWANSEA, built at the lowest crossing point on the river Neath (Nedd) before it enters the sea in Swansea Bay. The Romans were the first to note the crossing here. The foundations of one of the gateways to their fort, Nidum, are preserved on the roadside near the Dwrfelin Comprehensive School. The town grew up around the castle, built by Richard de Granville in the 12th century. Both King John and King Edward I visited it, but it fell into ruin in Tudor times. The gatehouse, with its twin towers, is the only part of the castle ruins that remains impressive. The ground before it has now been laid out as a lawn, and a small café, well built to blend with the castle walls, stands at the entrance to the green. The centre of Neath is grouped around the open space of Victoria Park and, in addition to the neo-Gothic Gwyn Hall, the town is well-equipped with modern assembly rooms and leisure centres. A new road joins it to the M4 motorway, with a bridge across the Nedd.

The ruins of Neath Abbey lie on the west side of the river, on the road to Skewen. Neath was a Cistercian foundation, and was visited by the traveller Leland just before the Dissolution. He described it as 'the fairest in all Wales', while the roof of the church was like the sky over the Vale of Hebron. A sad contrast to the state of the Abbey today, hidden among industrial plants alongside the Tennant Canal. CADW, however, has seen to it that the remains of the Abbey and the domestic buildings have been well cared for, and surrounded by green lawns. You can recapture the old serenity of the place and catch a glimpse of its original splendour once you pass through the gatehouse.

The valley of the river Nedd runs up behind the town towards the high hills of the Fforest Fawr, and still has traces of the natural beauty which once made it a place of pilgrimage for artists at the beginning of the 19th century. At Aberdulais, the waterfall inspired a fine Turner watercolour, and the Dulais Ironworks nearby have been restored – a fascinating piece of industrial archaeology. Across the road, the junction of the Neath and Tennant Canals is still a place of charm, although a new road may eventually drive through it.

The Neath Development partnership has been responsible for many of the area's new attractions including the Tonna workshops, the Pelenna Mountain Centre, and restoration of sections of the Neath and Tennant Canals, in association with local volunteers.

The Nedd valley is deeply wooded up to Aberpergwm, and at Resolven, a former colliery village, a track leads up to the ravine which holds the impressive waterfall of Melincourt. Medieval banquets are held at the Melin Manor. There are opencast coal workings at Glyn-Neath, but you are now on the edge of the coal measures. Ahead of you lie the hills of the Fforest Fawr and the surprising and secret wonderland of the waterfalls, to which PONT-NEATH-VAUGHAN is the gateway.

Two miles north-west of Neath, at Cilfrew, is the Penscynor Wildlife Park with its extensive collection of exotic birds as well as a wide variety of animals and fish. At nearby Crynant in the Dulais valley industrial history is interpreted at the Cefn Coed coal and steam centre.

Nevern (Nyfer), *Dyfed* (3/3A) A small village 8 miles south of CARDIGAN where the river Nyfer, trout and salmon filled, flows under an ancient bridge and the church, dedicated to the Irish saint, Brynach, is surrounded by dark yew trees. An evocative place, for although the church is mainly 15th-century it contains stones, and is surrounded by monuments, that take you back in spirit to the mysterious Dark Ages. Near the porch is the Vitalianus Stone which dates back to the 6th century. But the most remarkable monument is St Brynach's Cross, with its intricate Celtic decorations that rival those on the cross at CAREW. St Brynach's bird was the cuckoo, and tradition maintains that the first cuckoo of the year used to arrive on the saint's day, 7 April, and perch on the top of the cross. Legends naturally cling to Nevern Church. One of the yews has a broken branch, and the red sap constantly drips from it; a symbol, some people say, of unrequited love.

In the churchyard there are gravestones with delightful epitaphs. One to two children of the Bowen family of Llwnygwair reads:

> They tasted of life's bitter cup
> Refused to drink the potion up,
> But turned their little heads aside,
> Disgusted with the taste, and died.

Visitors can retain the out-of-the-world atmosphere of Nevern if, after seeing the church they drive, following the signposts, from the main road between NEWPORT (Dyfed) and Cardigan into the foothills of the PRESELI HILLS to the great cromlech of Pentre Ifan, which must rank among the finest of the prehistoric monuments of Wales.

Newcastle Emlyn (Castell Newydd Emlyn), *Dyfed* (4/1A) A small market town on the river Teifi, 10 miles east of CARDIGAN. The 'new' castle, from which the town takes its name, was

Above: Neath Abbey

Below: Robert Owen's grave, Newtown, *see p. 158*

built in the 13th century by the Welsh, but subsequently passed into English hands. Only a ruined arch remains, overlooking the Teifi, where the river flows over a weir. The church is comparatively modern, built in 1840 with considerable use of slate from the quarries at nearby CILGERRAN. The town itself consists basically of one curving main street, with pleasant 19th century houses, and a market hall with a tower. Newcastle Emlyn comes to life on fair days. It is the sales centre for the cattle and sheep of a wide surrounding area of farmland. Over the river is the suburb of Adpar, where a tablet on a house near the bridge commemorates the setting up of the first printing press to operate in Wales, by Isaac Garter in 1717.

At Cwm Cou, about 2 miles from the town centre, the water-powered Felin Geri Flour Mill has been restored and is once again producing stone-ground flour of quality. A unique water-powered sawmill is also being refurbished here.

Newport (Trefdraeth), *Dyfed* (3/2A) An interesting little town, on the lower slopes of Carn Ingli, an outlier of the main range of the PRESELI HILLS, with the river Nyfer going out to the sea between sandbanks. It was once the administrative centre of the barony of Cemaes, and succeeded in retaining its mayor and burgesses when the boroughs of England and Wales were reformed in 1888. The town received its charter from Nicholas Martin, the Lord of Cemaes, around 1240, and the mayor is appointed 'in conjunction with the Lord Marcher' and presides over the Court Leet. The castle looks down on the main street. It remained in ruins until 1859, when the gatehouse and one of the towers was reconstructed as a residence by Sir Thomas Davies Lloyd. The church has a 13th-century tower and a spacious interior, with some interesting monuments.

The Parrog, on the west side of the estuary, was the 'port' of Newport. It has a quay and the remains of an old warehouse, and a view of the bar across the river mouth that prevented Newport from developing on the scale of Fishguard. Nevertheless, the town had a great sailing and trading tradition throughout the 19th century. The wide, sandy beach of Newport Sands lies across the river. It has a 9-hole golf course among the dunes. On the road leading across to the beach is a fine cromlech hidden among some new houses: Newport must be the only little town in Britain with prehistoric remains in back gardens! In August, when the Court Leet meets, the ceremony of Beating the Bounds of the borough takes place, in which visitors are invited to join. The route takes you along the sea front, and then up along the ridge of Carn Ingli. A strenuous but delightful march.

Newport (Casnewydd), *Gwent* (5/5C) Newport is Wales' third conurbation – only CARDIFF and SWANSEA exceed it in size. Like the other two cities, Newport is a product of the industrial growth of the 19th century. It grew rapidly as a port for the coal, steel and tinplate of the eastern mining valleys. The Normans built a castle here, which was an important point of departure for their drive into West Wales. The castle ruins still stand on the banks of the tidal Usk. The castle walls were pierced by elegant windows in the 15th century when it became more a dwelling place than a fortress. The ruins have been carefully preserved, but they are rather cut off from the rest of the town by the roads built along the banks of the Usk, for Newport went through an intensive period of reconstruction and modernization during the 1960s and 1970s, with new shopping centres and sports and leisure buildings. There remain large areas of the town, however, that still retain their old appearance. The church of St Woolos at the top of Stow Hill became a Pro-Cathedral when the Church of England was disestablished in Wales in 1921, and the new Church in Wales created the diocese of Monmouth. Woolos is a corruption of the Welsh St Gwynllyw. the church has an impressive tower and an interesting Norman doorway.

There is another reminder of Newport's past history at the foot of Stow Hill. The Westgate Hotel still has the pillars which show the marks of the bullets fired at the rioters by the military, when they crushed by force the mass march of the Chartists on Newport in 1839. The marchers were led by John Frost, the radical mayor of Newport, and memorials of this stirring event are preserved in the excellent museum in John Frost Square. The event is also commemorated in the bright murals in the entrance lobby of Newport's Civic Centre, erected just before the Second World War. Newport has a busy dockland at the mouth of the Usk, and draws trade through being the nearest Bristol Channel port to the English Midlands. The docks have a unique feature in the Transporter Bridge over the Usk, now the only working example of this type left in Britain. A good view of Newport can be obtained from it at 242 ft above the river. A recent addition to the town is a multi-million pound leisure centre

The Transporter Bridge, Newport, Gwent

which doubles up as a concert hall.

Special events such as the Newport Show take place in the grounds of Tredegar House. The earliest surviving part of the house is *c.* 1500, the rest was subsequently rebuilt and is a fine example of a Charles II mansion. It is now being restored to its former glory, and is open to the public. In the grounds, now part of a country park, are a children's farm and a boating lake. On the Henllys road north of the town is the 14-Locks Interpretive Centre which demonstrates the development of the canals system in Gwent. The locks of the old Monmouthshire Canal have been restored, and the towpaths have been repaired to create a pleasant walk.

The country behind Newport has some delightful landscape surprises. Once past CAERLEON the Usk valley is particularly attractive up to Usk itself. To the west rises Newport's own mountain, Twm Barlwm, nearly 1400 ft high. It can be reached by a walk from Cwrt Henllys and gives a splendid view over the surrounding countryside. Twm Barlwm is also accessible through the Cwmcarn scenic forest drive, which has been developed by the Forestry Commission, with miles of waymarked walks, picnic sites and even barbecues for hire. The coastline on either side of the town is flat fenland (*see* Caldicot). Its character may be profoundly changed if the scheme for a great Severn Barrage comes to fruition.

New Quay (Ceinewydd), *Dyfed* (1/2C) A small fishing and trading town on the coast of Cardigan Bay, between CARDIGAN and ABERAERON. In the 18th and 19th centuries, New Quay was a busy little port, with a reputation for building good sailing ships for the coastal trade. The houses on the steep streets overlooking the harbour were full of retired sea captains. They have long gone, and New Quay in summer is crowded with visitors, in spite of parking difficulties. The Quay itself is a solidly built pier which gives shelter to the numerous yachts, although the harbour dries out at low tide. A fine sandy beach stretches for 1 mile to the north, giving excellent and safe bathing (but do not swim at New Quay Head). It extends to Llanina, from where you can look back at the curve of the bay and see how New Quay is sheltered from the prevailing south-westerly winds by the high 300 ft headland of Pencraig. Llanina Church, built in 1830, is

The river Severn, Newtown

perched on the cliff edge.

Dylan Thomas lived in New Quay during the Second World War. Some critics claim that New Quay, not Laugharne, is the true Llaregyb of 'Under Milk Wood'. The poet would, perhaps, be hard put to recognize the place today.

Just south of New Quay is the secluded beach at Cwm Tudu surrounded by spectacular cliffs. The beach is shingle with rock pools and caves. It is accessible down a steep hill from Llwyn Dafydd.

Newtown (Y Drenewydd, *Powys* (2/2B) Newtown, in the centre of the Upper Severn valley in Mid Wales, is the market town for a wide and fertile area, but it owes its growth to the woollen trade that developed during the 19th century. The wide central street leads down to the river, recently banked with new defences against the flooding which was only too prevalent in the winter. The new banking gives a pleasant riverside promenade. The old church stands near the bridge. The fine tower remains but a new church was built in 1847 on the main road. The original church, however, has in its grave-yard the tomb of Newtown's most famous son, Robert Owen. He was born here in 1771 but spent his career in other parts of Britain. He was a pioneer of enlightened capitalism in his New Lanark mills in Scotland, but gained his greatest fame as one of the fathers of the cooperative movement in Britain. He was also the founder of nursery schools. He returned on a visit to his native town and died in the Bear Inn in Broad Street in 1858. There is a Robert Owen Museum in Broad Street, and a small textile museum in one of the old hand-weaving factories in Commercial Street. The width of Broad Street is tested to the full when the stalls go up on market days. The grounds of Newtown Hall are now a spacious park, with leisure facilities and walks along the river bank. It also gives Newtown a convenient parking place near the main streets.

'New town' seemed to take on a new meaning in the 1980s when a grandiose scheme was proposed for a vast new conurbation in the upper Severn valley, which would lead to the regeneration of the whole area of Mid Wales. It was toned down to a more realistic size and Newtown has benefited by the establishment of new industries, including a Laura Ashley factory and housing estates on the road towards CAERSWS. It has still retained, however, its air of a busy market town. It also still has its railway station, on the line that goes to ABERYSTWYTH. Next to the station is the large Royal Welsh Warehouse where, in 1859, Pryse Jones started the world's first mail-order scheme, selling Welsh flannel products. The beautiful 32-acre Dolerw Park lies over the river from the town, and is reached by a new footbridge across the Severn. The Tourist Information Centre is near the car park. Newtown also has its own little theatre.

Behind the town, on the road to LLANFAIR CAEREINION, is the church of Bettws Cedewain with its 14th-century roof. From Bettws you can traverse the complicated and narrow roads to Gregynog Hall, 4 miles north of Newtown. It was the home of the Davies sisters who made it a centre of the arts and music in the years after the First World War. Here they established the Gregynog Press, producing editions much sought after by lovers of fine printing, and accumulated the remarkable collection of French Impressionists which is in the National Museum at CARDIFF. The Press has been reinstated with assistance from the Welsh Arts Council. Gregynog is now a conference and study centre for the University of Wales. A nature trail starts from the car park.

Neyland, *Dyfed* (3/2B) Neyland is on MILFORD HAVEN and close to the town. It is a little township that always seemed to have a promising future that never materialized. When the railway was extended from HAVERFORDWEST in 1856, Brunel planned to make Neyland an Atlantic terminus. The streets still bear names like Brunel Avenue and Great Eastern Terrace that remind you of a great dream that did not come to fruition. Although the *Great Eastern* herself came to the floating pontoon that Brunel had constructed, the Atlantic trade did not develop. The Irish packets, instead, left from Neyland, but this crossing came to an end in 1906. Neyland was left with a ferry across the Haven to Hobbs Point on the other side. Even that has gone now. The High Level Bridge spans the Haven instead with Neyland far below it. The bridge had its problems, too. A section collapsed during construction in 1970, but it is fully operative and is the way the walkers along the Pembrokeshire Coast Path make a diversion to cross the Haven.

Neyland Point, however, has a flourishing yacht club, and as an added asset for the visiting yachtsman a purpose-built marina has been created here. The nearby church of Llanstadwell has fine Norman work, the only church in the region besides St David's Cathedral to show such early Norman architecture. The vicar of Llanstadwell had the expensive honour of entertaining Richard II when he crossed to Ireland in 1394. Neyland has a sheltered beach of shingle, as does Hazelbeach at Llanstadwell.

Offa's Dyke (Clawdd Offa), *Gwent and Powys* (2/3A, B, C) This celebrated earthwork runs for 142 miles from Sedbury at the mouth of the Wye to Prestatyn on the coast of North Wales. There can be no question but that it was completed under the orders of Offa, the great Mercian king, in the later part of the 8th century. It was not intended to be a permanently manned barrier like Hadrian's Wall, but rather a demarcation of the frontier between the Welsh to the west and the Anglo-Saxons of Mercia to the east. It would also hamper cattle raiders and give a lookout over the hill country which the Mercians felt dangerous. The deep ditch lay on the Welsh side. Above the ditch the earthwork was 12 ft high and, in places, 70 ft wide, including the ditch. The Dyke is not continuous. Gaps were left in certain river valleys where the forests were thick at the time of its construction and so presented an impenetrable barrier in themselves. It is especially well preserved over the hills of Mid Wales. In the long passage of time, the administrative boundary between England and Wales has wavered on either side of the Dyke, but it has remained a surprisingly permanent racial barrier. To this day, Welshmen can speak of going to England as crossing 'Clawdd Offa'.

The Offa's Dyke long-distance footpath was opened by Lord Hunt in 1971. It is one of the two permanent trackways for ramblers in Wales, the other being the Pembrokeshire Coast Path (*see* Introduction). It was designed to include interesting places on the way apart from the Dyke, and to be traversed in convenient sections for overnight accommodation. There is a good information centre at KNIGHTON, roughly halfway along its length.

Pembrey *see* Burry Port

Pembroke (Penfro) and **Pembroke Dock** (Doc Penfro), *Dyfed* (3/2B) Pembroke, on a tidal creek of MILFORD HAVEN, was built around its castle, which remains the finest in Dyfed and is only exceeded in size in South Wales by CAERPHILLY. The first castle was built by Richard de Clare, who placed Gerald of Windsor in charge of it – he was the husband of Nest, the 'Helen of Wales' (*see* Cilgerran). Pembroke became the real seat of power in the 'little England of Wales' and, throughout its long history, it was never captured by the Welsh. From here, Strongbow launched his invasion of Ireland in 1169. The castle was repeatedly strengthened through the 13th century, and William Marshall built the great 100 ft high Round Keep, the finest example of its type in Britain. Henry VII was born here and the birthplace is claimed to be the tower to the right of the Great Gatehouse. The Castle ended its career as a fortress after a memorable siege by Cromwell in the second Civil War. Pembroke Town is, in essence, one long widening street running eastwards from the castle. The walls can be traced on the south side. The gardens of the houses that face the street run down to the line of the walls. Many of the houses are Georgian, but the eye is caught by the strange-looking building with its curious clock tower standing out from the centre which now accommodates a stationer's shop. The parish church of St Mary's stands opposite the castle, and is 13th-century but was restored in the 19th century. Monkton Priory was a Benedictine foundation founded in 1098, to the south-west of the castle. It was dissolved in the Reformation. The church was restored in the 19th century, and the priory dovecot has been incorporated into the Priory Farm.

Pembroke Dock lies just over the hill 1 mile north of the old town. The Royal Naval Dockyards were transferred here from Milford in 1814. The streets are laid out on a grid pattern, and the dockyards had an active career for 100 years. Many notable naval vessels were built here. The last ship was launched in 1922. In the dockyards, the solid defences of the Martello-type towers were built against the threat of a French invasion in mid-Victorian days. Cruises on the Haven depart from Hobbs Point pier. Fishing is excellent in the area. The boundary of the Pembrokeshire Coast National Park is only 2 miles away and within 6 miles are sandy beaches.

Penarth, *South Glamorgan* (5/5C) Just south of CARDIFF where a bluff headland marks the point where the Taff and the Ely finally enter the sea, Penarth was the creation of the great days of Cardiff's coal trade. Successful men could build their substantial houses overlooking the Bristol Channel and the view across to FLAT HOLM and Steep Holm and the Somerset coast. The place still has a spacious Edwardian air, with its pier and promenade and quiet roads, lined with trees

and discreet villas. It is a popular resort for sailing and fishing. Opposite the railway station is the Turner House Art Gallery, now a branch of the National Museum of Wales. Penarth has naturally expanded in recent years and the houses stretch ever westwards to where Dinas Powis still retains a country village flavour in spite of all modern developments. Plans are now afoot to build a barrage across the Taff estuary from Penarth Head towards Cardiff docks. This will alter the whole scene to the east of Penarth – it is to be hoped for the better! In fact, development plans lie heavily over the whole of the Bristol Channel eastwards from Penarth and Cardiff. The Severn Barrage Scheme has long been mooted by engineers and is receiving serious consideration in government circles. If it is proceeded with, it will bring profound changes to the whole coastline eastwards from Cardiff to the SEVERN BRIDGE.

On the outskirts of the town a country park has been created around Cosmeston lake which is used for recreational purposes. A medieval village, where special events are regularly held, also attracts the visitors.

Penclawdd, *West Glamorgan* (4/1C) A village in north-east GOWER on the Loughor estuary, Penclawdd is the cockle capital of Wales. The women of the village control it. For 200 years they have been following the falling tide out on to the wide sands of the estuary to rake up the cockles. In the old days they drove out donkeys with panniers on their backs. Now they use light carts. Men also go out on these watery flats, but they stick strictly to mussel collecting. Penclawdd is a very tight-knit community, and not so long ago the women, as the main money earners, decided exactly who should marry whom. There was a period when the oystercatchers, the black-and-white birds that swarm over the sands, were allowed to be officially culled for fear that they were damaging the cockle beds. A graver threat to the industry has recently appeared in a demand from the official inspectors that the cockle gatherers should modernize their cottage industry and old-fashioned methods of boiling the cockles. Modernization will mean extra expense that the gatherers may not be able to afford.

Pendine, *Dyfed* (3/3B) Pendine, on the west side of the united estuaries of the Tywi and Taf, is famous for its beach which in the early days of motor racing was the scene of a series of attempts at the world record. Today, Pendine relies on its bathing for holidaymakers and the village is crowded with caravans. A section of the sands – about 3 miles – is reserved as a Government Experimental Station. The sands are splendid and are a place of pilgrimage for motor enthusiasts. The great names of pre-Second World War racing all tried their luck here, including Sir Malcolm Campbell. But, for Welshmen, the sands are forever associated with J. G. Parry Thomas, the only Welshman who held the world speed record. He was tragically killed when his car, *Babs*, skidded on the wet sands. It was buried in the sandhills. But in 1969, Owen Wynne Owen, a motoring enthusiast, exhumed it and set about its restoration. The car, which has run again on local airfields, is at his house on the edge of the Nant Ffrancon Pass at Capel Curig in North Wales. He hopes to give it a worthy national setting one day.

Picton Castle *see* Milford Haven

Plynlimon (Pumlunon), *Dyfed and Powys* (2/1B) This great moorland wilderness, south of the Dyfi valley and east of ABERYSTWYTH, has always acted as a barrier between North and South Wales, and has thus been an important factor in Welsh history. The easiest ascent is from Eisteddfa Curig, on the highest point of the road between LLANGURIG and Aberystwyth. The route is well marked by posts and goes at a gentle angle. The northern side of the mountain is another matter. It drops steeply from the summit among rock faces to the mountain tarn of Llyn Llygad Rheidol – the Eye of the Rheidol – where the river rises. The summit ridge runs eastwards for 4 miles over the rounded top of Pen Pumlumon-Arwystli. Both the Wye and the Severn rise along this ridge, which is extremely boggy in places. The Severn source can be reached from the east side by a path, indicated on the road through the Hafren Forest from Stay-little (*see* Llanidloes). A great deal of the moorland, to the east and on the north-eastern section, is covered with the conifer plantations of the Forestry Commission, but enough open space remains free from trees and reservoirs to remind the walker of the loneliness of this wild track of country.

See also Dylife and Ponterwyd.

Pontardawe, *West Glamorgan* (4/2B) The Swansea valley runs back into the hills north-east of the city. Its first township is Clydach, with the big ICI works, founded by the German chemist Dr

Ludwig Mond, whose statue stands at the gate. Pontardawe is 3 miles further up the valley. Nearby, is the well-known Abernant Colliery and the Cefn Coed Coal and Steam centre at Crynant. Pontardawe has lost the big steelworks which led to its growth – the site has been levelled into a wide green stretch of land – and has sought compensation in a new trading estate. The little town is a crossroads. The road north-west takes you up into the hills, and a side road at Rhyd-y-Fro opens up a secret moorland country, with prehistoric remains like the circle on Carn Llechart, a megalithic circle of 24 stones and a chambered tomb, lonely chapels and great views. The south-easterly road leads to NEATH, but the main road continues up the valley to Ystalyfera and Ystradgynlais. These once busy mining villages are quiet now. The mines have closed and conifers cover many of the tips. At Abercraf the road curves south-east over to the upper Neath valley, past Onllwyn and Banwen, which deserves mention as the centre of the only official foxhunt run by miners. It is entered in Bailey's Hunting Directory. There is a Roman fort at Coelbren.

Pontardulais, *West Glamorgan* (4/2B) Pontardulais, an industrial village 8 miles north-west of SWANSEA on the river Loughor, has now been bypassed by the M4 motorway to West Wales. As it approaches the bridge over the river, the motorway passes the two structures that created the first settlement here – the motte and bailey mound flung up by the Normans, and the old church of St Teilo, now sadly ruined. The modern village developed a little further upstream. The big tinplate works, which brought wealth to Pontardulais in its heyday, have now been replaced by other industries, but the choral tradition, which has been the glory of the village, still persists. The Mixed Choir repeatedly swept the board at the National Eisteddfod, and the Male Voice Choir continues the singing pre-eminence of Pontardulais. Visitors can sample its quality if they drop in at the Fountain Inn, which can be found where the Swansea road enters the village. The choir relax here after practice. The Rebecca Bar at the Fountain commemorates the destruction of the old tollgate destroyed in the Rebecca Riots in 1843.

Ponterwyd, *Dyfed* (2/1C) Situated 12 miles east of ABERYSTWYTH marking the point where the river Rheidol emerges from PLYNLIMON and then begins its plunge into the spectacular gorge which ends at DEVIL'S BRIDGE. The most

Ponterwyd

prominent building is the George Borrow Inn, where the sturdy old tramper stayed after he had traversed Plynlimon in mist and approaching darkness. A mountain road takes you north from Ponterwyd into the heart of Plynlimon past the big Nant-y-Moch Reservoir, which is not a storage for drinking water; the dammed waters are, instead, dropped down through a long tunnel to work the power station lower down in the Rheidol valley. The road from Ponterwyd to Aberystwyth takes you past the exhibits of the old Llywernog Silver Lead Mine, which has been turned into an open-air museum of lead mining. Here you can see the great waterwheels that drove the pumps, and walk through some of the old mine workings. There is also a Miners' Trail walk. There are many fascinating exhibits on the 6-acre site and an interesting exhibition called the 'California of Wales'. It is open from Easter to the end of September.

The Forestry Commission's Forest Visitor Centre is at Bwlch Nant-y-Arion, just west of Ponterwyd. It has an interpretative centre, picnic sites and wonderful views.

Pont-Neath-Vaughan (Pont Nedd Fechan), *Powys* (4/3B) This small, scattered village at the top of the Neath valley, where the coal measures end and the limestone begins, is the gateway to one of the most surprising complexes of waterfalls in Britain. The somewhat drab approach through Glyn-Neath does not prepare you for the delights that Pont-Neath-Vaughan has to offer. Four streams – the Nedd Fechan, the Mellte, the Hepste and the Pyrddin – have cut their way down through the moorland in deep, densely wooded gorges and each of them has a string of fine waterfalls along their secret courses. They all have different characters: the elegance of Scwd Gwladys, the swirling cauldrons of the Nedd Fechan cataracts, the power of the Middle Clungwyn fall on the Mellte, and Scwd yr Eira (the Fall of Snow) on the Hepste, where you can walk behind the veil of falling water. There are a score more falls and cascades, and they have remained comparatively unknown because this is strictly walkers' country. None of the falls can be reached without walking. The best way for a motorist to obtain some idea of the splendours of this waterfall wonderland is first to drive up to the strange Dinas Rock just north of Pont-Neath-Vaughan, and then return and take the road that climbs out of the village to Ystradfellte on the slopes of the Fforest Fawr. There is a point where you can leave the car and take a path that will bring you to the Middle Clungwyn, the easiest of the falls to reach. A mile further on, a narrow side road turns down into the Mellte valley. Here the river disappears into a huge cave, Porth yr Ogof, which is most impressive, but it is dangerous to follow the watercourse into the dark recesses of the cavern. There is a car park close by. The road continues to the little mountain hamlet of Ystradfellte and its quiet church. From Ystradfellte you can drive over the impressive pass into the Senni valley and the upper Usk.

Pontrhydfendigaid, *Dyfed* (2/1C) The name of this village in Welsh indicates the reason why tourists turn off the TREGARON road at this point. The 'Bridge of the Blessed Ford' leads to the ruins of the abbey of Strata Florida. Founded by the powerful Lord Rhys, the ruler of Welsh-speaking South Wales in the 12th century, this Cistercian abbey in its quiet valley among the hills was always a favourite with the Welsh – a centre of learning and national feeling. The great sheep walks, on which the abbey depended, stretched far back into the moorlands of the 'Green Desert of Wales'. The abbey suffered

The river Mellte at the cave of Porth-y-Ogof

grievously during the Glyndwr rising and, after
the Dissolution of the Monasteries under Henry
VIII, the great church became a quarry for building material for the surrounding farms. The most
impressive part of the ruins is the doorway with
its subtle mouldings. Under a large yew tree
Wales' best-loved medieval poet, Dafydd ap
Gwilym, is allegedly buried. The ruins have been
beautifully laid out and are under the care of
CADW. There is a small but comprehensive
exhibition of the abbey's past history at the
entrance. A modern church stands near the
abbey, which blends into the atmosphere of quiet
serenity that still seems to enfold Strata Florida
among its lonely hills. In contrast, the huge
festival hall at Pontrhydfendigaid was presented
to his native village by the Welsh millionaire, Sir
David James. It is the scene of an important
annual eisteddfod, usually held at Whitsun.

One mile north of Pontrhydfendigaid, a narrow winding road twists up into the moorlands to
the cluster of small lakes known as the Teifi
Pools. This is wild Wales with a vengeance – a
beautiful wilderness, where a track, impassable
for cars, leads across to the Claerwen Dam and
the ELAN VALLEY.

Pontypool, *Gwent* (5/5B) A historic industrial
centre 8 miles north of NEWPORT (Gwent). The
Usk valley is not far away, but Pontypool draws
its industry from the eastern mining valleys of
Gwent. The Hanbury family were the first to
establish the pre-eminence of Pontypool in the
18th century. Their lacquerware, known as Pontypool Japan, is much sought after by collectors.
They were also pioneers of the tinplate trade. The
Hanbury mansion has now become a splendid
public park, with notable wrought-iron gates by
the celebrated Jones brothers of Bersham, near
Wrexham, and a curious summerhouse in the
shape of a shell on a hill in the park, which also
gives a fine view over the valley of the Usk. Here
also is the Valley Inheritance Centre which
demonstrates the story of industrialization. It is
housed in the restored stables block. Pontypool is
the starting point of the navigable section of the
Brecon and Monmouthshire canal which runs for
30 miles.

Anyone interested in industrial archaeology
will want to visit **Blaenavon,** at the head of the
valley of the Afon Llwyd, 6 miles north of Pontypool. It was at Blaenavon that Gillchrist and
Thomas conducted their experiments on the lin-
ing of the Bessemer Converter that revolution-
ized the steel industry. The 18th-century iron-

works are being carefully restored, together with the row of workmen's cottages on the site. In these works were cast the cannon balls fired at Waterloo. Blaenavon can also offer a rare tourist experience. The Big Pit has been kept in working order. Visitors can descend the shaft in the cage and enter the underground workings several hundred feet down. It gives a vivid glimpse of the way colliers worked in the late 19th century, with the whole spectrum of the Industrial Revolution in this part of Wales.

Pontypridd, *Mid Glamorgan* (5/4C) At the junction of the rivers Taff and Rhondda, 12 miles north of CARDIFF, Pontypridd grew up in the 18th century around the remarkable bridge (1756) thrown across the united streams by William Edwards, a self-taught mason who succeeded where others had repeatedly failed. His bridge consists of one elegant arch, and is still preserved alongside a modern structure. Pontypridd is the busy market centre of a whole complex of valleys. The town has equipped itself with a new shopping precinct. Ynysangharad Park, close to the town centre and reached by a bridge across the river, is a surprisingly large open space, complete with the usual leisure facilities. It contains statues, by Sir William Goscombe John, to the memory of Evan and James James – father and son – who composed the words and music of 'Hen Wlad fy Nhadau', (Land of my Fathers) the Welsh National Anthem. Music is a tradition in Pontypridd, for the singers Sir Geraint Evans and Stewart Burrows, who have both achieved world renown, were born in the same street in the Pontypridd suburb of Cilfynydd. Pop star Tom Jones came from nearby Trefforest, now more famous for its industrial estate, one of the first in Wales.

Porthcawl, *Mid Glamorgan* (4/3C) A popular seaside resort which grew around the little harbour towards the end of the 19th century to cater for the holiday needs of the mining communities behind BRIDGEND and in the RHONDDA VALLEYS. It now draws its patrons from a far wider area for it is well provided with all the attractions of a seaside holiday centre, though it is still popular with the local populations during Miner's Fortnight in the summer. The Grand Pavilion stands on the Esplanade, above a sandy bay, and Rest Bay leads to the Royal Porthcawl Golf Club, where the links are up to international standards. A more popular part of Porthcawl lies east of the harbour where Coney Beach has a big

funfair complex and a vast caravan park, probably the largest in Europe. The popular beaches are to be found at Rest Bay to the West, Sandy Bay and Trecco Bay. Swimming should be avoided near the headland. The dunes of MERTHYR MAWR close the development of Porthcawl on this side. To the west beyond the golf course the wide sands extend towards distant PORT TALBOT. In the dunes is the rather gaunt Sker House, featured in R. D. Blackmore's novel, *The Maid of Sker*. Newton village has a fine ancient church and a remarkable well which, although inland, rises and falls with the tide. Porthcawl, to the west of the Ogmore river estuary, looks out to an ever-widening Bristol Channel and yachtsmen are well aware of the presence of the Tuskar Rock offshore.

Port Talbot and **Aberavon,** *West Glamorgan* (4/3C) An important steel-producing town on the coast 14 miles east of SWANSEA. The town is laid out between the hills, which here are the nearest to the sea in the whole of South Wales, and the wide sandy plain that stretches behind the dune-protected beaches.

The old settlement was Aberavon, at the mouth of the Afan valley, but it has been overwhelmed by car parks, arterial roads and the rest of the modern improvements that have accompanied the ever-increasing growth of Port Talbot. The great steelworks, with their blast furnaces and rolling mills, are well seen from the M4 motorway at the foot of the hills and, when in full production, present a memorable spectacle of industrial power. The new wharf for unloading iron ore has eclipsed the old docks, and can take ships up to 200,000 tons.

All this obscures the fact that Port Talbot possesses long sandy beaches that would be the envy of many an English south coast resort. The western part of Aberavon beach has been developed as a popular seaside holiday centre, complete with wide promenade and the Afan Lido – a large sports and entertainment complex which has an Olympic-size swimming pool, ballroom and conference hall. The eastern beach is a complete contrast for here the wide sands lie undisturbed, with the steelworks half hidden behind the high dunes.

From Port Talbot (*see also* Margam) the Afan valley, known locally as 'Little Switzerland', cuts deeply back into the hills of the coalfield. This is the narrowest of all the Welsh mining valleys. One mile from Port Talbot is Cwmafan, once a famous copper-working centre, and next to it

Presteigne, see p. 166

Pontrhydyfen with its many bridges, the birth-place of the actor Richard Burton. The valley gets narrower as it winds its way towards Cymmer. It is now heavily wooded and, as industry and mining have departed, seems to be returning to its old beauty. The road continues past Cymmer and Blaengwynfi to make a spectacular exit over the mountains to the Rhondda.

The Afan-Argoed Country Park at Cymmer, 5 miles inland from Port Talbot, has a series of walks and an interesting Welsh Miners' Museum with simulated coal faces.

Preseli Hills, *Dyfed* (3/2,3A) This attractive range of hills dominates the skyline of the north-ern part of the old county of Pembrokeshire. They are not exceptionally high – the highest summit, Foel-cwmcerwyn, is 1760 ft. But the Preselis are the highest ground in the whole of West Wales and thus command outstanding views over a vast expanse of country. On excep-tionally clear days you can see the Wicklow Mountains in Ireland, Dunkery Beacon across the Bristol Channel and Snowdon in the north. It must be admitted, however, that such days are exceptional on these misty hills. As the old rhyme puts it:

> When Preseli weareth his hat,
> All Pembrokeshire gets wet from that.

Carn Ingli is the nearest summit to the sea. It rises to just over 1000 ft behind NEWPORT (Dyfed) and is crowned with a fine Iron Age fort. It is separated from the main range by the deep, wooded Gwaun valley. The next peak is Foel Eryr – the Hill of the Eagles – and from it a trackway known as the Fleming's Way runs east-wards for the whole 6 miles of the ridge to come down at Crymmech, where the old railway line crossed the Preselis. The main road between HAVERFORDWEST and CARDIGAN also climbs the range and the top of the pass, the Bwlch, is a favourite place from which to walk the range. The slate quarries of Rosebush lie under Foel-cwmcerwyn, and the Preseli Hotel at Rosebush is a connoisseurs' piece for the lover of curious country pubs. The hills are rich in prehistoric remains, from the stone circle at Brynberian to the rocks of Carn Meini, from which came the bluestones of Stonehenge. The legend of Arthur is echoed in many of the place names on the ridge – such as Carn Arthur and Cerrig Meibion Arthur.

A leaflet available from the office of the Pembrokeshire Coast National Park in Haverfordwest details a 6-mile walk with numerous Stone Age and Bronze Age relics.

Presteigne (Llanandras), *Powys* (2/3C) This gracious little town, on the west bank of the river Lugg, is administratively in Wales. It has a Welsh name, Llanandras, but it may be doubted if many of the town's inhabitants have ever heard of it. Presteigne is a border town, which takes its atmosphere and its architecture from the English county of Hereford and Worcester just across the river. Like so many of these small border towns, Presteigne grew up around a Norman castle. The castle has disappeared, but its site is now a public park known as The Warden. Broad Street has its Georgian houses, but the building that really catches the eye is the half-timbered Radnorshire Arms Hotel. It was built as a private house in 1606, became a coaching inn in 1792, and contains a priest's chamber, a Tudor doorway and secret passages. Presteigne received its first charter as a borough in 1223 and remained the official county town of Radnorshire until the reconstruction of the counties in 1972. It lies on the English side of OFFA'S DYKE. The countryside, like Presteigne itself, must be one of 'the quietest places under the sun'. The Lugg, which rises in moorland north of RADNOR FOREST, passes Pilleth where Owain Glyndwr won an important victory over the king's commander, Mortimer.

Pumsaint, *Dyfed* (4/2A) The 'Place of the Five Saints' is a hamlet in the upper valley of the Cothi, best known for the Roman gold mines at Dolau Cothi. The hillside above the stream has been honeycombed with tunnels, and a Roman bathhouse and small fort have been uncovered nearby and also in the village. The area has now been carefully restored as a picnic site owned by the National Trust and two special trails have been marked out which take you to the best section of the workings. There is an interpretative centre on the site. It is inadvisable to explore the tunnels off the official route. The modern museum at Abergwili, in CARMARTHEN, has a good display relating to the Roman gold mines and exhibits material found on the site. Remains of the Roman aqueduct lie along the Cothi hillsides. The valley becomes ever more wild and attractive as it goes to its source. Look out for the red kites that sometimes soar over this lonely countryside. Caeo lies over the hill south-east of

Old Radnor

the Roman gold mines. It has a church with a strong tower, dedicated to the Virgin and St Conwill. Caeo is a deadend but an attractive one. Beyond are the plantations of the Forestry Commission.

Radnor Forest, *Powys* (2/3C) This is the highest ground near the border and dominates the countryside east of PRESTEIGNE. The highest summits are the Black Mixen and the Great Rhos, which reach 2000 ft. The north side is heavily planted with conifers almost to the top, and the best walk starts from the south, behind New Radnor. This takes you up the Harley Dingle and the rounded top of the Whimble on to the level summit area. You can return via the valley which holds the expressively named waterfall of Water-Break-Its-Neck. Its 90 ft plunge is splendid in wet weather but has a disconcerting habit of almost disappearing in dry spells.

Radnor – Old and **New,** *Powys* (2/3C) New Radnor (Maesyfed) is a village in the shadow of RADNOR FOREST in Mid Wales, and visitors will probably only remember it as the place where the main road makes a right-angled turn in the centre of the village. It has charm, however, and the title 'new' is somewhat of a misnomer. In the Middle Ages it had a castle now represented by the high earthworks above the village and even town walls. The church has two interesting medieval effigies in the porch. The hill opposite bears the curious name of the Smatcher and is planted with even more curiously shaped plantations.

Old Radnor, about 3 miles east from New Radnor, demands attention for its fine church, perched on a hill and containing such treasures as a beautifully carved medieval screen, a megalithic stone as the font, a splendidly panelled roof and an organ case dated *c.* 1500, reputedly the oldest in Britain. The road south-west from Old Radnor will take you into fascinating country. From Gladestry the road west passes Colva and its interesting little church and continues over the pass to drop into the deep valley that holds Glascwm. Other typical examples of the small old Radnorshire type churches are within range – like Cregrina and Rhulen. The road west from New Radnor leads you into equally attractive country, as it climbs the pass at Llanfihangel-nant-Melan, with its small lake and, beyond, the romantically placed castle mound of Crug Eryr.

Raglan, (Rhaglan) *Gwent* (5/6B) Raglan lies just off the A40 main road between MONMOUTH and ABERGAVENNY and the A449 from NEWPORT (Gwent). This little village owes its existence to

the castle, one of the largest and most interesting in South Wales. The Normans built the first castle on the site, but Raglan did not come into prominence until the 15th century. It was then that an ambitious Welsh gentleman, Sir William ap Thomas, acquired it by marriage. He had fought in the French wars – his second marriage was to the daughter of David Gam, who was killed at Agincourt. He brought back a fortune from France and used it to create a strong position for himself in the Gwent borderland. He built the Great Tower, surrounded by a moat, and furnished it with gun ports for the artillery that had become essential for castle defence. The Great Tower is one of the finest examples of military architecture of the period. Sir William's son, William Herbert, further developed the family fortunes, becoming the Earl of Pembroke and, like his father before him, set about building a castle worthy of his position. He built the great gatehouse, with its machiolations on the top, and the domestic buildings around the fountain court. Raglan was further beautified and reached the peak of its fame under the Marquess of Worcester, one of the richest men in England. His son, Lord Herbert, devised a series of hydraulic inventions at Raglan, which delighted

Raglan Castle

Rhayader

his contemporaries. But, in the Civil War, the Marquess spent the whole of his vast wealth in the King's cause. At last, Raglan Castle fell, after a long siege. You can stand at the window in the now ruined Great Hall where the Marquess himself stood on the day of surrender, when he heard Fairfax and his men rushing into the courtyard 'as if the flood gates had been opened'. The castle was given up to the sack, and its treasures scattered. Raglan became the ruin we see today, with its wounds now carefully bound up by the officers of CADW and soothed with green lawns. A castle not to be missed.

Ramsey Island (Ynys Dewi), *Dyfed* (3/1A) This attractive island, 1½ miles long and ¾ mile wide, is separated from the mainland of St David's peninsula, by a wide sound through which the currents run fiercely at full tide. A string of rocks, known as the Bitches, project into the channel from the island and the sea pours over them in a boiling cascade when in full flood. Ramsey turns its most spectacular side to the open sea to the west. Here the great cliffs plunge impressively from the island's highest point, Carn Llundain, which is

over 400 ft. Further out to sea is a welter of savage rocks and small islets known as the Bishop and the Clerks, marked by the lighthouse on the South Bishop. Ramsey, unlike SKOMER on the other side of St Brides Bay, has lost its puffins; destroyed, it is said, by rats that came ashore after a shipwreck, but in compensation it is the greatest breeding ground for the Atlantic grey seal in Wales. The island was leased by the RSPB, but is now again privately owned. Access is permitted, however, and a circuit of the island by boat at seal-breeding time is a memorable experience. Boats leave from the lifeboat station at Porth Stinian 1 mile from ST DAVID'S. The seals are there in numbers from late August to October. There is also a small deer park on Ramsey.

Rhayader (Rhaeadr Gwy), *Powys* (2/2C) The Welsh name of this little town in the upper reaches of the Wye means the 'waterfall on the Wye', but the falls have largely disappeared with the construction of the bridge in 1780. The town itself is mainly a crossroads, with the leading inn at the corner and a decorative clock tower in front of it. Rhayader is very much a tourist centre today. It is the gateway to the ELAN VALLEY reservoirs, and a centre for fishing and pony trekking, with good caravan accommodation on a well-disguised park along the river. Waun Capel Park beside the Wye is claimed to be one of the most beautiful in Wales. The suburb of Llansantffraed Cwmdeuddwr, on the way to the Elan, has an ancient inn set above the rushing waters of the Wye. The road south from Rhayader to BUILTH WELLS passes through Newbridge-on-Wye. Here a side road, the B4358, turns off to Beulah and LLANWRTYD WELLS. It skirts the edge of the Green Desert and the high lonely moorlands which climax at the summit of Drygarn, the loneliest and least-visited summit in Wales over 2000 ft. It is also crowned with the biggest summit cairn in Wales. The side valleys off the Newbridge–Beulah road are equally unfrequented and attractive for anyone anxious to get away from the crowds.

Rhondda Valleys, *Mid Glamorgan* (5/4B) The valleys of the Big and Little Rhondda unite at Porth and then go down to join the Taff at PONTYPRIDD, 12 miles north-west from CARDIFF. With their long rows of terraced houses crowded into the bottom of the deep and narrow valleys, they present one of the most dramatic industrial landscapes in Britain. Up until the First World War, this was the Welsh Klondyke, supplying the steam coal which drove the engines of the world. Oil power slowly undercut the demand for Welsh steam coal. Today no colliery is still working at the top of the Rhondda Fawr. The air, once thick with lucrative smoke, is clear. The Rhondda has had to turn bravely to other things. These valleys can still hold surprises. You would not expect to find a centre of archery in the Rhondda, for example, but the Glyncornel Field Archery Centre set in 50 acres at Llwynypia has 28-target World Championship field courses. Archery, of course, is no substitute for coal, but at least it proves that the old defiant spirit of the Rhondda is still alive. There is even a plan to exploit the tourist possibility of the Rhondda with the creation of a Heritage Park interpreting the life and work of a coalmining community on the site of the Ty Mawr and the Lewis Merthyr collieries. There are two impressive roads into the valleys. One comes over the mountains via Bwlch-y-Clawdd from the Afan valley. And the exit from the Rhondda Fawr climbs to near 2000 ft and reaches a splendid viewpoint at Rhigos, with Llyn Fawr below and the whole range of the mountains of the Fforest Fawr and the BRECON BEACONS on the skyline.

Rhymney Valley, *Mid Glamorgan* (5/5C) The Rhymney valley runs north from CAERPHILLY, and the river enters the sea in the suburbs of east CARDIFF. It still has working collieries, including the Penallta, near Hengoed, between Blackwood and Bargoed. Lewis School, Pengam, now a comprehensive, is one of the oldest educational establishments in the valleys. At Gelligaer, on the hills behind Blackwood, is one of the biggest Roman forts in South Wales. Its outlines can still be traced and it has also been carefully excavated. A reconstruction of it can be seen at the National Museum in Cardiff. The church nearby is interesting and contains one of the few Anglican examples of a baptismal tank used in place of a font. The old Roman road ran north from Gelligaer on the mountain ridge that separates the Rhymney valley from that of the Taff and its tributaries. A modern road now follows the Roman route and gives a high level way to the MERTHYR TYDFIL area.

At Butetown, just off the Heads of the Valley road, is a beautifully restored hamlet with artisans' cottages dating from 1802. The cottages housed the workers of the nearby Union Ironworks. The Maesycwmmer Viaduct at Hengoed, 5 miles north of Caerphilly, is one of the valley's outstanding industrial monuments. The 15-arched viaduct was designed in 1857. At Ystrad Mynach is one of the few working smithies in Wales with a restored corn mill adjacent.

Rudbaxton, *Dyfed* (3/2B) Connoisseurs of the curious in church monuments should make a short diversion from the HAVERFORDWEST–FISHGUARD road to Rudbaxton Church, 4 miles north of Haverfordwest. The church itself, with its squat tower and weathered stone, and set among the trees, is attractive, but the sensation of the interior is the monument to the Howard family of Fletcher Hall. The style has been well described as Rustic Baroque. Five members of the family clad in their best clothes stand under an arcade – these effigies are life-size and coloured. Four of the Howards carry skulls in their hands, as symbols of mortality. One lady has her hands free; she is Joanna, who erected the monument. The statues date from *c.*1668. They confront the bust of General Sir Thomas Picton, who was born in Haverfordwest and was killed at the head of his division at Waterloo. There is also a brass plate commemorating Archbishop Laud, who once held the living as a young man. It nicely supplemented his income as Bishop of St David's.

Tylorstown and tip, Little Rhondda Valley, see p. 169

St Brides Major (Saint-y-Brid), *Mid Glamorgan* (4/3C) A village on the road between BRIDGEND and Southerndown, which still retains some of the air of a typical Glamorgan village of the 19th century. The road from Bridgend enters St Brides Major through a little valley with limestone outcrops on the slopes, for, geologically, this area of the Vale of Glamorgan lies south of the coal measures. The fine grove of trees on the left-hand side was planted to commemorate the visit of General Picton. He was staying with his brother-in-law, the vicar of St Brides, when he heard that Napoleon had landed from Elba. He immediately set off to rejoin the army and met his death at Waterloo. The church, with its Norman tower, contains some interesting memorials of the Butler family. Inevitably, a certain amount of villa building is now transforming St Brides, as it has so many of the other old villages of the Vale.

St Clears (San Cler), *Dyfed* (3/3B) A small township on the river Taf, between CARMARTHEN and WHITLAND. It was once a notorious bottleneck for tourist traffic to the West, but has now been bypassed. Today St Clears is a modest trading centre serving the rich surrounding agricultural district. It cut a bigger figure in the Middle Ages when it was a borough attached to a castle and had a Cluniac priory as well. The priory has gone, leaving behind a few earthworks in Priory Park. The castle mound remains, with St Mary Magdalen's church near it. The walls of the church show a tendency to lean outwards, but it contains some strong Norman work, including the fine chancel arch. Two miles south-west from St Clears on the road to TENBY is Llanddowror, with a restored church that holds memories of the Reverend Griffiths Jones, vicar of this parish, who first lit the torch that began the 18th-century Methodist Revival in Wales.

St David's (Tyddewi), *Dyfed* (3/1A) St David's is unique. Who would expect to find a great cathedral tucked away in a hidden valley at the end of a rocky, cliff-girt peninsula, filled with the sound of the sea? Yet this is the spot – the Land's End of Wales on the northern arm of St Brides Bay in Dyfed's far west – that the patron saint of Wales chose, when he established his monastery 'far from the haunts of men'. St David's still retains its feeling of insularity even when the visitors arrive in summer. And when they come to the little square of the village with its market cross – or should we say 'city', for the cathedral, the inhabitants claim, gives St David's city status – the visitors may well wonder where the cathedral stands. The only evidence of its presence is the top of the tall tower peeping up over the houses around the square. But as you pass through the medieval gateway and descend the long flight of steps (known as the 39 Articles) into the cathedral precinct, the full splendour of the great church is revealed. The exterior is not lavishly decorated, but the weathered purplish stone seems to fit in perfectly with the rocky valley. The interior surprises with its charm and beauty. The strong Norman arches of the nave lean outwards, due to a shift in the foundations soon after they were built, and the floor slopes up to the choir screen, which somehow adds to the impression that you have come to a very special place. The roof of the nave, 15th-century and fashioned out of light Irish oak with elaborately carved pendants, is a delight. The screen shelters the tomb of the 14th-century bishop, Henry de Gower, who built the splendid Bishop's Palace near the cathedral. The choir stalls are 15th-

The Bishop's Palace, St David's

century and the misericords on the seats of the stalls are enchanting – the scenes are carved with great humour and skill, and form one of the treasures of the cathedral. The presbytery is Early English in style, and contains the tomb of Edmund Tudor, the father of Henry VII. In Holy Trinity Chapel, with its elegant fan vaulting, a casket behind a grille in the wall contains relics which may well be those of St David himself. They were discovered in the 19th century during repair work. The bones are those of two men, one tall and one small. Tradition maintains that while St David was a small man, his faithful companion, St Justinian, was tall. The bones may have been hidden in the recess when the iconoclasts of the Reformation broke up the original shrine. It is good to think that the bones of the saint still rest in the great church that rose on the the site of what was his simple, early monastery far back in the 6th century.

St Mary's College on the north side of the cathedral was founded by John of Gaunt. Only the tower and the chapel remain. The cloister has been almost obliterated by the great rough buttresses put up in the 16th century to support the leaning walls of the nave. From the cathedral itself, you cross the little trout stream that runs

past the West Front, rebuilt in 1862 by Sir George Gilbert Scott. St David's must be the only cathedral with a trout stream at its doors. Beyond are the extensive ruins of the Bishop's Palace. This is one of the finest medieval ruins in Wales; the building was completed in the 14th century by that busy building bishop, Henry de Gower. The arcaded upper storeys, the rose windows and the private chapels and halls, still elegant in their ruin, give a vivid idea of the way a princely bishop could live in the Middle Ages. The Reformation Bishop Barlow would have none of this splendour and allowed the palace to fall into irrevocable decay.

The rocky and windswept St David's peninsula contains other memorials to the patron saint of Wales. His mother, St Non, is commemorated in the Holy Well, now restored, near the coast path at St Non's Bay. The little stream that flows past the West Front of the cathedral comes to the sea in the harbour of Porthclais, with its ancient protective pier. This was the way the monks sailed to Ireland in the old days. Further round the point is St Justinian's Chapel, near the lifeboat slipway.

The best and most popular bathing beach lies 1 mile north-west of St David's. Whitesand Bay, with its firm sands and good surfing beach, gives a fine view of RAMSEY and the other, smaller islands that end with South Bishop and its lighthouse. From Whitesand, the coastal path owned by the National Trust takes you to the point of St David's Head, the 'Octopitarium promontorium', or the cape of the Eight Perils in the Roman geographer's survey of the then known world, written in AD 140. The perils are evident if you look out from the head on a windy day and see the waves breaking over the hosts of islets and hidden rocks that stretch westwards from Ramsey. Old George Owen, in Tudor times, echoed Ptolemy's warning of the dangers of the rocks of the Bishop and the Clerks when he declared that, on winter's nights, they 'preach deadly doctrine to their winter audience' of poor mariners. Behind St David's Head rise the two miniature mountains of Carnllidi and Penberi. They are not high – just under 600 ft – but they add the final touch of rugged remoteness to this rare, western land of St David's.

St Donat's Castle and **Nash Point,** *South Glamorgan* (4/3C) Situated in the Vale of Glamorgan on the coast of the Bristol Channel, 6 miles south-west of COWBRIDGE. The earliest part of St Donat's Castle was built by the Strad-

lings around 1300 and the family occupied it for the next 400 years. The Tudor Stradlings were particularly notable for their literary interests and patronage of the arts. The last male heir died in 1738 and the castle passed into other hands. In 1925 it was bought by the American newspaper millionaire, William Randolph Hearst. He spent lavishly on St Donat's and filled it with a choice collection of medieval armour besides embellishing the gardens that stretch down to the sea. However, he only occupied it himself for a month. In 1960 it became Atlantic College – an international, co-educational sixth form school with special emphasis on outdoor pursuits. The castle consists of the outer 13th-century walls, with the 14th-century and Tudor buildings within the defensive circuit arranged around an inner courtyard. The Great Hall is a fine example of a baronial hall of the 15th century.

The coast, now known as the Heritage Coast, runs westwards from St Donat's with layered strata which reach 100 ft in places. At Nash Point, where the coast turns northwards, stand the two white towers of the lighthouses. Only one is now in use. The architecture of the lighthouses, the subsidiary buildings and the white-walled enclosure are in the best traditions of the early 19th-century Trinity House, which combined elegance and simplicity with practicality. Offshore, the sea breaks on the treacherous Scarweather Sands, which give ample proof of the necessity of a lighthouse on Nash Point. They are separated from the cliff by the narrow channel of the Nash Passage. On clear days, you can look across the Bristol Channel to Exmoor and the high tors behind Ilfracombe on the Devon shore.

St Florence, *Dyfed* (3/2B) A village on the Ritec stream 3 miles west of TENBY, several times winner of the Wales in Bloom award. The houses are grouped compactly around the church and many have the so-called 'Flemish' chimney – large and round, leading down to a wide fireplace. The church is solid rather than graceful in architectural style, with a tall Norman tower. Until the 19th century, small ships could sail up the Ritec, but in 1820 an embankment was raised across the mouth of the stream in order to reclaim land from the sea. The embankment was used by the railway in 1866. The result was the formation of a marsh behind the embankment and dunes along the coast in front of Penally – a case of well-meaning improvements going astray.

Just outside the village is the Manor House Wild Life and Leisure Park.

Old Beaupre Castle

St Hilary and **Beaupre** (Saint Hilari a'r Bewpyr), *South Glamorgan* (5/4C) To reach St Hilary, turn off the CARDIFF–COWBRIDGE road just before you get to Cowbridge, by the St Hilary television transmitter. The village is small but delightful, for it has preserved a large number of its thatched houses. The inn, also thatched, looks across at the church, which is 14th-century and contains a tomb with a full-scale effigy of a knight in armour. It probably represents Richard Basset of the powerful local family who built the nearby Old Beaupre Castle. The name Beaupre comes from the old French *beau repaire* ('beautiful retreat'), locally pronounced as 'bew-per'; at the end of the 16th century the Bassets certainly decided to try and make their family seat live up to its title. The place was never a real castle but rather a fortified manor house, and in 1600 Richard Basset added a classical portal to the outer gatehouse. But he expended his greatest effort on the gatehouse of the inner courtyard. Here he built a three-tiered porch of elegant proportions, decorated with classical columns. It is one of the finest examples of its type, fashion-able in late Elizabethan and Jacobean times. Unfortunately, the Bassets were ruined in the King's cause during the Civil War, and their fortunes never recovered. The house fell into decay and became a farmhouse. It has now been partially restored and is open to the public.

Saundersfoot, *Dyfed* (3/3B) Saundersfoot, 3 miles east of TENBY along the coast, under a sheltered, wooded hillside, developed its little harbour for the export of anthracite coal during the 19th century, when the South Pembrokeshire coalfield was in its heyday.

The collieries have closed, but the harbour remains and has allowed Saundersfoot to develop a new career as a popular holiday centre. The harbour is packed with yachts and the excellent sands draw the crowds in summer. Saundersfoot has laid itself out to meet the visitors' needs with hotels, cafés and souvenir shops. The place has completely recovered from an extraordinary explosion of the gas mains in the main street. In addition to its extensive yachting facilities, Saundersfoot is also a centre of deep sea fishing for shark and tope. The parish church of St Issell's is nearly a mile inland. It has an embattled Norman tower, and a fine 14th-century font. The coast continues north from Saundersfoot, past Hean Castle, to the popular holiday beach of Wiseman's Bridge, once the scene of a rehearsal for the D-Day landings which was watched by Churchill.

Severn Bridge (5/6C) This most graceful and impressive of suspension bridges is an elegant and most worthy entrance to Wales – but, strictly speaking, it is not in Wales at all.

The main span across the Severn is in England and the roadway does not reach Welsh soil until it has crossed the river Wye. But the two bridges over the Severn and the Wye form a unity, and both are fine engineering achievements. The main bridge is carried on two great steel towers which rise 445 ft above the water. The roadway is formed from hollow steel boxes which were floated down the Wye from the construction yard at CHEPSTOW. The Wye Bridge has a main span of 770 ft, and is of the stayed girder type, the first of its kind to be built in Britain. The Toll Plaza and the Service Area are on the English side of the bridge. The Severn Bridge has become vital to the industrial future of South Wales and the volume of traffic over it has grown to such an extent that plans are now agreed for the second bridge.

Skenfrith (Ynysgynwraidd), *Gwent* (5/6B) Situated on the beautiful river Monnow, which here marks the boundary between England and Wales, and on the road between Ross-on-Wye and ABERGAVENNY, where it crosses the border. Skenfrith is on the Welsh side of the stream. It has a castle, set on the river, with a round keep in the centre of a walled circuit. Skenfrith was part of a border defence scheme known as the Trilateral, which included GROSMONT to the north and WHITE CASTLE to the west. The church, with its curious, squat tower, holds a treasure in the 15th-century Skenfrith Cope, a masterpiece of medieval embroidery. The Monnow flows over a weir and the water drives the wheel of the old mill, where corn is still ground. A pleasant inn completes the picture of a charming hamlet among green hills, which gives a delightful introduction to Wales.

Skomer and **Skokholm**, *Dyfed* (3/1B) These two islands, off the southern peninsula that guards St Brides Bay on the west coast of Dyfed, are now famous for the wealth of their seabirds during the breeding season. These are the places to see the Manx shearwater, the enchanting puffin, and a host of other rare seabirds. The islands are under the care of the Nature Conservancy and the West Wales Naturalists' Trust and can be visited by the public. Skomer is the closer to the mainland. The departure point is Martin's Haven near Marloes on the mainland, but the crossing of the notoriously turbulent Jack Sound can be difficult in rough weather. But the rewards of a visit for ornithologists are great. Apart from the birds, Skomer has its special vole, which shows no fear of man – it must be the most trusting little animal in Britain. The Skomer Island Nature Trail is 2¼ miles long and has 16 viewing points for bird and seal life. Skokholm has an equal wealth of bird life, but lies further out and is separated from its sister island by Broad Sound. In strong winds, the expressively named Wild Goose Race can be wild indeed. The distinguished naturalist R. M. Lockley established Britain's first bird observatory on Skokholm in 1933. Geologically, the grey shales of Skomer contrast with the warm Old Red Sandstone rock of Skokholm.

Further out still lies GRASSHOLM, with its colony of gannets, the third largest gannetry in Britain. Plans are well advanced to make the waters around Skomer the first Marine Reserve in Britain.

Solva (Solfach), *Dyfed* (3/1A) Three miles east of

ST DAVID'S on the road from HAVERFORD-WEST, Solva is a classically picturesque ex-fishing and coastal trading village, on a winding creek that gives a safe harbour in St Brides Bay. It is so attractive that it has inevitably changed character in recent years. It has become a haven for yachtsmen, artists and retired folk who now outnumber the original Solvaites. But its charm remains. Two rocky islets guard the harbour, and on its east side the narrow ridge of the Gribin, with its Iron Age fort, is ablaze in season with yellow gorse and rare flowers.

The attractions of Lower Solva have been increased by the installation of a Nectarium in a disused chapel. 'Nectarium' is a useful word, devised by two enthusiasts who have established a centre here for breeding rare tropical butterflies and moths. An exotic but fascinating enterprise to find in a Welsh village.

From Solva a road runs north through a lush, rocky valley to Middle Mill, where the small woollen mill still works. Eastward the road back to Haverfordwest passes the big RAF station of Brawdy before dipping down to the wide sands of Newgale and its huge pebble beach. Looking down on Newgale is Roch Castle, a tower perched on a rock. The story goes that the builder of the castle, Adam de Rupe, placed it on the rock for safety, since he was told that he would die from the bite of a viper. His precaution was in vain, for a viper was carried into the tower in a bundle of firewood and crept out to kill him. In the 17th century the castle passed into the hands of the Walter family, and in 1630, Lucy Walter was born at Roch – she was Charles II's mistress and the mother of the Duke of Monmouth.

Strata Florida *see* **Pontrhydfendigaid**

Strumble Head, *Dyfed* (3/2A) This fine headland west of FISHGUARD, with its lighthouse on a small islet connected to the mainland by a small suspension bridge, is the climax of a rocky peninsula which entered history when the French landed here in 1797. The landing is commemorated by a memorial stone on the cliffs of Carreg Wastad. The church of Llanwnda, on a boulder-strewn common, has a lonely, primitive feel about it, and the farmhouses on Pen Caer peninsula all have their memories of the French landing. The area is rich in prehistoric remains, and Garn Fawr, the highest point on the peninsula, has a fine Iron Age fort. The best way to see Strumble is to walk the Pembrokeshire Coast Path, but motorists can drive to the Strumble

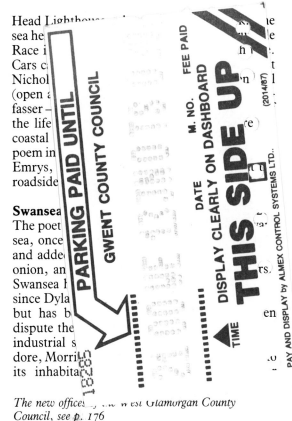

Head Lighthouse...
sea he...
Race i...
Cars c...
Nichol...
(open a...
fasser –...
the life...
coastal...
poem in...
Emrys,...
roadside...

Swansea
The poet...
sea, once...
and adde...
onion, an...
Swansea h...
since Dyla...
but has b...
dispute the...
industrial s...
dore, Morri...
its inhabita...

The new offices ... west Glamorgan County Council, see p. 176

through all the changes it has retained its reputation of easy friendliness.

As far as history is concerned Swansea claims that its name, at least, goes back to the days of the Vikings. It is derived from 'Sveinn's Island'. As far as the place itself is concerned we are on surer ground with the Normans who built the first castle here. The present castle, in the centre of the town, is mainly 14th-century and it owed its arcaded parapets to Bishop Henry de Gower, who used the same features in his palaces at LAMPHEY and ST DAVID'S. Little else survives from this early period and Swansea remained a small market town and port until the beginning of the 19th century. There was a short period, around 1808, when the town had ambitions of development as a fashionable seaside resort. The Industrial Revolution soon put a stop to such dreams. Swansea became the world's greatest copper-smelting centre, using ore, first, from the Parys Mountain mines in Anglesey and then from as far afield as Chile, brought back by a fleet of wind-jammers which made the dangerous voyage around the Horn. The copper trade faded at the end of the 19th century and left behind it a wasteland at Llandore. Swansea developed further as a tinplate centre and a big coal-exporting port, with new docks at the mouth of the river

Tawe. Tinplate and coal have faded in their turn, but resilient Swansea has totally reconstructed its industrial areas. A model restoration scheme has cleared the old industrial scars from the Lower Swansea valley. New, bright and clean industrial estates have been created around Llansamlet and Morriston. Swansea has successfully held the Depression at bay.

Swansea has always been divided into three parts – industrial Swansea behind Town Hill and Kilvey Hill in the lower Tawe valley, the Dockland and commercial area in the centre, and the residential parts on the hills and along the lower ground that confronts the long curve of the bay. The centre of the old town – the Swansea that Dylan Thomas knew – was largely destroyed in the blitz of the Second World War in which Swansea suffered as severely as any town in Britain. Some of the old features survived, however. The Royal Institution, near the docks, with its dignified classical façade, houses an excellent museum with exhibits to interest all ages. The Glynn Vivian Art Gallery in Alexandra Road has an important collection and a progressive policy; it also has an excellent display of the Swansea and Nantgarw porcelain for which the old town was once celebrated. The Grand Theatre, with its splendid late Victorian

Swansea Marina

auditorium, is now extensively enlarged and improved by the Council. The old market was destroyed in the blitz, but a spacious new one has replaced it, where you can still buy that Swansea speciality – laverbread, made from the seaweed collected from the Gower cliffs and cockles from nearby PENCLAWDD. The blitz also allowed the buildings that concealed the castle to be cleared, and now a spacious lawn marks the centre of the city, and new roads run towards the sea front, past the spacious City Hall and Law Courts. Erected before the war to the designs of the eminent Welsh architect Sir Percy Thomas, this impressive complex with its tall white tower contains the Brangwyn Hall, which houses the British Empire Panels by Frank Brangwyn, commissioned for the House of Lords but rejected because of their bright, vivid colouring. They have a perfect home in the Brangwyn Hall, which is also the heart of the important annual Swansea Music Festival in October.

The sea front of Swansea is, again, a part of the city that has been vastly improved in recent years. The old North Dock has been filled in, and the South Dock has become a yachting marina, as part of a major maritime development, which includes a Maritime and Industrial Museum. It has a working woollen mill and a gallery devoted to the docks. The new offices of the West Glamorgan County Council look out over the bay, and a wide road has replaced the track of the old Mumbles Railway – that famous line that could proudly claim to be the oldest regular passenger service in the world. The promenade has been extended past the home of the Swansea Rugby and Cricket Club at St Helen's and continues towards Singleton Park. Here the University College has been lucky in having space to expand, with the new Singleton Hospital close to it. A recent addition to the University is the Taliesin Arts Centre. The sweep of the bay continues in its graceful curve to Oystermouth and The Mumbles. Oystermouth has its old castle perched on a hill. Below, a line of hotels and houses face the bay under the shelter of a high limestone headland. A cutting takes you out towards The Mumbles, with a pier, the two pleasant little bays of Limeslade and Bracelet and the gleaming white islets of Mumbles Head, crowned with a lighthouse. Watersports are popular here. From the head of the pier you can see how Swansea is growing along the wide sands of its bay, with the houses on the 400-ft Town Hill, and the mountains of the Glamorgan coalfield forming an impressive background to the

Laverbread stall in Swansea market

east. As dusk falls, and the lights come on around the graceful curve of the bay, you can understand why Walter Savage Landor once compared Swansea Bay to the Bay of Naples. Of course, there were no docks or PORT TALBOT steelworks in his day! Oystermouth and The Mumbles mark the beginning of the GOWER peninsula, Swansea's special holiday playground. The city has the advantage of a remarkable area of natural beauty on its very doorstep (*see also* Bishopston).

For an increasing number of literary-minded visitors Swansea remains Dylan Thomas's town. The Heritage Committee of the Swansea Council has produced a special guide to the old haunts of the poet, Dylan Thomas's Uplands Trail. It takes you to the poet's birthplace at No. 5 Cwmdonkin Drive in the suburb of the Uplands, Cwmdonkin Park and some of his favourite still-surviving pubs. The small Dylan Thomas Theatre is in the restored area of Regency houses near the South Dock. A bronze statue of the seated poet stands before it. To those who knew him, it is hardly flattering.

In Lower Swansea is the Valley Industrial Trail demonstrating the area's rich industrial past. The trail starts at the Royal Institution and ends at Llandore railway viaduct. There is a coalmining trail in Llansamlet and Birchgrove. Details of these and other industrial trails are available from the Swansea City Council's Information Centre in Singleton Street.

Talgarth, *Powys* (5/5B) A small market town, reached by turning off the HAY-ON-WYE–BRECON road soon after it leaves the Wye valley. You pass the strong round tower of Bronllys, built on the site of a former motte and bailey castle. The castle doorway is at first-floor level and is reached by a steep wooden staircase. Talgarth itself is also built on a slope, with its solid houses crowded together. The little square is tilted towards a 14th-century tower. The church has been restored and contains the grave of the great leader of the 18th-century Methodist Revival in Wales, Hywel Harris. An inscription on the chancel wall describes him as 'the first itinerant preacher of Redemption'. He was born near Talgarth, and at the height of his career founded a remarkable religious community called the Connexion at Trefecca, 1 mile south of Talgarth. The building is in a style described as Strawberry Hill Gothic. It is now a college of the Methodist Church, with a memorial chapel attached, built in 1873. The College contains memorials illustrating Harris's career and houses the Hywel Harris Museum. South of Talgarth you are surrounded by the fine scenery of Mynydd Troed and LLANGORSE LAKE. And then, if you are still in the mood for some ecclesiastic research retrace your steps past Bronllys and cross the main road to Llandefalle, which has a three-tiered tower surmounted by a pyramid and contains a rood screen decorated with the same dragon motifs as the screen at Patrishow (*see* Crickhowell).

Outdoor enthusiasts will enjoy exploring the BRECON BEACONS on foot or by ponies from the many trekking centres in the locality.

Talley (Tal-y-Llechau), *Dyfed* (4/2A) A genuine beauty spot, with its ruined abbey, two small lakes and green hills all around, Talley is 7 miles north of LLANDEILO. The abbey was founded by the Lord Rhys, the Welsh Prince of Deheubarth, and the monks belonged to the Premonstratensians, who wore the white habit of the Cistercians and followed their rule, but who also undertook parish duties. Talley was the only abbey of the order in Wales. It shared the fate of all Welsh monastic institutions in the Reformation, and the ruins were pillaged for building materials until only the two central arches and a portion of the tower remained. The parish church, which still contains its box pews, stands beside it. The pews

Talley Abbey

of the squire, the squire's agent and the vicar's family are arranged in a descending order of precedence. On the lawn that now marks the nave of the abbey lies a memorial stone to the members of the Edwinsford (Rhyd Edwin) family, the Williams-Drummonds, who lived in the great house over the hill from one of the lakes beside the Cothi river. Sadly it has now fallen into ruin, but there are signs of the ancient splendour of the estate everywhere in the neighbourhood, including a fine avenue of native oaks along the side road around the lake.

Tenby (Dinbych-y-pysgod), *Dyfed* (3/3B) Tenby is a delightful combination of Regency houses and hotels along the cliff tops, a ruined castle and a snug little harbour, all surrounded by medieval walls and girded by yellow sands. The whole makes an unforgettable impression of holiday elegance and charm. The Welsh name of Dinbych-y-pysgod – Denbigh of the fish – indicates that the little town began life as a fishing centre. The Welsh were driven out when the Anglo-Normans and their Flemish mercenaries turned southern Pembrokeshire into a 'Little England beyond Wales'. The castle stood on the small headland that guards the harbour. It was finally destroyed in the Civil War and the sparse ruins now house one of the best small museums in Britain. In Regency and early Victorian days Tenby developed as a fashionable seaside resort, the hotels with their bow windows looking down on the sands, which give excellent bathing. The

medieval walls have retained their round towers; the most prominent is known as the Five Arches. Apart from the walls and the castle, the most important survivals from Tenby's past are the Tudor Merchant's House with its early wall paintings and the Plantagenet House next door, both of which belong to the National Trust and the parish church of St Mary's. This must be one of the largest parish churches in Wales. It has a tall spire, a fine roof and interesting monuments, including a richly decorated Jacobean tomb. There is also a memorial to the Tenby mathematician Robert Recorde. In Queen Elizabeth I's day, he invented the equals sign and was the first man to work out square roots. South of Castle Hill is St Catherine's Island, which can be reached by walking across the sands at low tide. It has a fort, built in the mid-19th century as part of the outer defences of MILFORD HAVEN. From the harbour, with its lifeboat station, the safe and shallow North Sands stretch towards the cliffs that lead round to the little cove of Waterwynch. Offshore is the Goscar Rock. Tenby was the birthplace of the artist Augustus John, and there are several art dealers and also the North Beach Art Gallery. The South Sands stretch westward for 1½ miles to Giltar Point backed by the dunes which have a fine 18-hole golf course. Penally village lies behind the Burrows. It is mainly composed of modern bungalows, but the church is 13th-century and contains a Celtic cross, with a wheelhead and elaborately carved patterns. The Penally Nature Trail is 3½ miles long with 13 viewing stations. A leaflet is available locally. CALDEY ISLAND is in full view, for Giltar is the nearest point to it. At ST FLORENCE, 3 miles west, is the Manor House Wild Life and Leisure Park.

Boat trips run regularly from the picturesque Tenby harbour to and around Caldey.

Tintern (Tyndyrn), *Gwent* (5/6B) Tintern has been famous as a beauty spot since the end of the 18th century. Turner painted it, Wordsworth wrote a poem about it, and now the crowds flock to it. It does not disappoint. The graceful walls of the ruined abbey stand by the tidal waters of the Wye surrounded by deeply wooded hills. Small wonder that the Cistercians chose the spot for their abbey, although the inevitable tourist traffic has banished the utter seclusion and quiet that the old Cistercians sought. Perhaps the most impressive part of the ruins is the 60 ft east window of the choir. After the Dissolution Tintern was used for industry. The dense woodlands around the great church supplied charcoal for iron smelting. A plaque on the wall as you enter the abbey informs you: 'Near this place in the year 1568 brass was first made by alloying copper to zinc'. An exhibition in the Visitor Centre traces the history of the abbey. Below Tintern the Wye cuts deeper into its limestone gorge on its way down to CHEPSTOW. The Wyndcliffe is the most celebrated viewpoint, looking across to the white cliffs rising above the woods on the Gloucestershire side, as the river makes a wide sweeping curve. There is a car park on top of the Wyndcliffe on the Welsh side of the Wye. From here you can make a circuit of the Wyndcliffe by following the path, cut by lovers of the picturesque in the early 19th century, which works

Tintern Abbey

Tretower

its way among the beech woods and up the face of the cliff. The scene is glorious here in autumn, when the woods turn yellow and gold. All the woodlands around Tintern are a splendid adjunct to the beauty of the scene. You can follow two forest trails from the car park at the old sawmills – the Chapel Hill and Barbadoes Forest trails give you views of the Wye Valley. Walkers can also start a series of explorations on foot through the valley from the old Railway Exhibition centre. From the village around the abbey you drive up the steep hill through the woods to Trelleck. The name is from the Welsh for 'Three Stones'; they stand rather mysteriously at the roadside. They are known locally as Harold's Stones, commemorating a victory over the Welsh by the famous Anglo-Saxon leader. They are, however, survivors of some prehistoric stone alignment. On the road into the village you pass the Virtuous Well, once a place of pilgrimage, and still carefully maintained. The main valley of the Wye continues north to Llandogo, with the rich woodlands lying all around, and then crosses over into England.

At Llangwm, some 4 miles west, is the Wolvesnewton Model Farm Folk Collection.

Tregaron, *Dyfed* (1/3C) A market town in the upper valley of the Teifi 12 miles north-east of LAMPETER. Tregaron is built around a square which has a statue of Henry Richard, 'The Apostle of Peace', in the centre. He was the Radical MP for MERTHYR TYDFIL for 20 yeas and died

in 1888. Behind the statue is the Talbot Hotel where George Borrow stayed after he had tramped into Tregaron in the dusk and felt that the place reminded him 'of an Andalusian village overhung by its sierras'. The hills are certainly close to Tregaron, for it is on the edge of that great open wilderness that stretches for 20 miles eastwards to ABERGWESYN. It is thus a great centre for pony trekking. Just north of Tregaron is the great bog of Cors Caron, which rivals Cors Fochno near BORTH in size and interest. The river Teifi works its way through its peaty mazes which are treacherous for unwary walkers. If visitors wish to explore its wealth of bird life and flowers they should follow the Nature Trail, details of which can be obtained at the Tourist Office in Tregaron. The bog is 2 miles from north to south and 2 miles across. Its name on the Ordnance Survey map is Cors-goch Glan Teifi – the Red Bog of the Teifi valley – but in summer the Red Bog can turn almost white with the tassels of the cotton sedge. The bog is a National Nature Reserve.

Tresaith *see* Aberporth

Tretower, *Powys* (5/5B) A village in the upper valley of the Usk, situated just off the ABERGAVENNY–BRECON road as it prepares to climb over the Bwlch pass. Tretower Court, the home of the Vaughans, is an excellent example of the fortified manor house of the 15th century. The setting is splendid, with the high hills of the BLACK MOUNTAINS all around. Tretower Court, now in the care of CADW, is built around a courtyard, rather like the quadrangle of a small Oxford college. It has a fortified gatehouse and the domestic buildings around the courtyard have been restored. The Great Hall, with its screen and oak beams, although now empty of any furniture, gives a vivid impression of the way a local magnate lived in the later Middle Ages. The poet, Henry Vaughan, was a member of the family, although he was born in nearby Llansantffraed and was buried in the local church near Talybont. You pass it as you drive over the Bwlch from Tretower on your way to Brecon. Tretower has an older fortress than Tretower Court. In the fields behind the 15th-century Court Bernard de Neufmarche, the conqueror of the old Welsh kingdom of Brycheiniog, granted land to a Norman knight named Picard. He threw up a motte and bailey castle, which was later replaced by a stone circuit. In the second quarter of the 13th century Roger Picard built the circular stone keep, to the same pattern as that at Bronllys (*see* Talgarth). The greatest of these round keeps was built by William Marshall at PEMBROKE.

Trevine (Trefin) *Dyfed* (3/1A) This large village, on the coast 7 miles north-east of ST DAVID'S, stands a little back from the sea, though its long main street eventually leads down to a little rocky cove, where the ruined mill inspired the poet Crwys to write one of the best-loved poems in the Welsh language. Until recent times, Trevine was famous for its fair, which lasted three boisterous days. All is quiet now, and even the retired sea captains, who were once the pride of the village, have been replaced by the holidaymakers. Trevine was once the site of one of the palaces of the Bishops of St David's but all traces of it have disappeared.

Usk, *Gwent* (5/5B) Usk is exactly where you might expect to find it – on the river Usk, around 8 miles north of NEWPORT (Gwent). This pleasant town, which never seems to be in a hurry, was an important Roman station called Burium on the road from the main Roman base at Isca (CAERLEON). In the Middle Ages the Normans naturally saw that it was provided with a castle. It played no dramatic part in history and it is now a picturesque ruin with a modern mansion within the walls. It looks down on the wide market square. Near the bridge over the river is the Three Salmons Hotel, with a name to remind you that the Usk is a famous fishing river that rivals the Wye. The dual carriageway from Newport to MONMOUTH passes the town on the eastern side. The church was formerly a priory of Benedictine nuns before the Dissolution during the Reformation. It cannot compete in interest with some of the small churches in the surrounding villages. Three miles to the east is the church of Llangwm Uchaf, where the screen rivals that of Llananno, in Powys, in the richness of its decoration. Here also is the Wolvesnewton Model Farm Folk Collection. The whole country between the Usk and the Wye is full of low, green hills and quiet villages – nothing spectacular but with the attraction of being off the beaten track.

Welshpool (Y Trallwng), *Powys* (2/3B) Welshpool, not far from the Shropshire border and placed on a beautiful section of the Severn as it prepares to leave Wales, is a prosperous market town, with a wide central street containing some Georgian and half-timbered houses. The church

has a handsome medieval timbered roof and a tomb of one of the Herbert family – good Jacobean work. Nearby is the small but interesting town museum. Welshpool is a terminus for the Welshpool and Llanfair Light Railway, one of the 'great little trains' of Wales (*see* Llanfair Caereinion). Immediately to the south of the town is Powis Castle, one of the great border strongholds, which was in the hands of the Herbert family from 1587 until 1952 when it was bequeathed to the National Trust. The castle has been reconstructed over this long period, but the 17th-century State Apartments and the terraced gardens are notable. The castle is open to the public from Easter to October. The 18th-century gardens and parkland are open daily. A museum to Clive of India is to be developed here. A section of the old Shropshire Union Canal runs through Welshpool. It has been restored and gives a most attractive, tranquil waterway through the town and the adjoining district. Enthusiasts dream of eventually restoring the whole length of it, but there are still problems with road bridges. Across the Severn from Welshpool is the Long Mountain (1338 ft). A road runs along the ridge and OFFA'S DYKE also follows it. As you climb up the steep rise onto the Long Mountain from Kingswood you pass a grassy lane on the left-hand side. This leads you to the famous Redwood Grove of the Royal Forestry Society. These must be among the tallest trees in Britain, and as the sunlight filters down through the branches high overhead and touches the reddish massive tree trunks, you feel that you are standing in a Cathedral of the Woods. In a field on the east side of the ridge is the curious church at Trelyston which is surrounded by great yew trees; it is half-timbered and has an old-fashioned barrel organ that still functions. There is a fine view eastward over Corndon Hill and the Shropshire hills.

Close to the town is Trelydan Hall, an impressive example of Tudor black-and-white architecture, typical of the Welshpool and upper Severn district. It is open to the public by appointment.

Wentwood, *Gwent* (5/5C) Four miles north-east of busy NEWPORT (Gwent) you can drive through the quiet wooded avenue of the old royal hunting forest of Wentwood and walk the forest trails. The forest occupies the hilly country that slopes down to the river Usk and is surrounded by interesting villages. Prominent among them is Llanvair Discoed, where the church wall is inscribed with a now-celebrated verse which seems to sum up the views of the 18th-century reformers, who disapproved of those happy games that the old Welsh peasantry had played in the churchyards of their parish churches from time immemorial:

> Who ever hear on Sunday
> Will practis playing at ball
> It may be before Monday
> The Devil will have you all.

White Castle, *Gwent* (5/6B) White Castle, together with SKENFRITH and GROSMONT, formed a group of castles known as the Trilateral, which acted as the main defence for this north-east corner of the old county of Monmouthshire. White Castle is the most impressive of the three.

Powis Castle, see p. 181

It was erected originally in the 12th century but remodelled in the early 13th, and shows an interesting stage in the development of castle building, when the concept of the keep was becoming outmoded and greater emphasis was being placed on the towers which provided flanking fire along the walls. There are two outer works, and the main central castle is surrounded by a deep moat, which still has water in it. A curious and rather sad little piece of history concerns Rudolf Hess, Hitler's deputy, who was imprisoned in an asylum at ABERGAVENNY and was brought here occasionally to feed the ducks. The castle has great views across to the Skirrid around Abergavenny, and north-east towards the hills that guard Grosmont. While at White Castle it is worth visiting the church at Llantilio Crossenny which is built among ancient earthworks, and the old moated manor of Hengwrt – the Old Court. The manor once belonged to the celebrated David Gam, who was slain at Agincourt. The manor house has gone, but the square moat remains as evidence of the troubled times of the Wars of the Roses in the 15th century.

Whitland (Ty Gwyn ar Daf), *Dyfed* (3/3B) Whitland, on the river Taf, has an important place in Welsh history. The present market town hardly gives a hint of it. It is mainly Victorian and the most prominent building is the big creamery, which serves the dairy farmer over a wide area and is the town's chief industry. Whitland is also a railway junction. Here the line to West Wales divides, one branch going to HAVERFORDWEST and FISHGUARD, the other wandering around south Dyfed via TENBY to Pembroke Dock. But in the 10th century, the great Welsh ruler Hywel Dda (Hywel the Good) called a conference of all his wise men here, where he had a hunting lodge called Ty Gwyn a'r Daf – The White House on the Taf. Tradition has it that they laboured for six weeks and codified the laws of Wales. Forty manuscripts of the laws survive. How much of their contents goes back to Hywel's day is a point still debated by historians, but he cannot be deprived of the credit for making the first attempt to bring order into the chaos of Welsh customs. His work has recently been commemorated in Whitland by the creation of the Hywel Dda Gardens on the site of the old market in the centre of the town. This is an imaginative concept, with a hall containing an exhibition illustrating the history of the laws. One mile to the north of Whitland are the scanty remains of Whitland Abbey, the first Cistercian foundation in Wales. A road goes north of Whitland into country not much frequented by visitors. It is a land of wooded valleys, of solid villages like Meidrim and LLANBOIDY, and constantly rises towards the higher ground which culminates to the west in the PRESELI HILLS.

Wolfscastle (Cas-Blaidd) *Dyfed* (3/2A) This village with a dramatic name on the road between HAVERFORDWEST and FISHGUARD has, unfortunately, nothing to do with wolves. It marks the spot where a Fleming called Wolf built his motte and bailey castle during the Norman conquest of Pembrokeshire on the very edge of the Landsker, the line drawn between the English and Welsh parts of Pembrokeshire. The remains of the castle mound are hidden in the trees above the village. South of Wolfscastle, the road enters the miniature gorge of Treffgarne, with the railway on the other side of the Eastern Cleddau river escaping from the gorge through a tunnel. Behind Treffgarne rise the strange rocks of Maidens Castle which form a striking object on the skyline. They are outcrops of the hard igneous rock rhyolite and they are weathered into curious shapes.

North of Wolfscastle the road to Fishguard passes through Letterston – Treletert in Welsh – where the rebuilt church has some monuments of interest. The village is placed on high ground and the area around it is known locally and jokingly as the 'Letterston Alps'!

Ystrad Meurig, *Dyfed* (1/3C) A hamlet set in lonely country north of TREGARON in the upper reaches of the Teifi valley. It looks south over the wide expanses of the Great Bog of Tregaron. There are the remains of the castle mounds, but Ystrad Meurig is best known for its school, founded in the 18th century by a scholar of genius, Edward Richard, who attracted pupils from all over South Wales. Many distinguished Welshmen were educated here at St John's College in this unlikely spot, where the bleak hills roll away north towards PLYNLIMON. The school no longer exists but was next to the much-restored church. There is a fine waterfall, rather difficult to find, behind Ystrad Meurig. The Caradoc Falls form a triple cascade and are most worthy of a visit after rain.

Bibliography

A Glimpse of the Past: A Tourist's Guide to the Industrial Trails. Wales Tourist Board, Cardiff 1981

Ancient Monuments Guide No. 4: Wales. HMSO, London 1954

Barrett, J. H. *The Pembrokeshire Coast Path.* HMSO, London 1974

Borrow, G. *Wild Wales: Its People, Language and Scenery.* Collins, London 1977

Brecon Beacons National Park Guide. HMSO, London 1967

Cadadar. *Welsh Made Easy.* Hughes & Son, Wrexham 1969

Conran, A. *The Penguin Book of Welsh Poetry.* Penguin, London 1967

Dillon M., and Chadwick, N. K. *The Celtic Realms.* Cardinal, London 1973

Gerald of Wales. *A Journey Through Wales and The Description of Wales.* Penguin, Harmondsworth 1978

George, N. *South Wales: A Regional Geology.* HMSO, London 1970

Houlder, C. *Wales: An Archaeological Guide.* Faber & Faber, London 1974

Houlder, C., and Manning, W. H. *South Wales: A Regional Archaeology.* Heinemann, London 1967

Humphries, E. *The Taliesin Tradition.* Black Raven Press, London 1983

Laing, L. *Celtic Britain.* Granada, London 1981

Lloyd, D. M. *A Book of Wales.* Collins, London 1953

Marsh, T. *The Mountains of Wales: A Walker's Guide.* Hodder & Stoughton, London 1985

Mason, E. J. *A Portrait of the Brecon Beacons and Surrounding Areas.* Robert Hale, London 1975

Miles, D. *A Portrait of Pembrokeshire.* Robert Hale, London 1984

Morgan, P. *The Eighteenth Century Renaissance.* Christopher Davies, Llandybie 1981

Noble, F. *The ODA Book of Offa's Dyke Path.* ODA, Knighton 1972

North, F. J. *The Evolution of the Bristol Channel.* National Museum of Wales, Cardiff 1955

– *The Waterfalls of the Glyn Neath District.* National Museum of Wales, Cardiff 1955

Owen, T. M. *Welsh Folk Customs.* National Museum of Wales, St Fagan's 1974

Pembrokeshire Coast. HMSO, London 1973

Sotrell, A. *Early Wales Recreated.* National Museum of Wales, Cardiff 1980

Thomas, D. *Miscellany Three: Poems and Stories.* Dent, London 1978

Vaughan-Thomas, W. *Wales: A History.* Michael Joseph, London 1985

– *A Portrait of Gower.* Robert Hale, London 1976

Wales: A Leisure Atlas. Wales Tourist Board and Hamlyn, London 1981

Williams, G. *Religion, Nationality and Language in Wales.* University of Wales Press, Cardiff 1979

– *Henry Tudor.* University of Wales Press, Cardiff 1985

Williams, G. A. *The Welsh in Their History.* Croom Helm, London 1976

Kennexton Farm House kitchen, showing the 'cupboard bed', St Fagan's Folk Museum

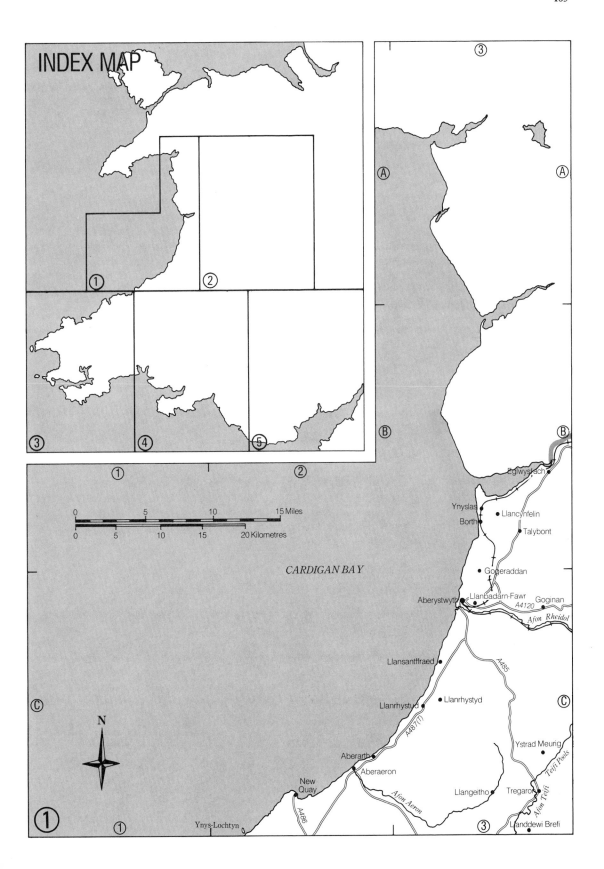

INDEX MAP

① ② ③ ④ ⑤

① ②

③ ④ ⑤

① ②

0 5 10 15 Miles

0 5 10 15 20 Kilometres

CARDIGAN BAY

③

Ⓐ Ⓐ

Ⓑ Ⓑ

Eglwysfach

Ynyslas • Llancynfelin
Borth • Talybont

• Gogeraddan

Llanbadarn-Fawr
Aberystwyth • A4120 Goginan

Afon Rheidol

Llansantffraed •

A485

Ⓒ Ⓒ

Llanrhystyd • Llanrhystyd

A487(T)

Ystrad Meurig •

Teifi Pools

N

Aberarth •
Aberaeron •

New
Quay Afon Aeron Llangeitho • Tregaron Afon Teifi

① ① A486 ③
Ynys-Lochtyn Llanddewi Brefi •

①

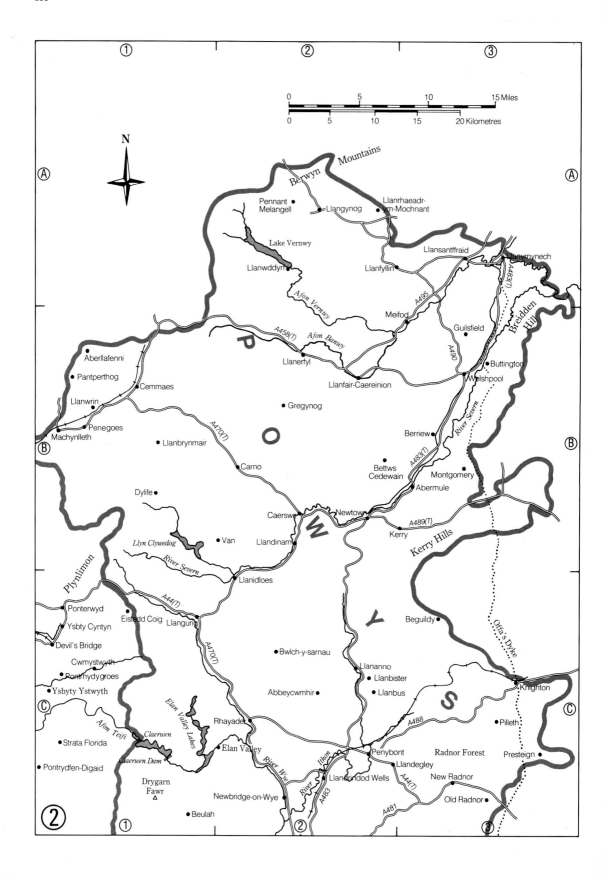

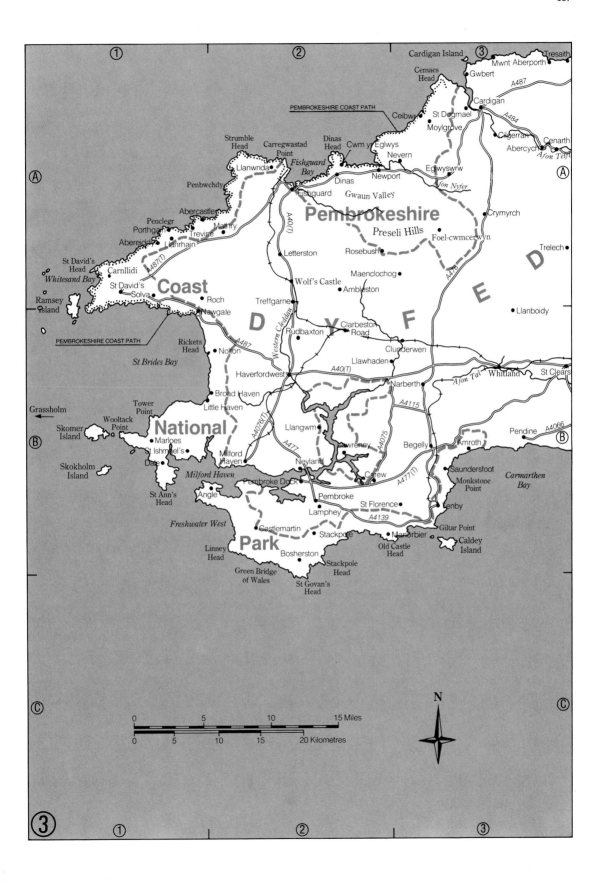

Cardigan Island
Cemaes
Head
Mwnt Aberporth
Gwbert
Tresaith
A487
Cardigan
PEMBROKESHIRE COAST PATH
St Dogmael
A484
Ceibwr
Moylgrove
Cilgerran
Abercych
Cenarth
Strumble
Head
Carregwastad
Point
Dinas
Head
Cwm yr
Eglwys
Nevern
Edwyswrw
Afon Teifi
Llanwnda
*Fishguard
Bay*
Newport
Crymych
A
Penbwchdy
Dinas
Fishguard
Gwaun Valley
Afon Nyfer
Abercastle
Pembrokeshire
Preseli Hills
Foel-cwmcerwyn
Penclegr
Mathry
Trelech
Porthgain
Trevine
Letterston
Rosebush
Abereiddy
Llanrhain
St David's
Head
Carnllidi
Coast
Maenclochog
Llanboidy
Whitesand Bay
St David's
Solva
Roch
Wolf's Castle
Ambleston
Ramsey
Island
Newgale
D
Treffgarne
Clarbeston
Road
Y
F
E
D
PEMBROKESHIRE COAST PATH
Rickets
Head
Nolton
Western Cleddau
Rudbaxton
Clunderwen
St Brides Bay
A487
Haverfordwest
Llawhaden
A40(T)
Narberth
Whitland
St Clears
Grassholm
Tower
Point
National
Broad Haven
Little Haven
A4076(T)
A4115
A477
Llangwm
A4075
Begelly
Amroth
Pendine
A4066
Skomer
Island
Wooltack
Point
Marloes
St Ishmael's
Dale
Milford
Haven
Neyland
Lawrenny
Saundersfoot
Skokholm
Island
St Ann's
Head
Milford Haven
Pembroke Dock
Carew
A477(T)
Monkstone
Point
*Carmarthen
Bay*
Angle
Pembroke
St Florence
Tenby
Lamphey
Giltar Point
Freshwater West
Park
Castlemartin
A4139
Old Castle
Head
Manorbier
Caldey
Island
Linney
Head
Bosherston
Stackpole
Green Bridge
of Wales
Stackpole
Head
St Govan's
Head

0   5   10   15 Miles
0   5   10   15   20 Kilometres

N

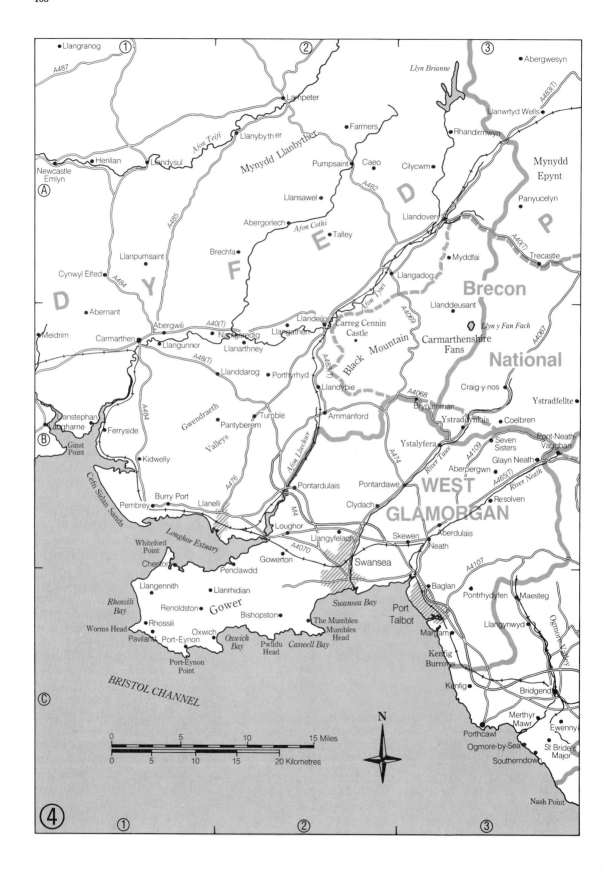

① ② ③

• Llangranog

A487

Newcastle
Emlyn

Ⓐ

• Henllan
Llandysul

Afon Teifi

Lampeter

Llanybyther

Farmers •

Mynydd Llanbyther

Pumpsaint • Caeo •

Llansawel •

Abergorlech Afon Cothi

Talley •

Llanpumsaint •

Brechfa •

Cynwyl Elfed •

A484

Abernant •

DYFED

Meidrim •

Carmarthen •

Abergwili

A40(T)

Llandeilo •

Llangunnor •

Nantgaredig

Llangathen

Llanarthney •

Carreg Cennin
Castle

Llanddarog •

Porthyrhyd •

A48(T)

Llandybie •

A484

Llanstephan
Laugharne •

Ferryside •

Gwendraeth

Valleys

Tumble •

Pantyberem •

Ammanford •

Ginst
Point

Ⓑ

Kidwelly •

A476

Pembrey •

Burry Port •

Llanelli •

Cefn Sidan Sands

Pontardulais •

Whiteford
Point

Chenton

Penclawdd •

Loughor •

Llangyfelach •

Gowerton •

A4070

Swansea •

Llangennith •

Llanrhidian •

Rhossili
Bay

Renoldston •

Gower

Bishopston •

Worms Head •

Rhossili •

Oxwich •

Paviland • Port-Eynon •

Oxwich
Bay

Pwlldu
Head

Caswell Bay

Swansea Bay

The Mumbles
Mumbles
Head

Port
Talbot

Port-Eynon
Point

BRISTOL CHANNEL

Ⓒ

Afon Tywi

A482

Cilycwm •

Llandovery •

Myddfai •

Llanddeusant •

Llangadog •

A4069

Llyn y Fan Fach

Black Mountain

Carmarthenshire
Fans

Brecon

A4068

Brynamman

Craig-y-nos •

Ystradgynlais •

Coelbren •

Ystalyfera •

Seven
Sisters •

Aberpergwn •

Glayn Neath •

River Tawe

A4109

A474

Pontardawe •

Pontardulais

Clydach •

WEST
GLAMORGAN

Resolven •

Aberdulais •

Skewen •

Neath •

Baglan •

Margam •

Kenfig
Burrows

Kenfig •

Porthcawl •

Ogmore-by-Sea

Southerndown

Afon Llwchwr

M4

Afon Tywi

A483(T)

Llyn Brianne

• Abergwesyn

A483(T)

Llanwrtyd Wells •

Rhandirmwyn •

Mynydd
Epynt

Panyucelyn •

A40(T)

Trecastle •

Ystradfellte •

Pont-Neath-
Vaughan •

River Neath

A465(T)

A4107

Pontrhydyfen •

Maesteg •

Llangynwyd •

Merthyr
Mawr

Ewenny •

St Bride's
Major

Nash Point

N

0   5   10   15 Miles

0   5   10   15   20 Kilometres

Ⓓ

PMYDDFED

National

Bridgend •

Ogmore River

④ ① ② ③

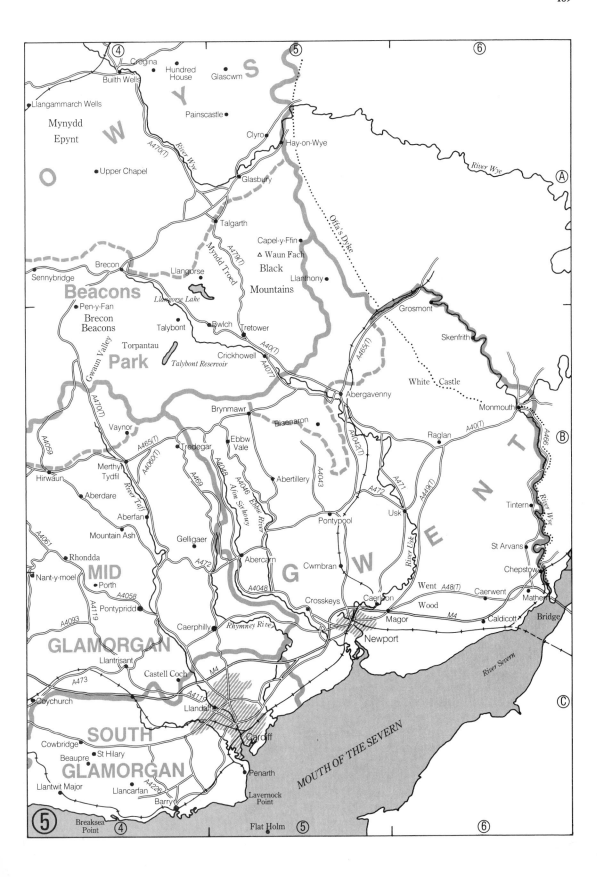

Index

Numbers in *italics* refer to illustrations